Capacity Building Series: Volume IV

Accelerating Adult Reentry

A Practical Capacity Building Model for Sustaining Post-Release Transitional Services

Books in Capacity Building Series

Volume I. *Building Capacity from the Bottom Up:
The Key to Sustaining Local Services (2024)*

Volume II, Second Edition: *Decriminalizing Mental Illness: A Practical Model
for Building Sustainable Crisis Intervention Teams (2024)*

Volume III. *Accelerating Juvenile Reentry: A Practical Capacity
Building Model for Sustaining Aftercare (2024)*

Volume IV. *Accelerating Adult Reentry: A Practical Capacity
Building Model for Sustaining Post-Release Transitional Services (2024)*

Capacity Building Series: Volume IV

Accelerating Adult Reentry

A Practical Capacity Building Model for Sustaining Post-Release Transitional Services

James Klopovic
with
Nicole Klopovic

AFFINITAS PUBLISHING

Capacity Building Series: Volume IV
Accelerating Adult Reentry: A Practical Capacity Building Model for Sustaining Post-Release Transitional Services
Copyright © 2024 by James Klopovic, DPP and Nicole Klopovic, PA-C

Published in the United States by

All Rights Reserved. No part of this publication may be reproduced, distributed, or transmitted in any form or by any means, including photocopying, recording, or other electronic or mechanical methods, without the prior written permission of the publisher/author, except in the case of brief quotations embodied in reviews and certain other noncommercial uses permitted by copyright law. Direct requests for permission to *jklopovic@gmail.com*, Affinitas Publishing.

Except as noted, the web addresses referenced in this book were live and correct at the time of the book's publication but may be subject to change.

Cover and interior design: Nick Zelinger, NZ Graphics
Virtual Assistance: Kelly Johnson, Cornerstone Virtual Assistance, LLC
Editing: Peggy Henrikson, Heart and Soul Editing

Publisher's Cataloging-in-Publication
(Provided by Cassidy Cataloguing Services, Inc.)

Names:	Klopovic, James, author. | Klopovic, Nicole, author.
Title:	Accelerating adult reentry : a practical capacity building model for sustaining post-release transitional services / James Klopovic, with Nicole Klopovic.
Description:	1st edition. | [Morrisville, North Carolina] : Affinitas Publishing, [2025] | Series: Capacity building series ; volume 4 | Includes bibliographical references.
Identifiers:	ISBN: 979-8-9850119-7-5 (paperback) | 979-8-218-57358-4 (hardcover) | LCCN: 2024925839
Subjects:	LCSH: Prisoners--Deinstitutionalization. | Ex-convicts--Services for. | Ex-convicts--Rehabilitation. | Community organization. | Organizational effectiveness.
Classification:	LCC: HV9275 .K56 2025 | DDC: 365.647--dc23

10 9 8 7 6 5 4 3 2 1

First Edition

Printed in the United States of America..

We dedicate this volume to all those who have worked towards building stronger, more resilient communities through local reentry and aftercare programming. You prove every day it can be done.

To those who have supported us along the way, your encouragement, wisdom, and especially friendship have sustained us. Now any community can build *Permanent Solutions to Permanent Problems.*

With humble appreciation,

James Klopovic and Nicole Klopovic

*The things you do for yourself are gone when you are gone,
but the things you do for others remain as your legacy.*
– N. D. Kalu

Acknowledgments

This project began with a discussion about how to construct grants that make a difference at the North Carolina Governors Crime Commission in the latter 1990s. Doug Yearwood, my colleague and friend, sparked the conversation and helped me define Capacity Building for the thousands of grants we were involved in for years. Then he encouraged me nearly daily through seven years of research and then writing the Capacity Building Series.

Many, many more people were involved in bringing about this book and its three companions. I interviewed dozens of people, and others commented on and critiqued the many new concepts. They were a test of fire for these pages. It would be impossible to name them all, but I still stand on those shoulders!

In addition, I must mention the remarkable publishing crew of Team Affinitas. They take this muddy clay of a writer and carefully mold him into an author. Peggy Henrikson is truly an editor extraordinaire. We've spent untold hours deciding the best way to explain, describe, and promote these ideas. Nick Zelinger is my great graphic designer—tops, really. He takes a plain manuscript and creates something beautiful, a treat to read. And my faithful virtual assistant Kelly Johnson is ever helpful with publishing details and internet technology.

Finally, I can't give acknowledgments without mentioning my daughters, Cindy and Nicole, who are in my heart every day, even when we are far apart. Nicole is the cofounder and CEO of The Nicole and James Klopovic Family Charitable Foundation, which we formed to support public programs that do good in the world. This Capacity Building Series will be its operating manuals. The Foundation and Nicole are the reasons I write.

Thank you all.
James Klopovic

A Note About Artificial Intelligence

We encourage you to use this remarkable tool to enhance your idea as you build your program's capacity. However, it must augment planning, operation, and sustainability. This book on Capacity Building represents years of work studying and documenting how outstanding people have made adult reentry and aftercare *work well in practice*.

Therefore, yes, take advantage of AI, but keep in mind the following: AI *does not and cannot* substitute for the extensive "street view"—even "worm's-eye" view—research covering what works in building this practical, proven model. AI cannot assess the local politics, personalities, processes, and procedures you will use to turn your good idea into a working, sustained program.

Secondly, and most importantly, AI can give you the sense of moving forward while hindering your progress. As a planner, you can get *stuck in analysis* with the *feeling* of moving forward. In the end, you must *act* to see what works for you, in *your* community, with *your* idea.

We wish you the best.

James Klopovic and Nicole Klopovic

Contents

Preface: The Birth of Capacity Building 1
    Chapter Previews 5
    List of Figures 6

Chapter 1. Introducing Adult Reentry Post-Release Services 7
    A Practical Way to Provide Post-Release Services—One at a Time 10
    The Essence of the Capacity Building Process 11
    Understanding Reintegration in Terms of Community Well-Being 12
    Discovering and Addressing the Unknown 13
    Beyond Reentry—The Overall Strategy for Reintegrating
        Former Offenders 19
    Basics for Building a Practical Capacity-Based Model for
        Post-Release Services 24
    Describing the Model of Capacity Building for Local
        Post-Release Programs 28
        This Study and the Subject Models 33
        What Do These Models Exemplify? 40
        The Life Cycle Concept 42
        How to Get the Most Out of This Book—A Checklist 44

Chapter 2: Facilitating Going Home Again 49
    Understanding the Task of Completing the Work of Reentry
        and Aftercare 52
    The Model—Connecting Reentry to Post-Release Aftercare Services 56
    Reentry Aftercaree—A Capacity Building Model and How to Use It 63
    The Process—Phases, Critical Features, and Effective Practices 65

**Chapter 3: Phase I of the Program's Life Cycle—
Plan and Implement** 73

   1. Nurture and Grow Key Leaders Who Know Post-Release
      Aftercare Services 77

   2. Integrate Capacity Assessment for Project Capacity Building 90

   3. Determine Project Scope to Focus on the Essentials of
      Transitional Services 98

   4. Design the Process Evaluation and Impact Analysis to Justify
      Reentry Services 102

   5. Nurture Relationships for Resources Development. 116

   6. Develop Performance-Oriented Service Providers as Part of
      Your Team 123

   7. Nurture Reentry Staff by a Process of Human Capacity Development .. 135

   Summing Up Planning for Your Reentry Aftercare Program 142

**Chapter 4. Phase II of the Program's Life Cycle—
Operate and Stabilize** 145

   8. Operationalize Your Reentry-Aftercare Plan 149

   Summing Up Operations for Your Reentry Aftercare Program 169

**Chapter 5: Phase III of the Program's Life Cycle—
Sustain and Expand** 171

   9. Sustain Operation 174

   10. Plot the Long-Range Strategy and Tactics for Expansion to Scale 179

   Summing Up Your Program Sustainability and Expansion 187

Chapter 6: Conclusion 189

   Lessons Learned 191

About the Authors 195

Appendix ... 199

Glossary ... 201

References ... 208

A Checklist for Your Adult Reentry-Aftercare Program ... 214

Intake Assessment and Risk/Needs Determination Chart ... 217

Reentry Skills ... 221

Memorandum of Understanding ... 223

Adult Post-Release Aftercare Resources and Key Contacts ... 225

    Foundations ... 225

    Funding ... 225

    Model Programs ... 227

    Organizations ... 230

    Reports and Publications ... 232

    Data and Analysis ... 235

    Internet Resources ... 237

Endnotes ... 241

PREFACE:
THE BIRTH OF CAPACITY BUILDING

I began thinking about Capacity Building in the early 1990s. After retiring from the U.S. Air Force in 1987, I joined the North Carolina Governor's Crime Commission (GCC) for a second career. Somehow, I was assigned to the Analysis Section that evaluated grants. It was light-years away from what shaped me growing up on a farm and two decades with the military. The GCC is the pass-through agency for federal grant funds, which are filtered through the governor to North Carolina's 100 counties and more. Every state has such an entity. Over time, billions are distributed throughout the country, a collective, massive, continuous stream of tax dollars. There is much room for improvement; a great deal is at stake.

Throughout my 25 years at the Commission, I observed and participated in the granting of millions of dollars in thousands of grants *just* for North Carolina. We managed well over 400-500 grants each year. The GCC processes more now, I'm sure. One year, one major committee of four received just over $70,000,000. All that money could have been spent much more effectively. . . . But how?

I noticed that some grantees "got it." They significantly changed their communities for the better and continued to do so. Others, not so much. I began to study what does and especially what doesn't work. Thank goodness enough goes right to be instructive, even illuminating. Their lessons learned had to be organized, told, and retold. I began to see that nearly *all* grantees never critically looked at the potential they'd have if they concentrated on building their idea to *last* from conception. They needed to evolve past the chaos and rapidity of continually implementing and not achieving permanency. Out of this musing, Capacity Building was born. Old ideas demanded novel rethinking, top to bottom and back again.

As I began my research on the topic, I visited the site of a highly successful juvenile aftercare, where I announced my intention to organize and explain how to do aftercare. The executive director, with the steely-eyed sternness and resigned but resolute voice of years of experience declaimed, "You can't understand, let alone organize, this thing we do. It's all chaos." Thus, he threw the gauntlet.

It wasn't far from the truth to say folks came to work, waited for the first thing to go wrong, then hustled to plug the dike with a longing eye to five o'clock. It was crisis management in action. So much time and potential wasted. Still, many local service projects made their ideas work out of sheer passion, brains, and intestinal fortitude. But largely, grant-funded projects lived for the next grant—*if* it came. It was a plan to fade away or fail outright. Success was achieved mostly by chance, a lot of work, and a little magic. Staff didn't know how to remove themselves from the chaotic crisis cycle of immediacy, which came at the expense of looking beyond it to permanency. More importantly, it prevented them from creating a success template for the next project—paying it forward.

Figuratively, I picked up the gauntlet. What now, thought I!? Capacity Building demanded an overhaul of the current approach, which began as a list of good things to do to deliver local public services—77 of them to be exact. However, all of these "good things" were an incomprehensible jumble that defied systematic organization and thus meaningful implementation. The order had no rhyme or reason.

Then it dawned on me that everything has a beginning, middle, and end—a Life Cycle. With this concept, chaos becomes a linear process. It bows to true planning, priorities, evidence, and *order*, increasing the effectiveness of collective talent and will. People could understand a Life Cycle. Better yet, they could apply a calculated sequence of proven practices with an eye to building an idea that lasts as long as the problem it addresses endures—finally to stable permanency. Moreover, stakeholders could muster a matrix of other essential talents and services to the cause of the idea. True synergy is possible where the whole becomes greater than the parts.

By then, I was focused on federal policy analysis and saw the need to do better granting—in fact, much better granting. Fortuitously, I pursued a doctorate in Public Policy. The topic was to define an evidence-based process to build *Permanent Solutions to Permanent Problems* at the local level. I demanded of myself to design a dissertation that was practical and would make a material difference in people's well-being, neighborhood by neighborhood. This was where problems and their solutions mingled, waiting for inspiration, sweat, and a *plan*.

Now great rigor came to play in studying how to accomplish govern*ance* (the how) not govern*ment* (the what)—through granting in this case. My goal was to help programs realize better results by doing more effective, sustainable program development. I spent seven years earning a degree devoted to Capacity Building, which took on new meaning and practicality with rigorous investigation.

I saw the sensible wisdom of this new approach called Capacity Building. Although a few programs are currently using it with great success, it's slow to catch on because it challenges the system of top-down government with bottom-up-and-back-again gove*rnance*. It's a new way of building lasting public programs that improve our neighborhoods with collaboration between all three levels of government (federal, state, and local), as well as the private and private nonprofit sectors. Capacity Building from the bottom up presents ways to build permanency using selected local services and talent to solve local problems. This collaborative matrix becomes focused and more—much more—than the sum of its parts.

To begin, I needed to define a universal, pervasive, and persistent problem to analyze and for which to suggest solutions. This problem had to be reentry, which is a concern, I can safely say, of *every* community in the country. Tackling it had to involve a community-wide strategy, and it had to start with prevention of the problem in the first place. Thus, it needed to include:

- Keeping our *children* in school and helping them be successful—by far the most successful crime prevention action we can take.

- Helping our *mental health consumers* to stay out of the criminal justice system and remain at home or in the workforce as productive members of their communities.

- Supporting our *troubled youngsters* to get back on the path to self-sufficiency and good citizenship.

- Helping t*hose who run afoul of the criminal justice system* to return to respectability and productivity as a part of community.

These steps represent a comprehensive strategy for reentry, township by township. Furthermore, a municipality can begin with only one element of the strategy, depending on their resources and especially their determination to succeed. This model for public services is based on prevention, intervention, and resolution of a universal, intergenerational problem. After all, having *no* reentry strategy is extravagantly expensive in public dollars and individual suffering, which these capacity-built programs could help alleviate. For those willing to address these issues, Capacity Building is the way.

Remember that discussion with the program director who said taming the chaos of services can't be documented? Well, this book is part of a four-volume set documenting just that—taming chaos, bringing order, and permanently solving a universal problem, one project, one community at a time.

This is a major life work for me—and its own reward. As Henry David Thoreau wrote in Walden, "If one advances confidently in the direction of his dreams, and endeavors to live the life which he has imagined, he will meet with a success unexpected in common hours." Who knows where these volumes will go and what effect they will have. I do know that whatever happens, it will be good. At least, these volumes in the Capacity Building Series can guide the generations that follow me in building local service ideas that are *Permanent Solutions to Permanent Problems*. If even one effective, lasting program results, it's been worth everything it's taken to realize these volumes and this dream of a lifetime.

– James Klopovic

Don't judge each day by the harvest you reap but by the seeds that you plant.
– Robert Louis Stevenson

CHAPTER PREVIEWS

Chapter 1. Introducing Adult Reentry Post-Release Services
The first chapter gives you a good idea of the Why and What of Adult Reentry Aftercare and explains that the current literature on the subject doesn't adequately describe the How. It then introduces you to the four successful model programs that freely shared their expertise for this study. It also explains the Life Cycle for these programs and how that concept is helpful in developing new programs and running current ones. Finally, it offers a comprehensive preview checklist of action items and effective practices for bringing your idea to fruition.

Chapter 2. Facilitating Going Home Again
This chapter delves into understanding the task of completing the work of reentry and aftercare. It includes the strategies and key features of the Capacity Building Model and the challenges of expansion. In addition, the chapter explains the process of developing a reentry aftercare program: its life cycles, critical features, and effective practices.

Chapter 3. Phase I of the Program's Life Cycle—Plan and Implement
Chapter 3 begins the in-depth description of the phases of the program's life cycles with the first phase of planning and implementation. It covers the major concerns that need to be addressed in the areas of leadership, capacity assessment, scope determination, process evaluation and impact analysis, resources development, service providers, and staff development.

Chapter 4. Phase II of the Project Life Cycle—Operate and Stabilize
This chapter explains how to effectively put each area of your planning into operation, discussing ways to minimize chaos and give order to the all-important process of implementation.

Chapter 5. Phase III of the Project Life Cycle—Sustain and Expand
Chapter 5 discusses how to sustain your program so it will reach its goal of permanence. It explains the importance of a continued focus on fundraising, staff training, planning for succession, and achieving results with clients. Those results are key to improving the safety and security of the community. With this, you will garner praise and appreciation for a job well done.

Chapter 6. Conclusion

The last chapter provides a summary of some of the main lessons learned by successful practitioners and shared throughout this guide. It also brings up questions to follow up on as more of these programs that support returnees and the community are initiated. Answers will arise as these solutions to permanent problems continue to be established.

LIST OF FIGURES

Figure 1-A. Capacity Building Checklist for Reentry-Aftercare Practitioners – PHASES I-III, with Key Action Items and Effective Practices 45

Figure 1-B (Appendix). Capacity Building Checklist for Reentry-Aftercare Practitioners – PHASES I-III, with Key Action Items and Effective Practices 215

Figure 2. Intake Assessment and Risk/Needs Determination Chart 217

Figure 3. Reentry Skills 221

Chapter 1

INTRODUCING ADULT REENTRY POST-RELEASE SERVICES

Chapter 1

INTRODUCING ADULT REENTRY POST-RELEASE SERVICES

Whether you think you can or think you can't, you're right.
– Henry Ford

The problem of *reentry* and how to go about resolving it are both misunderstood. The term reentry has been used for years and has lost its meaning. Reentry as current policy is an evidence-based program, a "best practice" (there's no such thing), and a continuum of what happens from incarceration back to the community. All these descriptors and many more confuse the main issue which, again, is how to sustain a local service idea. Instead of more nomenclature, reentry demands *a way to get it done*. Therefore, the task of this book is to delineate the *how*—the action of it all.

Post-release is a more accurate term to describe what is called reentry. *Post-release* considers parolees from the correctional system *and* the much wider group of probationers. In fact, in 2003, people on probation included twice as many as those on parole, in jail, or in prison combined.[1] In addition, the probation population is at highest risk of recidivating according to the practitioners interviewed for this model, because probationers are under closer supervision and tighter restrictions.

Considering this, the task of returning former prisoners to the community needs redefining.

Yes, it's necessary to plan for a prisoner's return to their community from the moment they're sentenced—but that's not enough. The community bears the burden of putting together and sustaining services to not only transition these individuals but support them in becoming productive citizens. This goes considerably and necessarily beyond the current modality of reentry.

The comprehensive plan for reducing recidivism and reintegrating returnees into the community should also have a preventive element. The community is much better served by diverting as many people as possible *before* they become involved in the criminal justice system. In fact, not involving the courts, corrections, and law enforcement in the *first* place is the surest, most productive way to reduce recidivism. This goes way beyond simply getting a post-release client into temporary housing and their first job, important as those things are.

That is why this Capacity Building Series includes suggestions for helping our youngest children be prepared for and remain in primary and secondary school, accomplished and capable, even happy (Volume I). It's why the series includes keeping mental health consumers in the family and community as productive members away from involvement in the criminal justice system (Volume II). When we can prevent it in the first place, it's also why the series encompasses programs for both juvenile and adult post-release services. These programs help put troubled youths and adults back on track to success in life after involvement with the justice system to prevent recidivism (Volumes III and IV).

> **The community bears the burden of putting together and sustaining services to not only transition these individuals but support them in becoming productive citizens.**

These models for local services are all based on capacity-built ideas for permanent, progressing, expanding public programs that have meaningful impact in their communities where it matters most. Such programs grow from one person with an idea and a will to see it through. It *can* and is being done!

A Practical Way to Provide Post-Release Services – One at a Time

The order to reduce prison populations and return former inmates to the community becomes necessarily taller, yet more realistic, when defined as post-release with a preventive element, not simply reentry.

The strategy then is to keep people from entering jail or prison in the first place. Then, if it happens, make sure they don't cycle back once they've been in the criminal justice system, whether after incarceration or while being court supervised. Now the task becomes one of devising a practical, manageable, and realistic way to reintegrate the more comprehensive post-release population to the community. The answer to that is the second part of the misunderstanding of reentry.

Most literature and advice largely discuss services and provide lists of suggested actions local stakeholders should take.[2] While these suggestions are quite helpful, they don't necessarily address specific local actions and how to accomplish those sequential actions efficiently and effectively. This begs the need for an organized way of building those services into the infrastructure needed to reintroduce clients to the community.

This problem is one of defining processes to organize the rather scattered advice. More and more communities are figuring out how to deliver effective transitional services by creating programs built on the infrastructure of sustainable, self-renewing resources. However, the process of how they accomplished this most difficult community development task is one of problem solving and winging it. Practitioners simply don't have the time or inclination to codify what they've accomplished when they do figure it out.

Even if the literature references successful sites, it makes unorganized observations from outside the sites mentioned. Referencing these sites is a far cry from the vastly more complex work of understanding how they operate. Nor do the references explain how to transfer that knowledge practically and successfully to a new site *and* make a difference in other communities.

What to do is not the problem. It is a matter of *how* to do a well-established array of post-release services such as housing, skills training, medical/therapeutic care, and employment—all tailored to the unique individual. The problem has been, is, and will always be how to go about *delivering* these services. This calls for a definition of Adult Reentry Capacity Building for Local Post-Release Transitional Services—what it is and, especially, what it is not. Let's have a look now at Capacity Building to sustainability.

The Essence of the Capacity Building Process

Capacity Building is a description of a *process* that follows practitioner-based suggestions for building an idea to stability, permanence, and self-renewal with specific, measurable, positive effect in the community. Ideally, it should also be replicable at another location, which is a critical test of its validity, reliability, and especially its viability. The delivery of reintegration services is presented as a practical, sequential progression, lending itself to organization and more effective work assignments. It helps identify problems, especially early on when solutions are relatively simple compared to delaying problem resolution and having a small bother morph into a crisis. Then it's the endless loop of crisis management, another term for chaos.

Capacity Building involves an understanding of the organic nature of the *network* of stakeholders, the decisions they make, and the evolving services they provide. The application of the process will still take years of work to tailor to each new site and the ever-increasing numbers of people going home after a court ruling, jail, or prison.

In fact, a process that works well is continually evolving. While the model is descriptively simple, it is based in proven, practical advice, not from this author but rather from those who know the job and are succeeding at it.

> **Capacity Building is a description of a *process* that follows practitioner-based suggestions for building an idea to stability, permanence, and self-renewal with specific, measurable, positive effect in the community.**

Understanding Reintegration in Terms of Community Well-Being

When the task of reintegration is understood as a process, goals change dramatically. For example, the present goal of reentry is to reduce recidivism. While that's certainly important, it's an interim goal in the overarching task of improving community well-being. Wellness assumes a community is sick and in need of cures. Well-*being* assumes the community has real strengths on which it can grow and progress.

When community well-being becomes the focus, decision making, for example, is not a one-time event. Rather, it becomes the daily nipping and tucking of actions aimed at establishing and nurturing relationships of service providers and program supporters that endure. Most everything is done with a look over the horizon rather than being absorbed by the inevitable and frequent crises that drain efforts of the day. Data can easily show that clients *can* be kept out of prison. More important is to ensure the means for the program's self-renewal. Thus, the task is one of building infrastructure—the process of capacity building—which is the basis of this model, this book, and this series of four volumes. Together, these books tackle comprehensive reentry prevention, intervention, and successful reentry. The mission then, is not simply to reduce the prison population. It becomes a more manageable task when the focus is on transitioning one former inmate at a time. This is quite realistic for any community according to the executive director of the Durham, North Carolina effort to reintegrate former inmates. Success is not just reentry; it's also assisting individual program candidates to become productive citizens. There is a difference.

Reentry just begins the process of returning home. This view of post-release means that institutions, especially governmental, are only *part* of the answer to reintegration. The community is where the entire equation of the problem and viable long-term solutions lie.

This book doesn't describe the scientifically proclaimed Evidence-Based Practice (EBP), which usually refers to, for example, a behavioral modification therapy which is rather academic. Capacity Building for transitional aftercare services is a practical sequence of milestones and activities for constructing service infrastructure, the business practices that support an EBP. Thus, it's not prescriptive, but rather descriptive. Capacity Building is a sequence of effective practices that confront and answer the everyday obstacles of delivering post-release services. This model is not theory. It's reality-based. As stated by post-release providers, "This stuff works." Not theoretical, it's very much practitioner-based, evolutionary, and organic. It's practitioner-based because only successful practitioners can realistically comment and advise on how to develop an idea. It's evolutionary because how it's applied will continue to improve with each application, as a major constructive theme of the process is that it encourages a learning, progressive environment. It's organic because with each application it will continue to redefine itself. Delivery capacity and services will be added, cancelled, and modified according to the needs of the individual client of the moment and the new partners each application involves. The model grows by individual applications. A local official observed, "Our mission has always been 'One at a time.'" When the job of sustaining a service idea is seen in this way, the totality of it becomes actionable and most possible.

Discovering and Addressing the Unknown

As much information as there is about reentry, much remains unknown and especially undone. A few unknowns are salient, the most significant of which is how to get beyond implementation.[3] The greatest struggle for practitioners at the local level is the chaos of startup according to the deputy director of the Durham reentry program. No matter how many sites tout success, there's no guarantee ideas will transfer. New practitioners who tackle the issue of returning inmates will confront old problems anew.

Nearly every reference on how to begin a project mentions the need for an advisory board, for example, even suggesting the titles of who should be on it. This is a far cry from approaching all these individuals and the many more necessary to the task of reentry aftercare to explain what's necessary, e.g.:

- the long-term work,
- maintaining their long-term buy-in,
- training them in their duties and responsibilities,
- producing productive agendas,
- enacting their suggestions and decisions, and
- explaining to them why certain ideas must be done and others cannot.

This detail only scratches the surface of the work and dynamic of building viable oversight, which is merely one aspect of building local services.

The next unknown is the lack of a practitioner-based model that builds sustainable capacity. The Michigan Prisoner Reentry Initiative (MPRI),[4] for example, is a popular model and is quite helpful in defining the sequence of services that transition an inmate from incarceration to the community. As stated on their website, "The MPRI involves improved decision making at seven critical decision points in the three phases of the custody, release, and community supervision/discharge process." It simplistically and inadequately links three popular governmental programs: the Serious Violent Offender Reentry Initiative, the Transition from Prison to Community Initiative, and recommendations from the Report of the Reentry Policy Council. It lists decision points for each phase and ends with the seventh point, an admonition really, to determine community responsibility to "take over" the case.[5] It's a program linking programs with no mention of *how* to build support for those services. It raises myriad questions with few practical answers.

> **Why capacity? Because the service mix will always be in flux due to near daily adjustments to what reality demands.**

Arguably, the work of reintroducing a former inmate to productive and long-lasting community membership begins just where the MPRI ends. It's a theoretical model, as it provides little about application. The thread for an effective process is new thinking and actions regarding capacity building with matrix solutions, which is not mentioned at all. Why capacity? Because the service mix will always be in flux due to near daily adjustments to what reality demands. What matters is that program support is in place no matter what shape it takes. That support will be as unique as every community in which ideas for post-release services take hold. This also implies that service matters more than capacity, which is a salient point missed by the literature.[6] If you can't deliver the continuously effective service, why try. Another offshoot of models without capacity is the idea of Evidence-Based Practices (EBPs), which needs to be understood before their lessons are applied.

Evidence-based practices are much in vogue and with good reason; science and application are better in concert.[7] As with any advice, the use of evidence-based practices needs to be tempered with an understanding of their strengths and weaknesses. The Center for Court Innovation studied the Harlem Parole Reentry Court to determine its effectiveness, suggesting reentry courts can be an EBP.[8] Following is a summary of their results:[9]

- *Dosage* – This references the intensity of transitional services. They found that if interventions were reduced in length, failure rates increased, so a returning inmate needs to have at least six months of services during which the day is filled, 40 to 70 percent at least, with structured activities. So, an EBP must be of sufficient duration to have the desired effect. What happens if EBP duration varies?

- *Community-based services* – Transitional services that begin during incarceration *must* continue in the community. Experience demonstrates this is not done adequately. Does this jeopardize the effectiveness of an EBP?

- *Sanctions* – Ex-offenders need very close supervision with the real possibility of sanctions if they fail to comply. Is control by sanctions, that is threat, compatible with EBPs? No. EBPs are usually strengths-based and nurturing.

- *Supervision effect* – By including parolees *and* probationers, more former inmates are under supervision, which increases the opportunity for violations and subsequent revocations. It's better to have graduated consequences, with revocation as a last resort. EBPs should be part of the mix of preparing an inmate for independent living but may not be included or done as comprehensively as they should be.

- *Addiction* – Most people run afoul of the law because of drug addictions. The most effective treatment begins at sentencing, continues with work release, and transitions to community aftercare. Inmates have many complications, which implies the need for multiple EBPs. However, EBPs are difficult and expensive to incorporate, thus they may not be adequate for the population of post-incarceration clients who come to a local municipality. In fact, many inmates have multiple complicating factors, not the least of which are mental and physical problems, lack of education, and little or no experience in the work force.

What we have here is a list of services. What holds them together? What directs their common purpose? What is the business of delivering these services—that is, what services capacity delivery systems support them? They are good services, floating on air, lasting until the next bit of unreliable funding. Let's return to the Harlem model.

The argument made for reentry courts is that these courts positively affect the above findings, and thus we have an EBP. Just being labeled an EBP, though, is little assurance it will work in another place. Let's turn a discerning eye to how an idea becomes an EBP and the utility. or lack thereof, of being designated so.

First, few good programs are properly evaluated to test overall performance and, by extension, its fidelity as an EBP. A methodologically sound evaluation is prohibitively expensive, very technical, and extremely time consuming. Thus, the lessons from numerous programs are never discovered nor explained. These evaluations are usually sponsored by large agencies, such as the federal government, which usually turn to the academic community for the study. The academic community applies strict methodology, which limits what a researcher can do. For example, for an analysis of results, researchers can compare program completions with and without sanctions. This would be a relatively simple calculation, and thus easier to do and better defended. Rarely are longitudinal studies done that extend years after a program. It's just too difficult to track program graduates for the years it takes to answer the question: Did a reentry-aftercare program effectively transition a former inmate to the community as a productive member free from crime?

The propensity is to choose measures that have a good chance of determining a positive effect. What about the rest of the story? Capacity Building flips that model. The desired effect determines measures. Ultimately, that effect is a person involved in the "system" is returned to the community, well and productive. With meaningful measures, a program can be detailed in a positive light. Measures are usually statistically significant or not. *And* appropriate corrective action can be better illuminated.

A program is considered successful *if* it shows a statistically significant positive effect. Even statistical significance is made more unrealistic by its underlying assumptions and methodological restrictions. Practitioners can conduct a client satisfaction survey, which is another way to determine if an idea is working. But what do they *do* with it and how do they apply what really works? *That* is the question.

These studies are usually not designed to aid the highly complex socio-behavioral nature of the implementation process, which doesn't easily lend itself to studies that need results relatively soon. The fact is, it takes years to plan, implement, and stabilize a single idea, let alone develop the complex network of services needed for post-release programming. And that's just to determine if the idea will work at all! Saying a project will be effective by incorporating EBPs is much different from achieving meaningful results.

Now for a quick comment on the results outlined in the Harlem Parole Reentry Court study. First, these results are from *one* court. Much more can and needs to be learned from several sites. Each result describes a narrow aspect of a service, while the actual, field-level description of it is far more complex and nuanced. The more important *practical* results would be understanding the details of how the Harlem practitioners realized these findings. Who were the key people and talents required? What, specifically, did they do? When did they do it? How were they networked and built into a results-oriented team? The multitude of questions a practitioner would ask remains unanswered. Yes, an EBP is a good start, but that's all it is.

Next let's consider detailed toolkits such as The Jail Administrator's Tool Kit for Reentry[10] and The Elected Official's Toolkit for Jail,[11] for example. Indeed, these toolkits are of some help in the field, but their application is problematic because the areas explained are limited to a few topics better suited to consulting or technical advising.[12] The Jail Administrator's Tool Kit for Reentry exemplifies this constriction by summarizing *essential ingredient*s: Leadership, Staff, Tools, Stakeholders, Public Relations and Inmates and Their Families.[13] These essentials are good for sparking solutions to specific questions or by being the conduit to fellow practitioners who will be eager to help tease out answers to questions of the moment. They may be essential, but they are quite limited in explaining *how* they work and especially work together, and, again, difficult to apply as stated.

Tools can be assessment screens for clients, for example. However, many more useful tools are available beyond client assessment, such as memos of understanding, data gathering instruments, and budget briefing templates. What about other essentials, such as capacity assessment to determine the gaps in services, evaluations of operational efficiencies, and analyses of impact to mention a few important considerations? Also, how do you put these tools together to justify budgets, access resources, and tell the story of your program as you publicize it to potential partners? Let's examine the situation more closely.

Reentry strategies in the Jail Administrators Toolkit for Reentry[14] mentions tiers of inmates and commensurate services. The Toolkit doesn't mention how to put together the delivery mechanisms. These would consider, for example, developing relations with providers, providing a place for training, transportation, client monitoring, data gathering, measuring effectiveness of each of the services, and assessing overall effectiveness, to mention a few concerns. Jail staff issues are listed as essential but are only part of numberless actions that must be taken, in sequence yet. Furthermore, *when* in the sequence of developing a program should these staffing issues be addressed, *who* should address them, and *what* provisions should be made to address them as they continually arise?

The Toolkit merely "Identifies the complicated issue of incentivizing your staff to support and participate in inmate reentry."[15] How does one apply that? The Toolkit also expressly states that it's designed merely to prompt the reentry discussion.[16] But when process is mentioned, a toolkit usually just *lists* services along a continuum of needs that follow an inmate from incarceration to the community. That's it, yet it is just a beginning.

This is just a quick wink into the difference between merely delivering a list of services for individuals and permanently integrating them to effect community betterment—permanently.

So, the first problem with present reentry programs is that the practitioner would struggle to put this toolkit into action. Several omissions from these aids to program implementation are obvious. One is the consideration of scope. A true reintegration strategy must encompass the entire population of post-release clients, even the most difficult to treat. (These progressive aftercare model sites are criticized for taking only the clients who are predisposed to succeed in transitioning home. The models studied for this book rarely exclude a returning inmate, much to their credit. Perhaps the only exclusions would be the serious habitual or sex offender.) It would also be extremely helpful to involve a preventive element in the transitional process.

Another issue is the minimal organization of suggestions. The lists of services usually found in toolkits only imply a rational, practical path to follow. They are lists, not a process. The success of a prescribed continuum of necessary transitional services lies in the success of their implementation, the roots of a good, sustainable service idea. Then, further work is needed to make them self-renewing with a steady stream of operational resources. Effective effort is better served with a logical series of actions organized by the major phases of project/community development, i.e., planning and implementation, operations to stability, and in its time sustainable expansion. It is the three phases of a project life cycle.

> Reentry into the community is a short-term goal, while reintegration as a productive citizen is much more long-term and the true aim of post-release aftercare

Then, further work is needed to make them self-renewing with a steady stream of operational resources. Effective effort is better served with a logical series of actions organized by the major phases of project/community development, i.e., plan and implement, operate and stabilize, sustain and expand.

Added to the lack of process and organization of actions is an oversimplification of the work of designing and developing the business of reintegration. It's paramount to thoroughly digest and understand how a program of services results in a productive former inmate. Plus, merely a listing of services implies the work is short-term, even terminal, when nothing is further from reality. Reentry into the community is a short-term goal, while reintegration as a productive citizen is much more long term and the true aim of post-release aftercare.

Finally, nowhere, it seems, is there mention of building support capacity and how an overall community reintegration strategy is constructed. How are the matrices of public and private services created? How do they lead to the common goal of successful aftercare? The work of reintegrating clients in post-release is perpetual and constantly changing. What must remain is the business infrastructure to accommodate the vagaries of politics and funding and a demanding and fluid target population.

Beyond Reentry – The Overall Strategy for Reintegrating Former Offenders

Thus far, the case has been made for having a continuum of reentry to post-release services and aftercare. Now the question is how to actualize the strategy. First of all, goals are necessary. The Second Chance Act of 2007 supports local municipalities in their efforts to improve reentry, reduce recidivism, and promote community safety and security.[17] It reflects national, state, and local policy goals, which seek to:

- Break the cycle of criminal recidivism.
- Rebuild ties between offenders and their families.

- Encourage the development and support of evidence-based programs.
- Promote law-abiding conduct by offenders.
- Establish a self-sustaining and law-abiding lifestyle for offenders.
- Facilitate reentry into the community.

These aims are a helpful beginning. But to be as effective as possible, public policy goals (and by extension, programming) should be communicable, practical, measurable, and transferable to any locale. We say transferable in that the process needs to be universally applicable where action defined by the unique locale can be taken. This process ultimately describes improvement of the public circumstance, beginning with the immediate goals of a post-release strategy to reduce recidivism *and* improve neighborhood safety and security.

The above goals are more policy pronouncements than statements that are easily understood and applied to (local) circumstances. They would not help build permanent solutions to the permanent problem. Still, they point us in the right direction by encouraging the discussion of what post-release programming should achieve. Capacity Building tells us what *can* be achieved.

Beyond these characteristics, it would be helpful if goals also guided efforts to strengthen problem-solving capability. Only with a process that explains how to establish permanent self-renewing programming—a primary purpose of this book—can a strategy achieve the sought-after long-term goals.

A continually growing body of literature points to what can be done to reduce prison populations, either by keeping offenders out in the first place or keeping them from recidivating, which happens most effectively at the community level.[18] Local officials know the importance of reducing recidivism while assisting former inmates in being productive citizens. As with most good ideas, the devil is in the process of realizing those aims. Just how can local stakeholders achieve the promise of reducing recidivism?

This model for community-based post-release aftercare services delivery is only one element in the mix of state and local efforts, systemic and non-systemic ideas, and programming and policy necessary to reduce correction recidivism and increase community reintegration. Let's consider the broad mix of what should be entertained to reduce prison and jail numbers while improving the lot of returning former inmates. The overall strategy follows the maturation to criminality and return to individual-specific success in the community after involvement with the criminal justice system.

- *Prevention* – First, we must make efforts to stop crime and victimization in the first place. The most productive crime prevention initiative is success in school. This is seen in local efforts to prepare children for a better classroom experience by, for example, well baby clinics, preschool, and before and after school programs.

- *Intervention* – More and more, local recidivism reduction efforts are proving to be effective when part of a broader strategy of reentry aftercare. For example, the Criminal Justice Resource Center in Durham does the following:

    o *Deferral at the call for service* – Local municipalities can design a post-release services strategy that encompasses deferring people from the criminal justice system in the first place. Proven ideas include having a social worker assigned to a police department to intercept eligible citizens at the time of the service call and channel them to local services and resources rather than to jail. How novel! How practical!

    o *Decriminalizing the mentally ill* – A community can build a law enforcement-based Crisis Intervention Team (CIT). The team refers mental health consumers facing arrest to community-based services, arresting only the very few who need the criminal justice system. The CIT movement holds great promise and is proving to be one of the most cost-effective programs a municipality can sponsor. (See Volume II in the Capacity Building Series, *Decriminalizing Mental Illness: A Practical Model for Building Sustainable Crisis Intervention Teams*.)

    o *Pre-booking diversion* – Judges can divert people via mental health or reentry courts,[19] for example. Judges are very effective with carrot and stick motivation for former inmates who generally are difficult to motivate.

    o *Post-booking diversion* – Court officials and jailers can also divert offenders in post-booking status to community resources. For example, Durham has a sheriff's deputy located in the jail dedicated to finding mental health services for appropriate court-involved people and referring them to those services.

- o *Focus where most recidivism happens: post-release* – Communities can focus services on the broader population of those in post-release status, probation, who are likely to recidivate.[20] Reentry characteristically focuses only on the term of probation where the threat of a judicial reversal of their status weighs heavily. However, true reentry focusses on reintegrating a former inmate into the community, after probation and usually without recidivating.[21] This is a much longer process than the timing of post-release.

- *Correction* – The criminal justice system can reform institutional responses by enacting policy and programming to be more efficient and effective.

  - o *Legislation* – States can legislate prison reform to redesign sentencing and release policy to, for example, mandate risk and needs assessment from the moment incarceration begins.

  - o *Funding reallocation* – Prison grant and general funding can be channeled to recidivism reduction strategies, for example, with funding via the Second Chance Act enacted in 2007. Or, the State General Assembly justice and public safety funds can follow a court-involved individual to local programs such as Triangle Residential Options for Substance Abusers. The program is self-sustaining by being based on enterprise industries such as a client-run moving company and picture framing business, offered at a fraction of the cost of a prison bed.

  - o *Policy* – States can also craft policy to manage prison populations by, for example, ensuring that reentry skills training begins at sentencing and continues through community-based programming to complete the transition to success in the community.[22]

  - o *Programming* – Correction departments that are involved in a reentry strategy generally have exemplary programs to start the reentry process at intake. This begins a continuity of programming to prepare the individual for a successful transition.

This overarching strategy encompasses prevention, intervention and correction, punishment and reward, policy and programming. Significant gains in efficiency and effectiveness will more than pay for measures that, over time, will have the greatest success. At first, these measures will decrease recidivism by minimizing it as much as possible; then, they will promote measurable community wellness via aftercare. Then the strength of a sustainable service idea becomes the strength of the community.

Furthermore, a way forward should encompass adult and child offenders.[23] The above strategy represents a new way of thinking by realizing that criminal justice systems must invite the community to participate with courts, prisons, and law enforcement agencies. And reciprocally, that communities need to invite the criminal justice systems to collaborate with their transitional strategies by sharing one other's services and especially talent.[24] The literature well documents what a comprehensive incarceration reduction strategy should look like. It's contrary to the present situation in which public departments are silos for their programs, policies, and procedures. Need I say, there is much duplication also.

One of the most insightful and realistic statements for what post-release intentions and goals should be comes from Chief Justice William Ray Price, Jr., Missouri Supreme Court:

> *I am not advocating that we reduce prison populations just to save money. Nonviolent offenders are still law breakers, and they will break laws until they learn their lesson. What I am saying is that we need to do a better job teaching nonviolent offenders the right lessons. That takes more than prison; it takes more than a slap-on-the-wrist-probation. Drug and alcohol addiction must be broken; discipline and job skills must be learned. When that can be done better, outside of expensive prison walls that is what we should do. Results matter, public safety matters, taxpayer dollars matter, saving lives and restoring families matter.*[25]

Local decision makers in our courts, corrections, law enforcement agencies, and nonprofits providing post-release services know the best ideas for strengthening and reforming our criminal justice systems, in particular corrections. Substantial evidence now exists about how to return inmates to the community as productive citizens.[26] Post-release and reentry programming work to halt the cycle of criminalization and crime by investing in human capital to address the deficits in inmate education and employability.[27] Most former inmates are ready to return to productive citizenry; they just need the reassuring path to do so.[28] What's most lacking in this strategy is a process of institutionalizing the ideas chosen for implementation.

Basics for Building a Practical Capacity-Based Model for Post-Release Services

Let's look again to the literature for guidance on what should be in a practical model for post-release services. It's helpful to see what's recommended, where gaps in the literature may be, and what would be helpful to implementing a post-release aftercare program.

The toolkits are a good place to start.[29] They suggest two overarching thrusts for a successful strategy:

- *System elements* – These include leadership, collaborations, data, targeted programming, evaluation, and sustainability.

- *Intervention elements* – These include system services that focus on what needs to be done for the former offender, such as screening and assessment, transition planning, and post-release services.

These toolkits suggest certain primary stakeholders need to be involved:
- Law enforcement
- Community service providers
- Victims
- The general public
- Employers
- The courts
- Probation and parole
- Released inmates and their families

This list is expanded to necessary support entities:
- Elected officials
- Community-based organizations
- Jails
- Prosecutors and defenders
- The federal government

The toolkits mention the necessity for collaboration, support, leadership, and cooperation. They reiterate the need for effectiveness, reduction of recidivism, and enhanced public safety and security. To be fair, these overviews of suggested general tasks are already well known by the local decision makers, service providers, and elected officials. However, they need to know much more to successfully implement ideas and programming. You need a good idea, a plan, a process, and an undying will to succeed.

In addition, these toolkits cite many good examples of successful programs. Hampton County, Massachusetts cited in *The Elected Official's Toolkit for Jail Reentry*[30] lists these key elements:

- Partnerships and collaboration
- Assessment of needs
- Mandatory in-jail programming and services
- Community in-reach
- Service and transition planning
- Post-release services in the community
- Lower-security options
- Self-evaluation

Yes, this information is helpful. However, every reference on a topic must pass a utilitarian test asking: How can this piece of advice be effectively put to work? Here again, we have lists with little rhyme or reason to the sequence of tasks and no instruction on the proper way to implement these recommendations. They end up being a bit confusing and give a false sense of security about the realities of mounting a meaningful post-release-aftercare services program. It's always tougher than it seems. Such sketchy guidance leads to more failure than success. Local stakeholders need a practitioner-based, ground-level, descriptive narrative about developing the specifics. These observations, suggestions, and lists need to be activated in a way that's as permanent and dynamically ever changing as the problem of returning offenders.

Expanding upon the above key elements, following are five characteristics of promising reentry programs that transfer to post-release programming:[31]

- *Collaboration* – No single community entity or agency can be held responsible for programming delivery; borderless working partnerships are necessary.

- *Access to benefits and services* – A client selected for transitional services must have access to employment training and opportunities for housing, food, counseling, medical and mental health assistance, social security/disability income and Medicare/Medicaid.

- *Sustainability* – This is the first and most important aspect of an effective program, because it must be built to permanently answer the problem at hand. Planning for program permanency needs to consider:
    o surpassing a temporary status,
    o consistent funding,
    o performance measures, and
    o becoming common practice in the locality.[32]

- *Cultural/gender components* – Gender-specific programming is an important element.

- *Community linkages* – The offender must be connected to appropriate community services and support that are most effective in addressing recidivism. This includes family reunification, general aftercare, and follow-up as part of the transition plan.[33]

A note on effectiveness: Evidence-based-programs are merely a statement of what may be working in at least one locale, with little explanation of what made it work nor how to employ lessons learned. The science is arguably suspect when it comes to practical application. We have promising practices, for example, from certain sites that claim results. Again, it's difficult to translate these claims to other locations. It's better to understand what is effective by defining it from the perspective of a practitioner. A suggestion or an idea is deemed effective if a local practitioner suggests that it works in the field. That definition of effectiveness passes the test of utility, and it usually can be connected to measurable results. In other words, it's an *effective practice* as determined by practical application with the desired results.

> The literature at the time of this writing is helpful, but it's misleading in its simplicity.

The foregoing suggestions are characteristic of the literature and thinking at the time of this writing on how to confront the difficulties of programming to address breaking the cycle of crime and bringing post-release individuals back into society as productive citizens. Academics and researchers take a detached view of programs that seem to work and relate what's largely obvious and identifiable and lends itself to categorization. Of course,]the literature at the time of this writing is helpful, but it's misleading in its simplicity. Nearly all suggestions usually found in the literature are focused on services, because services are easy to observe, analyze, and prescribe.

What is largely uninvestigated is how successful sites support and sustain their services—and *prosper.*

Looking at the literature critically, one finds it's most difficult to apply what it describes. For example, take Community Linkages: Just how *is* a former offender linked to services and support? This clientele is known to be unmotivated, recalcitrant, and trapped in a criminal cycle. Furthermore, services are maddeningly difficult to procure and maintain. Successful linkages are the hard work of months, even years, and are usually continuous operations. How is it done?

For example, more than an overhead view is needed to understand how the Criminal Justice Resource Center in Durham has established a network of service providers over years of developing relationships. It then matches these services to every program client according to a detailed profile developed *before* release from incarceration. This profile is designed to discover and document the success and failure factors for everyone they accept into their program. It illuminates what the formerly incarcerated person prescriptively needs and who specifically would best address their needs. Each client has a unique fit to the basic list of needs for housing, subsistence, family/neighborhood support, education, care, and a job.

Thus, a model must go deeper to elucidate how to be effective at the tasks of transition. Everything practitioners do is informative and teaches us. Every municipality, community, and practitioner considering post-release programming needs to know what works. For example: Who is on the Justice Services Center (JSC) team, what are their duties and responsibilities, how do each function, and how do they operate in a team? Or better yet, how do they function as a matrix of project-forward applicable local services who become partners? Then, there needs to be an understanding of how staff effectively interact with clients. For instance, they're in constant contact with clients, monitoring their intentions and attendance at meetings. They conduct medical and counseling visits, assist in job hunting activity, and monitor progress on the job. They also note whether clients are keeping away from old friends who contributed to their undoing in the first place. This is just to mention a fraction of the measures staff take to keep a client on track.

Much of the JSC's success is based on the nuance of the team's behavior and social interaction with a client. A practitioner also needs to have a concise worm's eye perspective, if not a contact at the JSC, to fully understand details of the monthly staffing meetings. Staffers drug check clients on the spot to ensure sobriety, monitor progress on all aspects of the reintegration effort, make new contacts to services, and check old ones for viability. During these meetings, staff award success with more services while a probation and a parole officer stand by ready to revoke clients if they backslide or fail a drug test.

Most important, JSC staff help their clients learn to trust and to develop hope then confidence that there's a path back to respect because many before them made it.

A basic misunderstanding of the problem of reentry is that it's largely concerned with parolees from prison. However, those on probation who have not yet been incarcerated are much more at risk for incarceration as they are more closely supervised, and their freedom can be revoked for nearly any reason and sometimes at the whim of probation officers, who have various philosophies and standards for revocation. The resolution of this misunderstood problem is one of the most urgent concerns of local government, because a former offender left to his or her own resources and devices will likely commit more crimes. The problem seems to defy resolution.

Resolution comes by understanding what can be done in small chunks and as a process via a network of local services, some of which may be designed and started specifically for the needs of the municipality. To try to solve this large undertaking any other way is to court failure. Post-release services delivery for parolees or probationers is just too big to grasp in its totality. Post-release after sentence completion programming must be constructed as only one part of an overall strategy to prevent crime, intervene in the crime and criminal cycle, and ultimately punish criminals or rehabilitate them to respectability and get them back home. No one program can have the desired effect of improving community well-being for the long haul. Thus, any neighborhood, community, or municipality needs to think about the basics of building problem solving and business capacity under their services in general if they are to evolve and survive for as long as ex-offenders will be returning home.

Describing the Model of Capacity Building for Local Post-Release Programs

The discussion thus far has been about the reasoning and justification for a community to take on the considerable commitment to help people coming from incarceration to transition back into the community. Not only is it the right thing to do, but it also saves considerable public resources and tax dollars. Now let's take transition from theory to practice.

To-do lists are not capacity building. Capacity Building focuses on institutional systems, social capital, networks of partners, building relationships, and proving processes aimed at goal accomplishment. It's about sustainability, not service lists. All these and more must come together to solve a social need or community dysfunction. None of the literature focuses on true capacity building, but that's the one thing that can be most helpful in establishing a strategy to transition ex-offenders.

> This model is an affirmation that beginning a project as massive as providing post-release services *can* be done because it *is* being done.

Note, however, that this model of adult reentry aftercare is largely a point of departure. It's impossible to capture every step, every nuance, every decision program staff have made that resulted in their evolving success. No document will ever capture the details of years of daily decisions and work. Therefore, this model is an affirmation that beginning a project as massive as providing post-release services *can* be done because it *is* being done by a relatively few far-sighted local pioneers. One of the rewarding parts of starting a post-release program is that staff will be building on what has been done before them and continue that building for those who will continue the work. While this undertaking has a beginning but no end, as the problem is perpetual, in the final analysis, the work is rewarding.

A Change of View

Again, practitioners generally know what they need to do; they just need to know how to go about it. Building service delivery capacity suggests a completely different and necessary view of resolving the volume and complex problems of returning ex-prisoners. The focus must change:

- *From prescriptive to the descriptive* – We need to stop merely telling practitioners what they should do, perhaps because an idea has worked elsewhere or shows some evidence of positive result under certain circumstances. Instead, they need detailed descriptions of how an idea or suggestion is made to work and become productive as quickly, effectively, and efficiently as possible.

- *From evidence to community betterment* – Evidence that a concept or even a suggested task works is only a start and may be headed down the wrong path, which can lead to unsatisfying or unintended results. Building capacity and the evidence of good effects have to result in community betterment. In the case of post-release aftercare services, that betterment is first reducing recidivism then transitioning a formerly incarcerated person out of the crime cycle into the community as a contributing citizen.

- *From personalities to process* – When ideas are prescriptive, their implementation tends to focus on the personalities involved, who tend to jockey for position and influence. Process tends to take personalities out of the work of realizing an idea. The focus of a proper capacity building process is less about who each leader or practitioner is, which is *de*structive, and more of how stakeholders function *together,* which is quite *con*structive.

- *From complex to simple* – Sweeping statements of what to do give way to simple sequences of action items with propositions of who should best do them and how they should make it happen. Yes, a proper vision is necessary, but it must lead to practical and productive action. Too many projects begin as a grand adventure and simply peter out when the far-ranging, long-term work of it must be done.

- *From pundit to practitioner* – Ultimately, project success rests with the local stakeholder. It stands to reason that how to provide post-release services should be advised by fellow stakeholders with an appreciation for the local dynamic. Experts should be consulted, but realistically so. Their advice is good only if it enables the practitioner to see the project through.

- *From pronouncements to proven practices* – Most suggestions for delivering a service tend to be idealistic statements, whereas it is much more productive to learn proven practices from practitioners. As currently characterized, the job of reentry focuses on general and largely dissociated or independent categories of services such as education, job skills, housing, and medical and psychological treatment. Much, much more needs to be done to have these services work as one seamless stream of aftercare tailored to each recipient. The particular definition of the face-to-face conduct of the service will be as unique as the township that delivers it.

The real change of view is from short-term toil and frustration to a far-reaching focus offering the sense that hard work will ultimately be rewarded. Staff at the Durham, for example, are continually improving processes, procedures, and services because they can see ex-offenders succeed, if not prosper, in their homes and neighborhoods. Evidence of this long-term mentality is seen in low turnover in a field normally wracked with people coming and going.

Another fact of a successful local aftercare program that's motivational is that everything must be practical. This results in staff being able to see the effects of their work.

Practicality Matters

The literature and field investigations at successful sites suggest the necessity of a practical guide, an outline describing the basics of how to design the delivery systems of post-release services. Practicality suggests the characteristics of this guide:

- *User friendly* – The goal should be to present ideas relatively simply and as easily understood as possible so project staff can grasp the essence and put the suggestions to work. For example, it isn't enough to suggest the need for an employment skills class. Ideally, that idea needs to be accompanied by a profile of the individual most likely to succeed, collateral support needed, a proven curriculum, how to get the individual to and through the training, and how to follow up. Descriptions should lead practitioners in the correct direction to figure out what's best for their particular situation.

- *Proven* – While scientific evidence of a practice is helpful, the best proof of an idea is that it works as determined by the people making it work. So, suggestions should have stood the test of application at a successful site and preferably have the endorsement of experienced program staff. This, of course, is quite different from maintaining the fidelity of a scientifically proven, evidence-based practice such as a therapeutic modality, i.e., conducting it as it was designed.

- *Long term* – The idea must have staying power. The problem of the formerly incarcerated returning to the community will continue with the existence of crime and consequences. The answers to that circumstance must be as durable as the need.

- *Measurable* – It's better if an idea has a quantitative aspect. That is, it has to scientifically prove itself to help accomplish overall programmatic goals, although, that isn't necessary in every context. It's unrealistic to assume every practice will have a scientific investigation to prove its worth. A good idea should not be held up for lack of a research scientist, math, and statistics, but the idea must be deemed sound by a consensus of practitioners.

- *Locally applicable* – Many ideas are top down and not grounded in the worm's eye view of service delivery. However, ideas, no matter where they come from, must work locally from site to site.

- *Transferable* – Because an idea works in one town is no guarantee it will work in another. Ideas in this guide should have some grounding in various communities so the nuances of implementation can be tested and captured in various environments.

- *Dynamic* – If there's any constant with tackling a community service need, especially a social issue, it is change. Therefore, ideas should stand the further test of being modifiable as the realities of service provision undergo inevitable adaptation.

- *Organic* – Ideas must fit neatly into the greater whole so hopefully that whole is greater than the sum of its parts. Thus, reentry aftercare services need to nestle into the array of services any municipality offers. This is to avoid the tendency to be or treat a service as a silo, insulated from true collaboration as a partner in reentry. This is an important point because post-release services will have to compete for limited dollars, most of which must go to structural needs such as community safety and security and education.

Making an idea practical and functioning well is true capacity building and the focus of this book—work that's basic to 21st-century governance.

A Focus on Process

The next aspect of this capacity building guide focuses on process—goal-oriented, effective, efficient processes to create a program that lasts. This is another great missing piece in the literature, which relates what works in theory and in fragments. That process or path must pull all the pieces together to realize stated goals. It must do two essential things:

- *Get beyond implementation.* – The model must resolve the considerable obstacles of implementation. In the public sector, these obstacles prevent good ideas from launching or stop them in infancy. This is to the detriment of not only the project in question but other projects struggling for a beginning. Let's face it; many critics look for a failure to justify denying further service adventures.

- *Lead to permanency.* – The model has to guide the service idea from concept to a state of self-renewal. Staying power must be an overriding daily concern, and it begins with the first meeting to decide if the project will be undertaken. Anything done has to be designed, enacted, and managed to last as long as the problem it answers endures.

The guide presented here for post-release services will answer all these concerns. It's based on models of how practitioners of successful local sites plan, operate, and stabilize their efforts to transition the formerly incarcerated back home.

This Study and the Subject Models

It's advisable to consider adult reentry as part of a comprehensive strategy. Much can and must be done to prevent individuals from becoming involved in the criminal justice system and public services. People can and want to be self-sufficient.

Promisingly, the literature yields a rich well of programming from which to define the practicalities of building a post-release program. We know what works and have examples of how they do it. What remains is to understand a viable reentry strategy . . . then do it. That is, we can move from the what and the why to the action of how. When we organize the how, people can do successful programming, change lives, and improve their communities. It's about:

Building permanent solutions to permanent problems.

This book presents a qualitative study to determine how successful post-release long-term aftercare programs deliver their services. I chose the study sites for convenience and proximity from 24 sites suggested by state reentry specialists at the North Carolina Governor's Crime Commission. I used a range of criteria for site selection. First and most important, they had to be self-renewing and socially transformative. That is, they had to be permanent, with the ability to generate reliable operational resources. Plus, they had to make measurable improvements, first in the clients, then in the community. They needed to be mature and had to have gone through the process of planning, operating, and stabilizing their programs to self-sufficiency. A bonus in that respect was that each site continues to expand according to its ability to do so and the need. Closing the service-to-needs gap is important. Lasting to do so is a primary concern for these programs. Only with permanency can the program begin to close the service-to-needs gap.

This book presents a qualitative study to determine how successful post-release long-term aftercare programs deliver their services.

Geographically, the sites are diverse. They are in the third, fifth, and eighth most populous cities in North Carolina, which represent about six percent of North Carolina's population. The professionals at the sites were quite willing to cooperate on extensive interviews with staff, board, and community members and shared how they worked. Interviewees were selected by being key staff or by having key insight or knowledge about the program in question. Two dozen people participated in nearly 40 sessions. Interviews were conducted with an extensive questionnaire. The questions covered the process of building and permanently establishing a new local service idea. The sites had to be focused on transitional services and model various ways of delivering post-release services (day and residential) that a municipality might wish to replicate or use to improve an existing program. Collectively, the sites represent many decades of program experience successfully effecting reintegration and measurably improving their communities.

Ideally, a site also had to have maturity:

- *Operational systems* – Their operational systems had to have sophistication demonstrated by having standard, established methods of running the business of providing services. For example, a mature site would most likely have late-version technology (hardware and software), such as a current financial management package.

- *Board members* – The board members had to be well established and understand their role in constructing and leading the effort. That is, they had to be actively working on program governance and expansion.

- *Leadership and staff* – Leadership and staff had to have a degree of sophistication about being able to assess capacity to determine the services-to-need gap, analyze impact, and evaluate processes. Preferably, site staff would be skilled in making the case to local budgetary officials and stakeholders for resources, especially monetary justification of the program.

- *Vision and mission* – Vision and mission had to be clearly stated, measurable, and used in daily operations. Also, staff had to have internalized their vision and mission. After that, it was preferred that they were well trained and educated initially and were getting regular technical and professional development.

Introducing Adult Reentry Post-Release Services | 35

- *Range of services* – The programs had to provide a range of services that were individually and collectively effective in serving the post-incarceration population.

Longevity reasonably assured a site had wrestled with and solved the problems of implementation, worked out the processes of daily operation, and were focused on expansion or were part of a wider expansion effort.

The youngest site was LINC, which had been in business for a decade at the time of this writing, and the oldest site was DISMAS, which was following a model started in 1964. The literature and calls to other sites served to round out the process of idea development as many experiments in post-release transitional services have *gotten it right*.

Let's take a closer look at our four model sites.

Durham County Justice Services Center (JSC), which previous to July 1, 2023, was the Durham County Criminal Justice Resource Center (CJRC)

The JSC in Durham, North Carolina, is an excellent and long-standing example of a nonresidential day program. It has established extensive community partnerships, which has taken advantage of considerable untapped local resources. It's a significant example of dynamic networks designed nearly on the fly to address problems large and of the moment. The department's services focus on three goals:[34]

- *Successful transitions* – They deliver transitional services to former adult offenders and at-risk, court-involved youth.

- *Improved public safety* – They focus on post-release transitional services which reduce recidivism and increase community safety and security.

- *Information sharing* – They have developed a simple, yet sophisticated, real-time database using off-the-shelf software, which is shared with stakeholders, especially court officials.

The most critical service needs of clients are for housing assistance, substance abuse treatment, and employment services—all provided by the 's connections to community resources. The Community-Based Corrections program served 1,964 clients from 2007 to 2010, and 75 percent of program graduates had no arrests in the year following case closure.[35]

Leading Into New Communities, LINC

LINC, Inc. in Wilmington, North Carolina, began as a small residential model that demonstrated how a 12-bed facility (on a shoestring) fit into a lower socioeconomic neighborhood where it thrived and was most needed. Modest, yes. Successful, to be sure.[36] It's grown into a self-supporting residential community with a much larger facility for men and women. In addition, LINC provides direct services and is networked extensively to community resources for essential transitional services. This allows staff to serve a large clientele base consisting of both adults and juveniles. Their therapeutic community offers connections to:

- housing,
- job skills and jobs,
- education such as GED and literacy,
- intervention services to reduce criminal behavior,
- substance abuse treatment, and
- mental and medical health services.

LINC staff report, "We served 578 individuals from 2002 to 2009, and of that number, only 55 went back to prison. Over the last three years, since 2012, we served 150 individuals and out of that number, seven went back to prison." Based on that success, LINC opened a state-of-the-art 40-bed full-service facility for men and women, summer of 2012.

Triangle Residential Options for Substance Abusers (TROSA)

TROSA began as the idea of one man who came to Durham, North Carolina, from San Francisco in the early 1990s with about $17,000, a credit card, an idea, and an indominable will. You should see it today! Now no one can say, "It can't be done."

A full-service residential program, TROSA is completely self-renewing due to its innovative income-generating enterprises, which teach career and life skills such as communication and leadership.[37] Residents learn responsibility via TROSA's therapeutic environment and motto of self-help and empowerment: *Each one teach one*. Staff understand that the transition from substance abuse and the criminal justice system to home in the community takes years. Therefore, their key programming extends from immediate needs through a lengthy recovery and aftercare process. TROSA works with

> **Key programming extends from immediate needs through a lengthy recovery and aftercare process.**

the most difficult clients, drug dependent with systemic involvement, usually the criminal justice system. Their clients are returned to sobriety, dignity, and a place in community. Their services are targeted yet comprehensive:

- *Vocational training* – Enterprises such as a moving company, a picture framing business, and contract labor, teach self-reliance and build career potential, while substance abuse is conquered. These businesses and in-kind donations provide most of the money to run the program at a profit, which is all returned to housing and treating more clients.
- *Education* – First, clients are offered a GED program, then the possibility of college, for which TROSA pays tuition and fees. They also have computer and continuing education classes.
- *Peer counseling/mentoring* – The therapeutic community model is based on peer-based counseling by upper classmen and women and professional services. This fits with their motto: *Each one teach one.* It's a brilliant concept—rebuilding lives with camaraderie.
- *Aftercare* – Recovery is not complete until and unless a resident assumes a place at home in the community, so TROSA provides housing, transportation, and support in the final stage of going home permanently.
- *Onsite medical clinic* – A clinic is available for medical care at no charge to residents. In fact, all services are free to residents. Note when TROSA states it's self-sustaining, it means for everything it does and offers.

This model has stable operating cash flows, a capacity-based process model for replication, and a program for leadership succession. This succession plan is even more remarkable as it's based on the *process* of replication, which describes not merely what to do but *how* to do it. It's also a notable example of social entrepreneurship, which supports a proven therapeutic community based on evidence-based practices. Again, they are mustered in a targeted matrix of services focused on the TROSA vision/mission.

TROSA was established in 1994 by Kevin McDonald with a credit card and little more. At the time of this study, he managed a $3 million annual operating budget. The program originally served nine former inmates. At the time of this study, it served close to 500, and it grew from there, expanding to a nearby city! This took 30 years.

TROSA works so well that judges sentence offenders to TROSA at *no* public cost. I must admit, my visits to TROSA were most uplifting.

Dismas Charities Inc.
Dismas Charities Inc., which began in 1964, is a unique alternative to the criminal justice system.[38] *Healing the Human Spirit* is their philosophy for both nonresidential and residential treatment and supervision. It offers a proven mix of cost-effective reintegration programming that involves:

- community services,
- local employers, and a
- therapeutic environment.

A premature focus on results distracts resources from systemic transformation and positive change in the community.

Dismas is a successful collaboration with the Federal Bureau of Prisons for community-based corrections. It demonstrates that a private not-for-profit can successfully partner with a governmental agency, where the work of the prisons to complete their reentry efforts is done by Dismas at remarkable savings in tax dollars. This demonstrates the efficiency and effectiveness of public/private partnerships.

Crucibles for Transformation
Each of these sites is a thriving crucible for transforming lives. They each uniquely attack and solve the same overarching obstacles. They've reached the point of stabilization with calculated expansion in mind.

For example, at the time of this writing, LINC was remodeling an old, condemned jail into a modern, full-service, 40-bed resident facility for men and women. It subsequently had its grand opening during the summer of 2012. By the way, they're renting the abandoned jail facility from the local municipality for *$1 a year for 40 years!* All the renovations and retrofitting will be paid for by creative financing and enterprises. The startup grant of nearly $500,000 is forgivable after the successful renovation. And LINC leaders are considering social enterprises, including sustainable aqua and agriculture. The $900,000 mortgage is scheduled to be repaid in *five* years. Work like this exemplifies extraordinary resourcefulness.

Each site has harnessed social capital in highly creative ways. Most of all, residents teach and mentor fellow residents through the life-changing work of recovery and redemption via a job with a living wage and, most important, a place at the home kitchen table.

Irrepressible Staff

The staff and consequently the residents at these sites hold a crystal-clear vision and a universal belief that it *will* work. Problems turn into opportunities. Key people understand it's all about relationships above, below, and laterally. Their most important partners are those they serve.

Gone is the stagnation of top-down, often disconnected, authoritarian oversight, although they may experience it from their external partners. The environment of openness creates leadership that's participatory and collaborative. However, staff in these programs realize it takes sternness from the program to instill rigor in a resident changing a life of many bad decisions.

While everyday life at these sites is the ultimate challenge for residents, it's quite wholesome and exudes the energy of mutual respect. This generates a *can do, no obstacles* energy in which residents know they are worthy and capable, a sense they may have never known.

Use and Multiplication of Resources

Resources from the inception of each of these programs were developed as dependable streams with a minimum of dependency on soft grant money. Leaders and staff can project budgets. Every dollar is treated as the last dollar and targeted to the purpose at hand. Little or nothing goes to waste. Cast-off or donated furniture from TROSA's moving company goes to furnishing residents' housing. In-kind donations of unused hard goods are repurposed or sold through the secondhand store. The cafeteria, which serves three ample meals a day, is supplied with good food from local restaurants and food supply outlets that would have otherwise discarded it. Part of the fiber of everything they do is building goodwill, which is palpable. People are always doing for each other.

In the process, otherwise "throwaway" citizens are returned home to the community, ready and equipped to make a new start, which sets an example for their families and children.

Strategic Planning

Staff evaluate evidence-based practices to adopt and painstakingly test them for effectiveness in the task of transition, their business sense, and their cost effectiveness. Business plans for an enterprise idea at TROSA are state of the art because they're accomplished by graduate students and faculty at Duke University's business school. This happenstance was a demonstration of the program's foresight, sophistication, and growth.

> These programs show how to develop a local service idea that can be a model for just about any other good service idea.

Another strategy regards the aspect of place. Each one of these aftercare sites is purposefully located in the neighborhood that struggles the most with people released from corrections, which is *the* way to address a local social need. It's as if staff *live* the problem at hand. It's about citizens accepting responsibility and being accountable to their fellow neighbors for addressing a common problem. It's "all for one and one for all." While the ultimate success of the returnee rests with him or her, the community produced these unfortunates, thus the community must bear a good bit of the responsibility to help them reach their potential. When it works out, everybody wins.

What Do These Models Exemplify?

Beyond being highly effective at the business of transitioning former inmates, these programs are examples of how to do effective services delivery with longevity in mind. They demonstrate how to spend wisely, how to develop funding, and how to build permanent infrastructure to continue services. Overall, these programs show how to develop a local service idea that can be a model for just about any other good service idea.

A Reform Movement and 21st-Century Governance

The sites studied for this capacity-building model are part of the movement to reform how agency/institutional public local services are delivered. Essentially, institutional reentry only starts what aftercare must finish in the communities involved. The sites that served as examples for this composite model for aftercare have several distinctive building blocks of 21st-century governance. For example, the service idea is comprised largely of local services, resources, and talent aimed at the problem at hand. They form an assembly in which the whole is greater than the sum of its parts.

Considering govern*ance,* what is old is now very new. The most successful innovators understand that top-down govern*ment* does not work to fulfill the potential. People don't like being told what to do by someone who doesn't "get them" or their community. Top-down ideas are arguably crippled or die a slow death as locals decide what and how much to do. People work best when they're part of the solution. Ideas, processes, and procedures flow in a circular, cyclical fashion. Yes, good programming can begin top down. However, it's best when collectively directed—digested at the foot-soldier level, worked out, and returned to the top enriched by hands-on experience and a street-level view.

> **People work best when they're part of the solution.**

The sites discussed here exemplify forward-thinking 21st-century *governance*:

- They are *decentralized, with bottom-up-decision making* – Participation matters. Each understood and practiced decision making that was flat and *decentralized*. This gave participants autonomy and ownership of their part of the task at hand and thus the vision. It also made necessary control, that is monitoring of the work, much easier and better because much of what is done is self- or communally governed. People are given responsibility, and they honor that privilege.

- They focus on *matrix solutions*. Each has a unique mix of stakeholders assembled according to the problem definition, local capacity to deliver services, and program needs.

- They've built a *continuum of services* across agencies. They recognize that transitioning is a long-term process. It requires a series of stakeholders—public, private, and nonprofit—to help a resident make serious lifestyle changes and ultimately succeed at reintegration into the community.

- They *multiply local resources*. A better allocation of local disparate resources results when they're focused on a single goal. The whole does indeed become greater than the sum of the parts. For example, TROSA's first-class moving enterprise gets cast-off furniture, which is refurbished and sold at the end of the year. This event, rather extravaganza, attracts buyers from the entire southeast coast! TROSA gets donations from bed linens to biscuits. And on it goes.

- They achieve significant *cost savings*. Matrix solutions are done with efficiency and effectiveness and notable cost savings. Their largest cost saving results from keeping people out of the criminal justice system. Many graduates of these programs not only renounce crime but resolve substance abuse and earn gainful employment in a self-supporting career.

- The programs exemplify how to build an idea into a *self-renewing entity*.

    o Leadership is *task- and process-oriented*. Senior staff and board members are selected for long-term work and individual experience and talents.

    o *Scope is limited and realistic.* Each site began serving only a few clients. Each grew incrementally and only when it was feasible to add additional clients.

    o *Service capacities are fully understood.* They understand the limits of what the community can deliver and work within those parameters.

    o *These programs are data based.* Program practitioners have a sophisticated grasp of measurement. Their impact and process data are self-generated. They use real-time data for decision-making nearly minute by minute.

    o *Resources are multi-sourced.* Resources are developed first by making friends based on credibility. Program staff deliver what they promise. Money is developed as reliable, permanent funding streams rather than as soft (e.g., grant) dollars.

    o Selected services are *performance-oriented* and contribute to overall goal accomplishment. Each service in the array of offerings needs to measurably contribute to the project purpose or it's cancelled if it can't be modified to provide necessary services.

    o Staff form a team of *goal-oriented professionals* in a "family" atmosphere. A real sense of camaraderie comes with a tough job well done. Staff are continuously challenged and afforded opportunities for growth through training, education, and professional development. Yes, the work is grueling, challenging, and underpaid, but they are largely happy doing it, which is a testament to finding reward in succeeding where others fail.

If there's a word to capture the work of these exemplary sites, it's *practical*. They do *less,* not more, no matter the temptation to assume more responsibilities, perhaps foolishly. Quality, performance, and staying power matter. They realize this work is vital and can be overwhelming in its intention and scope, or worse yet, scope creep, so they work on only what can be done well. Each site has variations on the theme of *one at a time*.

> **Successful practitioners send the message that to move reentry forward, we must call it what it really is**—*post-release long-term aftercare services.*

These programs provide us with superior examples for how to successfully confront a problem that affects every community in the country—people returning from incarceration or under court supervision. Many have drug problems and mental health issues. Yet, these people find resurrection in these programs.

The reentry numbers will only increase as corrections budgets are slashed and the courts reduce prison populations. The system will have to turn to the local community to transition people who run afoul of the law or who need help battling substance abuse and mental/health problems. More communities can and should emulate the work highlighted by these models. Staff at these sites have solved the problems of implementation that plague all public/private collaborations. So many great program ideas flag because stakeholders don't understand how to plan for stability. Now they have a model to do so.

The sites highlighted herein operate efficiently and effectively. They are stable, growing, and they significantly better the community. Stakeholders understand that the work is not only about reentry. It's about delivering a networked continuum of services to assist the formerly incarcerated in breaking the cycle of reincarceration. The responsibility for successfully reintegrating former inmates lies with the community, which has the problem and holds the solutions. The emphasis is on post-release aftercare. Successful practitioners send the message that to move reentry forward, we must call it what it really is—*post-release long-term aftercare services.*

The Life Cycle Concept

After many discussions at many sites and attending conferences and classes on community building, an idea emerged to organize the process of building a local service program by describing and explaining the phases of its Life Cycle. Everything—everyone, every animal, every plant, every car, and so on—has a life cycle, and so does an idea for a local public service. Everyone understands a life cycle, and more importantly, can make it work and communicate it. The concept establishes critical functions and sequences that practitioners can follow as they progress in building the program from planning to permanency.

Basically, the process includes three phases, and each phase includes two stages:

- **Life Cyle Phase I – *Plan an Implement*.** Of all functions, planning is the most important overall task. Yet it's where most public projects fail.

- **Life Cyle Phase II – *Operate and Stabilize*.** This is where staff figure out how aftercare works in *their* municipality. *All* are starkly different—from the people to the politics to the way things get done. But when a core of motivated people with a good idea focuses on making it happen, it does.

- **Life Cyle Phase III – *Sustain and Expand*.** This stage is the goal. It's when your idea becomes permanent and can begin to close the service-to-needs gap. In the case of reentry aftercare, this gap can seem like the Grand Canyon.

The Life Cycle structure of Capacity Building provides a logical way to think about and organize the entire process for delivering post-release transitional services. Not only does it offer a blueprint for starting a program, but it's a way for practitioners of a current program to organize their thinking as they grow their idea. Each phase of the life cycle illuminates key features and their subsequent best effective practices and how to properly conduct each one. The building blocks of an idea became practical, proven, and possible by any group of likeminded local citizens in any municipality.

How to Get the Most Out of This Book–A Checklist

Now you have an introduction to the work of post-release aftercare and good models that prove it can be done. Next, as a preview, please peruse the following checklist. It provides a "snapshot" of the how-to specifics of 21st-century Capacity Building organized by a program's life cycle. It lists what you need to take your idea to permanency. The rest of the book delves into the necessary details.

The checklist is just a few pages by design—simple but not simplistic. Following is your suggested procedure:

- Thoroughly review this action-oriented checklist—and think about it.
- Read the book, take notes—and think about it.
- Refer to sections in the book as you develop your program—and *act* accordingly.

The checklist gives you the sequential process of developing your idea. Correct process is fundamental. It's a proven path to success.

The following table in Figure 1-A is repeated as Figure 1-B on pages 215-216.

Figure 1-A. Capacity Building Checklist for Reentry-Aftercare Practitioners – Phases I-III, with Key Action Items and Effective Practices
Phase I of the Project Life Cycle: Plan and Implement – *Design and implement essential local reentry-aftercare operations.*
1. Nurture and grow key leadership familiar with post-release aftercare services.
Establish a stable leadership body focused on capacity building and transitional services.
Train your leadership body for effectiveness and efficiency.
Establish a functional committee structure for relationship building, goal accomplishment, and longevity.
2. Integrate capacity assessment for reentry project capacity building.
Profile returnee risk and needs factors to determine your mix of services.
Catalog local resources according to returnee needs.
3. Determine project scope to focus on the essentials of transitional services.
Develop measurable mission and vision statements that focus on the needs of your target returnee.
4. Design the process evaluation and impact analysis to justify reentry services.
Decide on a few initial impact measures that define results and can be easily gathered, analyzed, and reported.
Establish a learning environment based on data to evaluate and improve the efficiency of processes.

Figure 1-A. Capacity Building Checklist for Reentry-Aftercare Practitioners – Phases I-III, with Key Action Items and Effective Practices
5. Nurture relationships for resources development.
Map your services to identify resource development opportunities
6. Develop performance-oriented service providers as part of the local reentry team.
Muster your local transitional services and agencies.
Develop a targeted post-release services center.
Begin residential programs based on sustainable enterprises.
7. Nurture reentry staff by a process of human capacity development.
Build an environment in which staff keep skills current and feel free to apply lessons learned.
Hire and develop staff for your unique returnee and community needs.
Phase II of the Project Life Cycle: Operate and Stabilize – *Establish your idea to expand.*
8. Operationalize your reentry-aftercare plan.
Leadership
Ensure that the executive director emphasizes building external relationships.
Have the board assume responsibility for organizing and training themselves for the progression of roles from planning to oversight and preparation for the future.
Capacity assessment
Continually assess your clientele—especially their risk factors—to monitor and adjust your services delivery and mix.
Scope
Use performance data to support experiential decisions on how much can be done effectively.
Process evaluation and impact analysis

Reflect on what the data are telling you and adjust resources allocation for effectiveness and keep processes flexible for efficiency.
Resources development
Give partners ideas about ways to collaborate.
Train and develop your board and staff to network for and maintain essential resources.
Services
Court and shape service partners early.
Key staff
Develop a common sense of purpose immediately.
Phase III of the Project Life Cycle: Sustain and Expand – *Realize Reentry-Aftercare.*
9. **Sustain operations.**
Reassess, reform, and refocus agency functions for scaling up and out.
Build the therapeutic community.
10. **Plot the long-range strategy and tactics for expansion to scale.**
Refocus leadership as an Expansion Task Force.
Have a project development strategy.
Consider the residential option with socially conscious enterprises.
Formalize resources development with a development officer.

Now you have an overview of how the elements of Capacity Building fit together. The bugs have been worked out. This checklist is your personal consultant at your side. The rest of the book explains each step in detail to answer your questions.

Herein is *wisdom* attained from experience. Visualize the **Life Cycle** of your idea. This makes your vision real.

Herein is *logic*. Build your idea with **Critical Actions**—what you need to do when you need to do it. See your project taking shape.

Herein is *purpose*. **Effective Practices** are just that—*effective.* You must act, but not haphazardly without a mission.

Process matters. Moving relentlessly, productively, with this proven process is the antidote for confusion and failure. Again, the process is *simple* but not simplistic; it's *suitable* for any good local service idea; and it's *sustainable* as it builds permanency.

One of the best aspects of Capacity Building is that you will mold your program to your local circumstances, politics, and people—and especially to your mix of staff and partners. It will be *yours.*

As you progress, add, edit, and refine your path. That way, you're building your implementation plan of action for your *next* idea—or to help *others* make a permanent difference as well.

The aim is to help create communities where people can live, work, play, be content, and *thrive.*

Capacity Building is 21st-century governance. *Lead it.*

Chapter 2

FACILITATING GOING HOME AGAIN

Chapter 2

FACILITATING GOING HOME AGAIN

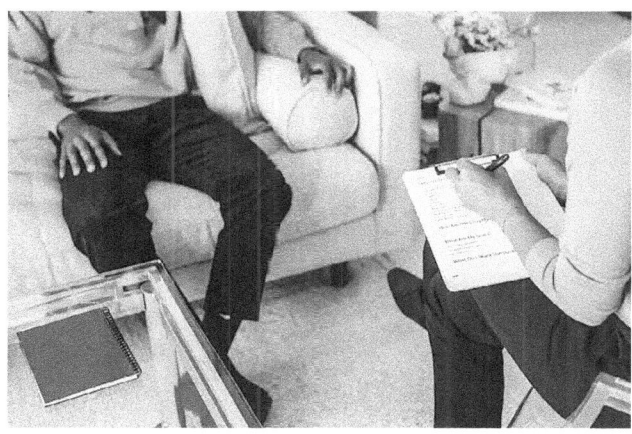

The demand for services that prisoner reentry generates overwhelms the meager resources that corrections administrators and local government leaders have available to them. Meanwhile, leaders [of churches and other faith-based institutions] want to meet this demand but are unsure how best to marshal the resources available to them.
– Chuck Colson, Founder, Prison Fellowship (VA)

This quote hits at the heart of the matter of returning home: Returnees cannot do it alone—and local agencies are struggling to provide their services. The services-to-needs gap is significant.

The greatest structural barrier to the success of services delivery is the disconnection between institutional efforts and the considerable but disparate and unorganized transitional resources in the community. This situation veritably shouts for a way to muster what is available, not to mention grow resources to make measurable improvements in the community.

"Reentry" while someone is serving a sentence does not connote the totality of post-release services. Yes, reentry does begin during incarceration. Still, the community is largely responsible for continuing an array of comprehensive post-release services exemplified by the model programs. Prison, for example, may sponsor education and training, counseling and rehabilitation, work-release programs, planning for release, and connection to community resources. Yes, these programs are good and necessary but post-released former inmates still flounder, as represented by their recidivism rates without these model programs. It remains to the community to complete the larger work of returning an inmate to the community—respectably, productively, with a seat at the family table.

> **We must have continuity between criminal justice reentry and community post-release services for reintegration to succeed.**

We must have continuity between criminal justice reentry and community post-release services for reintegration to succeed. The gap between what is offered and what is needed is cavernous. Thankfully, many examples demonstrate how to make the connection. In fact, the success of completing the cycle of crime, correction, rehabilitation, and return to the community rests on each municipality. Communities need to figure out how to combine public, private, and private nonprofit resources via matrices focused on post-release reentry.

Institutions and communities acting alone cannot address this permanent need. Together they can greatly improve prison overcrowding, overwhelmed courts, and recidivism. When our criminal justice agencies, communities, and local service providers work together, individuals released from jail or prison can become productive citizens. They can pursue careers, be good neighbors, and have a place at the family table, or at the head of it—home again.

Understanding the Task of Completing the Work of Reentry and Aftercare

Public institutions struggle with transitioning the formerly incarcerated. Correctional institutions' responsibility essentially ends when the former inmate leaves the door of prison or jail. Ultimately, our towns and counties have this duty to complete the transition. Regrettably, only a few of those needing transitional services are lucky enough to find them, and fewer still effect a successful transition to a career-worthy job. Significant reserves of local resources go untapped. The relatively small number of successful transitional programs provide the gloomy example of struggle with politics, bureaucracy, and funding for years and years. These obstructions can stifle others who have even the most ardent intentions to start a program.

The main problem is that these well-intentioned potential local champions lack an example process. They need to know how successful programs such as LINC and

TROSA have solved and are continuing to overcome these problems—while prospering in them as well. Local governments *are* beginning to construct the kind of transitional programs highlighted in this model. However, the true need will begin to be met when the public sector can partner with these programs. Public funds, ostensibly state and federal correction funds, need to be redirected to these well-working programs. This transfer can be done at a healthy return on investment as exemplified by our model programs.

The key to structuring your program and justifying support is a thorough understanding of the returning former inmate. "High incarceration and recidivism rates are related to broader social problems. . . . Jails often act as crisis intervention centers for people struggling with serious difficulties such as addiction (and) mental illness."[39] Substance addictions thrust people into criminality and make them squander what little they had. Worse yet, their family has probably given up also. They have no job and likely have never had steady employment because their skills are minimal or nonexistent. They're wholly dependent on charity, the public sector, or the street. Many such problems are exacerbated by having been incarcerated. The situation was best expressed by a resident of a local residential facility: "No home, no family, no job, no self-respect, no prospects, *and* I have a record. I had it all, and it all went up my nose."

Yet, a program such as TROSA in Durham, for example, serves hundreds of residents at a time. It has a 100 percent success rate placing people in jobs once they've successfully completed TROSA's *two-year* therapeutic program. The founder, Kevin McDonald, came to Durham in 1994 with a dream that he could make a difference in the lives of court-involved substance abusers—because he was one. He knew their monumental problems; he had lived them and knew there had to be a better way. There is, and he created it.

Now in only a little over 16 years at the time of this writing, TROSA is self-sustaining. It saves state and local governments millions of dollars by keeping people out of jail and prison. It does this by being an alternative to incarceration and reducing resident's recidivism to nearly zero! Amazingly, *judges* sentence people to TROSA not because it doesn't cost public funds but because it works better than the alternatives.

TROSA, may we say, is not "hug a thug." It can't be. It's as tough as the residents. At any time, a resident can self-eliminate just by sitting in a certain chair in the dining hall. Some do, as they prefer prison to the rigors of TROSA. Those who stick it out, however, provide the incalculable benefit to the community of a gainfully employed good neighbor. How did one man help so many realize their potential?

Getting a successful start is always most baffling; there are volumes of information and nearly uncountable issues with which to wrestle. Certainly, everyone has an opinion on what you should do. Whom do you turn to for advice that works? Which comes first? What is most productive? And what is just a waste of time? The idea is to avoid the failure so many projects soon meet.[40]

Even before committing to the task, it's necessary to think about a few smart things to do early on, for example:

- *Engage a few key people.* – Talk to people, local and otherwise, who are successfully transitioning the formerly incarcerated or have a vested interest in not seeing them recidivate. Your leadership—key staff and board of directors—will emerge from this. Every successful practitioner in this area said that getting buy-in and practical support must be won from the very beginning, nearly to the exclusion of doing much else.

- *Begin developing relationships immediately.* – Every successful person in this field said their success is rooted in making friends *every day*. It can be said that without the community, your efforts will fail, because it's the community that's ultimately responsible for its citizens. Promote your successes as soon as they can be measured. Make sure your measures are meaningful to your partners and friends. Who are they? Just about everyone. There's nothing like being a mainstay at the local chamber of commerce.

- *Inventory existing services*. – Know what you and your community can deliver to narrow the scope of what you do. The corollary of this is not to bite off more than you can not only chew, but *swallow*. Success is one client at a time. Start small to be able to control what can, at times, spin out of control due to unforeseen factors such as budgets that are summarily slashed.

- *Focus on what you can do.* – The problem of delivering post-release services in the volume needed to make a difference in community well-being is more than daunting. Pick a doable piece of the aftercare portfolio of services. The LINC founder in Wilmington, North Carolina, for example, began by assisting other community residential facilities, where he could talk to walk-ins to learn the business. He learned by doing.

- *Be aware of major obstacles and anticipate their answers.* – Actually, obstacles to transition and transitional services are the same. Primarily, they are problems involved in attaining/providing housing and medical and mental health services, learning/ teaching employment skills, and eventually securing/

> **Your program will evolve in direct proportion to its involvement of your residents.**

developing a permanent job with a living wage. All this is encompassed by independence and the most sought-after goal, self-respect, at home and in the community.

- *Treat everything as an opportunity.* – Nearly every community has difficulty, even tragedy, involving their post-release population. A big part of your success will be changing the mindset that "criminals don't deserve special attention" to one where the attitude is "some people make mistakes and need a chance at setting things right." Be ready to demonstrate that helping this population makes sense and is marvelously cost effective.

- *Focus on process.* – While services are important, the processes used to deliver them are more important. Services are what you do. Processes are how you do the work.

- *Involve your returnees, your clients, from the beginning.* – Only people needing and availing themselves of transitional services truly understand what works. Your program will evolve in direct proportion to its involvement of your residents. The more successful your residents are, the more successful your program will be. Remember, your clients *want* to turn their lives around. Furthermore, they see senior residents "making it"—and they want that.

Senior staff at TROSA while reflecting about what they would have done differently at the very beginning offer a few suggestions.

- *Develop staff.* – The criticality of having qualified, trained, and *motivated* staff was universally observed. As soon as you can, build staff to strengths, in quality and quantity.

- *Do more fundraising early.* – Fast forward to how these exemplary sites after years of working on development strategies have an array of funding streams. Begin to work on these strategies from the beginning. Even a bake sale done over time develops a reliable source of money in an endeavor where every dollar is well employed and earning impressive interest.

- *Get buy-in.* – This work cannot be done without public support. Get out and tell your story immediately. Also, work on getting support from all sectors—the public, private donors, private nonprofits, business, and government. These programs, especially TROSA, are not directly publicly funded. Yet these programs partner with public agencies as part of their defined services and available resources that augment reentry, if only because it alleviates some duplication of offerings. The job done by these nonprofit reentry organizations frees agency resources and monies for their defined services.

- *Make believers of your clients* – Day and residential clients must believe in the program and that they can succeed. Residents must become part of building a "community within a community."

- *Compose your leadership (board) for expansion* – The founders of these organizations highly recommend anticipating going to scale, as remote as it may seem during startup. This is vital to initial planning, which must anticipate stabilizing then sustaining your idea.

Concern for people being released from prison to succeed in community is a recent phenomenon. Not long ago, an inmate was escorted to the main gate with a set of clothes and a few dollars for a bus ride. While numerous successful transitional programs now offer examples, practitioners at new sites will have to do much experimentation. No site is the same. There's no guarantee a successful idea in one place will work in another. Yes, established sites can give you lessons they learned, but then you need to shape those lessons to your ground realities.

Luckily, every community can learn from the many prosperous transitional programs that have the job figured out. What are they doing right? How do they mitigate bad news? How do they avoid program-ending mistakes? What processes did they follow to remain standing after years of struggling to survive? It's all about process, which is the takeaway lesson from successful programs. Gleaned from extensive interviews at a half dozen sites, this process has certain characteristics.

The Model – Connecting Reentry to Post-Release Aftercare Services

The model is the story of what lies *beyond* the work of reentry, which is largely begun inside the prison or jail gate. The formerly incarcerated are best served if they own the work of stabilizing their lives after incarceration. However, ownership only *begins* the work of gaining health and earning respect. Most times, it's the work of years to regain a place in their homes and neighborhoods and in society. It involves much more than working toward dignity via a career.

> With relatively long-term residential programs, the chronic offender can make the necessary lifestyle changes to successfully reintegrate

These programs must reach a point where they are self-renewing. Then, the real work *begins* as they endeavor to be socially transformational and reach more and more of the target clients. This model attempts to relate how a few exemplary programs are doing both—becoming self-renewing *and* transformational.

Strategies to Muster and Multiply the Means for Successful Reentry

We'll consider several strategies the local community can take to build the infrastructure, the business, of reintegration. For example, we have day programs, reentry councils, and jail-to-community transition teams. However, the most difficult population that needs assistance is the chronic offender, who usually has a physical or mental handicap, a serious substance abuse problem, or all these complicating factors. While the process, critical milestones, and effective practices of this model can serve any idea, this model will dwell largely on residential programs for specific reasons.

With relatively long-term residential programs, the chronic offender can make the necessary lifestyle changes to successfully reintegrate. Many returnees, especially those with substance abuse problems, need a 24/7 regimen to make lifestyle changes. Otherwise, for most of these returnees, too many temptations and pressures lurk during a return to the community. Can you imagine them returning to the community that spawned their bad choices in the first place?

Also, an important reason to illuminate how successful residential programs came to be socially transformational is that any, yes any, community can put one together. Residential programs are a way to fill in the missing link in the success of a local effort. That missing link is a lack of continuity between what the courts and corrections are doing and what the community must do. The conduit from prison to community resources is not established the way it should and can be.

Our institutions are doing what they can, but they're limited because their major charge is legal, punitive, and regulatory. They are doing what they've been created to do—care, custody, and control.[41] In *Life after Lockup: Improving Reentry from Jail to the Community*, the authors describe what this book suggests, i.e., public agencies and communities co-investing in aftercare with matrix solutions:

At the same time, community-based agencies often do not consider the returning jail population to be a primary concern, and typically there is not a community-based organization with the responsibility, authority, or accountability to intervene after release. Community agencies will need to recognize the considerable overlap between the jail population and their human service caseloads in the community—and, therefore, that it is in their interest to work with these individuals, ideally before they are released from jail. Co-investing [with matrices of services targeted to the problem and need] in this population should, in fact, increase the odds that interventions will be more efficient and effective. For both jails and community-based agencies, a reentry focus will involve formalized working agreements, joint strategic planning and resource allocation, cross-agency leadership, and intra-organization culture change.[42]

Communities, while making progress with post-release programming, still struggle with "co-investing." Public services are structured to work within their defined "silos," or offerings. However, a collaborative effort is required. First, the work of a successful transition remains in rebuilding the individual for success in community *after* the formal debt has been repaid. The real repayment of personal debt begins when the people can call a former prisoner "neighbor." Second, this lack of continuity in services suffers from the misallocation of community resources that need to be recognized, organized, and focused on the task at hand. It's almost as if services are waiting to be asked to participate but don't know how to break the ice. For example, hundreds of people at great risk of recidivating can be reintroduced to the community by gathering or generating neighborhood resources for training, subsistence, jobs, counseling, treatment, and more as demonstrated by TROSA, LINC, Dismas Charities Inc., and The Durham County JSC.

Key Features of a Successful Adult Reentry Model

Let's begin with the end. In retrospect, what do experienced executive directors wish they would have done from the very start? What key actions do they recommend for success?

- *Plan.* – Invariably, the successful practitioners interviewed for this document said they had no plan when they began, and they could have been much further in their development if they had created one. Planning is the best insurance for successful implementation. An action plan focuses on the key issues that are the most difficult to put into action, such as how leadership leads and how a few nascent staff members are molded into a vision-inspired team, all moving in the same direction. The plan focuses on productive action by minimizing distractions. It's so easy to be busy about nothing and wonder why the idea is abandoned after "all that work." Having a path takes the negative behavioral/social side of people working together out of the equation. It results in less turfism, less jockeying for position, and less squabbling. Planning with a purpose mitigates the focus on personalities. Simply, a plan produces a greater sense of purpose.

Prospective partners, especially businesspeople, like a plan, especially when it materially, measurably improves their situation in the community and the community at large. Capacity building is just good business. Project practitioners and the board are less likely to take on too much when they understand that less is more and can make that approach stick. It's much more important to have little successes and *measure* them than to make blustery pronouncements. Resources are husbanded as precious assets that must show a "return on investment."

Staff may need to experiment with the exact mix of services needed to effect transition in each locale, for each client. However, an eventual plan of basic service categories, such as certain evidence-based therapies, housing, and subsistence, shapes how providers are developed. A plan even encourages creativity. Everyone knows the basics of what the plan demands, such as searching for in-kind donations, but how each demand is satisfied is left up to ingenuity.

So, the first thing you must do is write a detailed plan of implementation and operation w*ith the resolve* that transitional services *will work*. Do not skimp or cut corners with planning, practitioners admonish. As Ben Franklin warned, *"If you fail to plan, you plan to fail."*

- *Make friends.* – As previously mentioned, make friends early on. You'll need relationships that will sustain the work. Partnering with intention is the epitome of collaboration. It can be inter- and intra-agency, such as with nonprofits, police, trades training, and the like. Also look to your local municipality. How about churches? And set up communication channels with your partners. Frequently attend their major meetings to the extent that you (say, the executive director) are missed if you're absent.

- *Focus, focus, focus. Process matters.* – Vision, mission, beliefs, goals matter, providing you have a process to get there. Yet again, the message is that *process matters*. Most successful projects begin with a "wing and a prayer" and nevertheless manage to address critical issues. Having inspired leadership helps. In hindsight, practitioners bemoan what could have been with a little structure at the beginning of their journey.

- *Tailor services.* – Each client is an individual. You may have categories of services, but each person is best served as defined by the individual with their advocate. Such services can be getting a job or help with drug abuse, housing, and counseling. The goal is independence. Make sure the client is doing what it takes to get a life-sustaining job with dignity.

- *Become a good neighbor.* – Make sure the wider community knows what you are doing, how you are doing it, and how their support makes sense, usually in terms of business. Neighbors have surprising resources and ideas for support for those in transition.

Remember that community is a system—or can be. The forward movement of a township is in direct proportion to how they cooperate on a project and collaborate on the big ideas. Reentry is one of the most important. True collaboration enhances the success of reentry.

Yes, our model programs enjoy successes. That's one reason they willingly share their experiences—mainly about what not to do. At the root of their success is that they went about building capacity intuitively. They focused on the individual and building a holistic approach to addressing their needs. With this, the community is well served.

This model is focused on essentials; thus it hews to critical phases and features of capacity building argued previously. A proven path forward is the only bulwark against maddening bureaucracy, people issues, service ideas fizzling out, prejudices against such work, residents that recidivate in the worst ways, and a thousand other irritants. It focuses on the work that matters.

Let's look at what it takes to become a large-scale operation of transitional services.

Going to Scale

The next big challenge this model addresses is how to scale up. Consider the qualities of exemplary programs that have done so—LINC, TROSA, and Dismas Charities.

These programs are:

- *Socially transformative* – They are stable, self-renewing, and making measurable differences in community well-being. In other words, they are socially transforming their communities for the better.

- *Mature* – They are mature enough to warrant study. They've survived implementation and adjusted operations to the realities of the day, and they enjoy predictable streams of resources based on glowing respect from all corners.

- *Focused* – They have and continue to overcome project-ending obstacles such as lack of funding and lack of focus on well-defined principles and efficient, effective ways of doing work. They're doing the *right* work of aftercare the *right* way.

- *Respected* – They have wide respect in the community from elected and appointed officials, the public, private, and nonprofit sectors, staff, and the most important stakeholder, the resident-client.

- *Inspiring* – The models highlighted, usually the construct of one messianic leader, inspire real commitment. Everyone involved does more than they thought they could. They are as revolutionary as they are evolutionary.

- *Action oriented* – They get and practice the minute-to-minute necessary process of action-reflection-adjustment-action, from the top down, bottom up, and back again. It's participatory management and enlightened leadership.

- *Staffed by values brokers* – They're laboratories for local-level governance fashioned by value brokers of networked solutions to community dysfunction. These practitioners "sell" the value of their program to all their stakeholders, not the least of which are their neighbors, rather than trying to justify the cost of survival. In so many ways, they exemplify the modern social service enterprise.

- *21st-century governance* – These programs exemplify 21st-century services delivery. Primarily, they provide huge community betterment at no or little cost to the taxpayer, as in the case of TROSA.

They place themselves in our toughest neighborhoods because, as said by one key executive, "That's where the action is." They have grand goals and resolutely proceed to achieve them, though it will take years. Dynamism is evident in their organic nature, that is, they grow, morph, bend, twist and shape as needed. They target very limited resources to goal accomplishment and manage them to the penny—and every penny shows a profit.

> Hold that attitude that *success is the only option*. Success is far in the future, hard won, difficult to see entirely, *and* worth the struggle.

During operations, these programs continually court key stakeholders and develop staff comprehensively and closely. When TROSA residents, for example, learn the methods of reintegration, they become mentors to subsequent groups of residents. This fulfills the TROSA mantra: *Each one teach one.* Brilliant. What better way to become independent than to have the responsibility for another human being.

Staff are comprehensively groomed. They develop interpersonal skills and get professional development from on- and off-site workshops. Further formal education is encouraged, and training in technical skills is always in the works. Moreover, staff are cross-trained, as in LINC's case, to do the executive director's job! Staff development is up close and personal to the extent that they offer critique of one another on daily and personal experiences. LINC staff role play real situations of the moment to develop the skills to deal with a truly unique and demanding population.

All works well with these models, considering the significant path they chart, especially when they have respect for and from the community. When ample resources and support are dependable, they can begin to look at closing the services-to-needs gap. When they consider expansion, they do it in increments, small bites, to ensure success as much as possible. Any decision is the collective will. They do take risks, but nothing is left to chance if it can be anticipated. They know the value of considered action and don't fear taking a step forward, adjusting as circumstances dictate. While they give remarkable attention to detail, it's the correct detail, which focuses on the criticalities of taking their big idea to reality and importance.

Success Is the Only Option

Pause for a moment to consider wider, much wider implications. Success is vital, essential, far-reaching. Don't be timid in your reach for local ideas exemplified by reentry. Do be necessarily detailed and completely resolute to succeed. Hold that attitude that *success is the only option*. Success is far in the future, hard won, difficult to see entirely, *and* worth the struggle. Success is its own reward—but even one failure will *never* be forgotten. The implications are incalculably regrettable. Great ideas will remain stillborn—or worse yet, never even voiced in the face of the specter of failure. When something succeeds, others are inspired to try—again and again. The implications here are also incalculable, but in unimaginably bright ways.

Now, we're ready to consider a model you can use to build your own Reentry Aftercare program.

Reentry Aftercare – A Capacity Building Model and How to Use It

This model begins where the reentry programming of our courts and corrections systems ends. It extends beyond correction and reformation to transformation. The new Capacity Building model bridges the gap from incarceration to home by outlining how to build a successful business with transitional services. Nothing lasts if it's not on a permanent foundation. The model is also a compilation of the best ideas from the practitioners and professionals of successful programs of transitional services. It's targeted to the local decision maker or practitioner who needs to understand how to design a comprehensive effort and execute it for permanency.

> Few things are as motivating as having a home and a place at one's table.

Reentry is one of those municipal conundrums that will never be fully resolved. We'll always have people involved with the "system" who are ready to do what's necessary to return to productivity and respectability. Thus, we'll always need a community-wide capacity-built reentry strategy.

This guide first discusses the business supporting the services of successful rehabilitation. The ideas are gleaned from numerous interviews over several years at various sites. They're supported by direct and in-depth observation of residents making life changes via specific proven programming tailored to the needs of individual returnees. This model approach is meant to work in conjunction with myriad programs at the county and township level. All address the universal problem of what to do with the formerly incarcerated and/or those dependent on public services.

The model is summarized by a checklist of sequential actions, which are also explained in narrative form to facilitate necessary action. The checklist is in Chapter 1 of this book as a preview as well as toward the end on pages 215-216. Although the actions are presented successively, all the critical features discussed evolve nearly simultaneously; one grows with and from the others.

The model's primary use is a format for assembling the political will, resources, and existing services to effect the successful transition of clients from incarceration to civil productivity. Few things are as motivating as having a home and a place at one's table. Residents in these programs want to succeed, and they work at it.

Your reentry effort will be different from the model, as it will be *your* interpretation dictated by your ground realities. Therein lies another great advantage of Capacity Building and this implementation plan. It's fungible. Learn from the collective wisdom it charts. Take notes and make the model yours—now and for future capacity-built service ideas.

If you're in a position of leadership, use this guide to understand how your roles will change with the maturity of your program. Realize that your best contributions will come with longevity and the consistent application of your resources and talents. See how relationships are the foundation of *each* criticality.

The relationships you build in your community are vital to establishing your ideas. Your relationship with your clients determines how well you build services for them. Your relationship with your staff determines client progress and success. Your relationship with your matrix partners and friends matter! They are all "salesmen and women" for the collective effort. How well you do with people in general is paramount. And it is satisfying to make and keep new friends.

Approach what you build with an eye to permanency. Yes, it is rewarding to return a resident to full reintegration with home and hearth. But first your program must endure. It doesn't matter how many effective practices you try if your program fails. Approach work in the small bites suggested in the model. Iteration—incremental movement—works best. That's why effective practices are highlighted. Rewrite them for your own purposes. They can be assignments, but be sure that what you're doing contributes efficiently and effectively to your vision and mission. And don't fear discarding an idea when it appears not to work. In fact, the quicker the better. The worst thing you can do is become enamored with something that's not profitable in hard dollars, return on investment to the community. Gone are the days when public dollars can be spent on the program du jour to get the dollars for a quick fix to a tough problem. Calculate what it takes to get a precious, hard-won tax dollar in your hand.

Progress is based on the process of a thousand small things done right, not on the big idea. The people behind an idea are what matter. This is another way of saying that attention to detail matters. How efficiently and effectively you operate from day to day is huge. Start from day one to measure things. If anything, decide on one measure of effectiveness then make that number a saleable argument to your business partners. It's all about the return on investment. Everything you do must perform by the numbers to tell the story of efficiency, effectiveness, goal attainment, and betterment in the community. Likewise, your adjacent matrix service partners must perform by materially contributing to overall program successes.

Use this guide to keep track of the day with an idea of how the day's activities lead to the future. Know where you are heading. Use operations to test planning and ideas. Correct immediately. Be ruthless. When you are stable, which will take years, return to the basics of capacity building before you take on even the smallest of additional tasks or responsibility. Do only what can be done well. You are free to make this model your own. See it as a good start based on the suggestions and experiences of your peers and fellow practitioners. What matters is your success, the growth of your community, and the success of those you serve in your program. Truly, when one succeeds all succeed.

It's all about the return on investment.

The Process – Phases, Critical Features, and Effective Practices

The point was made earlier that a critical failing with the usual public sector services is a lack of documentation about project development based on capacity. To over-simplify, people get a bit of funding, usually a terminal grant. They find a small office, hire a staffer, and collapse after the grant ends, usually in a year or two. Planners may, at best, discuss critical success factors during project implementation[43] but say little about how to make them work. Plus, this is in reference to private sector enterprises; *public* sector application is quite different.

More specifically, implementation, operation, and project stabilization information on reentry-aftercare are good starting places but fall short in two areas. First, most "implementation" plans in the private sector don't hew to a process applicable to local implementation. Starting a project in the private sector is just different, and many of the processes, procedures, and methods don't apply to the local public project. The most glaring differences are how the two approaches are funded and measured. The private sector has profits, which are their measure of success, direct and to the point. You make a profit or you don't.

The public sector must largely depend on tax monies, grants, and donations, and their measures of success are improvement in individual and social well-being. Such improvements are very difficult to track and determine definitively as they're subtle, behavioral, and long term. Second, the information available is mostly applicable to institutional responses to this type of programming. The previously mentioned toolkits,[44] for example, address institutional needs such as transitional programs from jail or prison and provide what are essentially lists of recommended things to do. However, these lack continuity, sequence, and applicability to the work of reentry. The items aren't glued together by a logical, practical, proven course of action. Resources you may find from a literature search stop before explaining how the idea in question is institutionalized before it becomes transformational. In fact, they rarely address how to get past implementation. Yet, most of project development lies *beyond* detailed planning and startup activities.

These resources may discuss implementation and perhaps a bit about operations. They don't discuss how to permanently address the questions they were meant to address, such as prison overcrowding and unacceptably high recidivism rates. The model here addresses both those needs as well as the broader need to explain, as described by successful practitioners, how to build meaningful, enduring capacity. There's a big difference. The intention of this model is to be a guide. Much of the interpretation remains, as it should, in the hands of those tackling the task of building an enduring, comprehensive program of transitional services.

For example, the model may suggest forming a transitional team at the outset, with some explanation of what they should do and how they should conduct business. Detailed specifics are intentionally left to local determination. This is the defining characteristic of the process. Only the people on site, in the neighborhoods, on the street can determine program needs and answers to those needs. This book does, however, suggest the most productive way to proceed in critical areas as determined by program practitioners who have learned the trade. For example, Dismas Charities staff shared experiences and ideas proven over nearly 50 years of trial, error, and a lot of critical thinking. The plan is only a start and isn't, nor can it be, explicitly proscriptive. However, it's enough to help practitioners chart their own way.

> A minute spent in correct planning saves untold time, even failure, later. **Plan well to do well.**

Now let's consider an introduction of the life cycle, critical features, and the most productive effective practices for developing the right mix of transitional services for *local* application. I trust you'll agree that describing developing services delivery in terms of the program's life cycle makes the work of it understandable, very realistic, and much more productive. It makes your goal *attainable*.

The literature mainly discusses the life cycle of *product* development, which largely is initiation, planning, execution, and closure.[45] It's terminal. This obviously will not do to conceptualize post-release transitional programming. The life cycle of a reentry program is constant and potentially unending, as your project can and must continually grow. Therefore, the model will describe relevant planning, operations, and stabilization, with expansion and eventually permanency as the overarching goal. Don't start if you don't plan to stay the course. This moves the discussion from the terminal work of completing a definitive project, one with a defined end, to one of continuous program development that lasts as long as the problem lasts.

By way of introducing the model, certain observations about the critical features are helpful to chart the way ahead. These features are the criticalities of the first phase of project development, planning, that naturally progress with the maturity of the program. The strength of your plan determines its ultimate success. A minute spent in correct planning saves untold time, even failure, later. Plan well to do well.

- *Leadership* is designed to be inclusive from the first day the idea is conceived. Critical stakeholders, residents, staff, and partners need to have a vested interest. This comes only from an early understanding that transitional services are one of the most productive, cost-effective initiatives a local municipality can support. Everyone invited to help must bring talent and sweat to the idea.

- *Capacity analysis* is defined by the needs of the target population overall. Measure their improvements toward independence, and these quantitative and qualitative results are meaningful to all. Such measures of effect, behavioral improvement, are then applied to one unique resident at a time. Every site studied had an intimate understanding of the people they served as each was slightly different; each needed tailored services. While essential services were categorically the same, such as the need for immediate housing and subsistence, how each site provided the service varied. This again demands the necessity for local determination in the structure and direction of any programming.

- *Scope* is a matter of continually doing only what can be accomplished well. So many good ideas overreach, which is called scope creep. Resist it. Proceed slowly to anticipate contingencies, prove the next steps. All study sites began by serving only a few clients and only those who had the potential to transition successfully. They wisely understood that they had to learn a maddeningly complex program before they could expand even to a few more clients. The idea had to make monetary sense and measurable impact on the target population. Visions, beliefs, and missions that helped define scope were inspiring.

- *Analysis and evaluation* should be remarkably simple, understandable, and especially practical. Programs start out by measuring something simple and immediate, such as the effect on recidivism rates. Then, of course, they calculated return on investment, ROI. All staff always had an eye on the chain of outcomes to ultimate goals of individual and, by extension, community betterment. Once established with affordable automation and skilled staff, they migrated to sophisticated impact and monitoring systems. Practitioners of post-release services are expert in investigating process efficiency and program effectiveness. Their zeal for essential data is quite intense. Everyone kept their share of the numbers, having real-time numbers at the flick of a few keys.

- *Resources* are developed to be relatively dependable. These model sites have a history of streams of operational support. Sources of support are expansive if you know how to probe them. They should be sustainable and reliable. For example, consider in-kind donations and support from volunteers. Once targeted, resources must strengthen the stated mission. Conversely, money with requirements that aren't compatible with program goals are usually avoided. Now that's mission-critical thinking. Significant money was turned down because of attached strings or divergence from the program's vision and missio. Relationships are the basis of resources. Support comes from *friends* who are compelled to help because they want to be part of aftercare success and what it does for their communities.

- *Services* tailored to local circumstances effect successful transitions, but only if they are well supported by business infrastructure. While model sites have a similar array of services such as housing and substance-abuse therapy, the mix of services varies. The variations are according to how individual site practitioners interpret the needs of their clients and their local capabilities to satisfy those needs. They define services by the target client and budgeting capabilities, so behavioral therapies are similar from program to program. However, at the application level, they're interpreted accordingly.

- *Staff* display missionary zeal. The one element that most determines project success is those who do the work. Are they clock watchers counting the seconds down? Or are they sincerely involved no matter the hour or day? Staff at every site know they're doing vital work and are making an important difference. More than a few staff at the model sites gave up more lucrative jobs to be involved in this work. They were inspired, usually by a charismatic executive director and then by the residents themselves. They have energy for the job way beyond what one sees in most other working circumstances. Many staffers are former offenders who continue giving and strengthening the community to atone somewhat for past indiscretions. Some make careers out of helping. Mutual respect is palpable. Everyone has a purpose.

Each of these critical features are accomplished by effective practices at work at the various sites within North Carolina and nationally.

Planning, Learning, and Growing

Planning never stops. At TROSA, for example, at the time of the study, they were buying land for future development. LINC leased an old, abandoned jail and renovated it into a sparkling new, full-service 40-bed facility for men and women. Dismas is continuing its national expansion. Boards are working on and expanding their program capacity. Participants at the primary study sites were fairly bubbling over with what was next.

One of the many themes within operations is continuous, comprehensive, and close staff development. Oh yes, countless priorities vie for attention, but these successful programs put inordinate expense and effort into how staff adjust to their jobs.

Every site recognized it's the day-to-day work conducted by competent, inspired staff that realizes their dreams. Staff take charge of becoming highly competent by energetically pursuing their own education, training, and professional development. Every member of the program feels he or she is essential to the team, and everyone is a leader. Yet, that was not nearly enough.

Staff take responsibility for increasing the competencies of their fellow workmates! LINC, for example, held scheduled and spontaneous "what if" role plays about real circumstances of the moment. The workplace becomes a laboratory to investigate how to do things better and how staff can become better by understanding these insights. They teach each other the business of aftercare. What they were doing was intuitively constructing a learning organization.

This philosophy of staff development is best epitomized by the motto at TROSA: *Each one teach one.* Senior residents take responsibility for doing risk assessments of potential fellow participants and assume full responsibility to induct, orient, teach, counsel, and mentor new residents on how to succeed. I reiterate; this is a tough program, and I have seen residents self-eliminate to return to the "comforts" of jail. They learn personal responsibility as they exemplify responsibility in a wonderful virtuous cycle. This approach engenders mutual and collective responsibility for success. These programs are compelled to make a difference as all are vested. And those involved smile a lot.

Everyone, staff and residents, continuously improve and dream about doing more. While they truly struggle with implementation and survival, all staff, especially key leadership, have a firm idea of how they will expand. What a great and inspiring dream. So Dismas plans more aftercare sites or how to serve more residents at existing sites. LINC can see a gated community for former inmates where beautiful homes are owned by neighbors who were once without hope or a chance. This isn't simply wishful thinking about impossibilities because such communities exist. So, they ask with determination, why can't Wilmington have one?

> **Aftercare staff and partners ensure every decision pays dual dividends of ROI in dollars plus success for residents and the community.**

TROSA is expanding to house more residents and is constantly entertaining ideas for suitable income-producing trades—perhaps sustainable agriculture, for example. Site officials also consider the substantial issues of replication and succession. Perceptive, action-oriented visionary statements plan for long-term contingencies rooted in resolute, if cautious growth by analyzing every move. Every process is continuously improving. Aftercare staff and partners ensure every decision pays dual dividends of ROI in dollars plus success for residents and the community. Intuitively, all are building capacity for continuous improvement and planned, judicious expansion.

Expansion is also a product of action orientation; project staff are *always* moving ahead, despite a lot of trial and error. Unproductive ideas are jettisoned the moment they show fatal weaknesses or are uncorrectable. Decision making is anything but haphazard, and forward movement is incremental to make sure they're not assuming more than they can do well. Experience has made them aware that one failure, especially a public one, can set the program back significantly. All approach this work as the opportunity of a lifetime.

Returnees' State of Mind

Before we proceed to the model, allow me to make a pertinent comment about the state of mind of the returnee. I observed many and interviewed more than a few of the people in these programs. Simply put, those chosen for or who by luck find these programs *sincerely want to make a change in themselves* and return to the dignity of a place at the dinner table with family. They demonstrate this by word and deed. Take TROSA for example, residents commit to a very strict, much stricter than prison, regime of rebuilding themselves and others that takes *two years!* Their life from sunup to sunset involves learning to change, living that change, then giving back. TROSA is a beehive of activity. Residents learn that the way to get respect is to sincerely give it. They know how difficult life can be with bad choices and just do not want it anymore.

That's one of the many reasons these programs work! Hard work and one small success at a time are synergistic, self-fulfilling, motivating, and inspiring.

Moving into Chapter 3, we'll delve more deeply into the first phase of the Life Cycle—Plan and Implement.

Chapter 3

PHASE I OF THE PROGRAM'S LIFE CYCLE– PLAN AND IMPLEMENT

Chapter 3

PHASE I OF THE PROGRAM'S LIFE CYCLE – PLAN AND IMPLEMENT

A man will be imprisoned in a room with a door that's unlocked and opens inwards; as long as it does not occur to him to pull rather than push.
– Ludwig Wittgenstein

Just where does one begin to unwind the complexities of aftercare? Well, at the beginning—by defining the *how to* of essential planning. Now, planning is one thing, but action directed by Capacity Building is another. We're addressing the latter.

The study sites demonstrate that starting small is the best course, as in the cases of LINC and the JSC. Both began working in established transitional offices or by providing services to just a few returnees to learn and grow the business. Again, the LINC founder began as a counselor.

Alternatively, while TROSA began with a few clients, expansion to another fully functioning site required an investment of several millions of dollars. They needed to buy land, build or renovate a campus, and staff it with TROSA trained, qualified people. Now that TROSA is established, their business model requires certain infrastructure regarding office, residential, and workspaces. So, they had to begin by growing to a rather large number of clients to support opera-

> Now, planning is one thing, but action directed by Capacity Building is another.

tions with labor and the financial support from aid that may attend them. Now that these model sites are established, the argument is made that it's better to begin with a residential program of ample capacity. At TROSA, it was to build to support at least 100 residents at the next site. This seemed the optimal population—not too small, not too big—considering their 30 years of successful experience. *Think optimal and doable* is the new mantra. They're already thinking of the next and the next sites, building on their success.

Another idea is to begin with a one-stop transition *day service* for those who don't need a residential environment, then expand. Considering the multiplexity of transition, however, it's more reasonable to begin with *residential* post-release services. So, begin with a board comprised of local vested talent. Realistically, a local champion will rise to present a workable idea to community leadership; at least that has been the experience of the study sites.

Planning for capacity in the public sector moves considerably beyond the tasking that may be taught in business school. Well, school is school, a good start—but "the street" is reality. Transitional program development includes the classic tasks of organizing, managing, and budgeting—but these tasks aren't definitive enough. Need determines the shape of things. Project building in our local municipalities is simply not routine, formulaic, or mechanical. Everyone learns to multi-task from their first day on the job and never stops. Practicality is the watchword.

The executive director, for example, is usually a charismatic, natural leader. The job is to develop an atmosphere for learning and an aura of competency based on realities defined by a complex client and their wider community. The atmosphere is hurly-burly but not haphazard; each staffer has a place in the forward movement of the effort. But no matter how confusing and long the day is, no one loses sight of the future that can be.

Notice how critical success factors[46] take priority. The project leader understands the dynamics of local politics and continuously infuses project stakeholders with the urgency of the project and its common sense. The mission is clear and is supported by leadership that inculcates all stakeholders. Clients or residents are co-partners with the staffing mix and are continuously sought for feedback, if not actual labor, to make successful transitions.

Doing well and staying on vision, even guided by written beliefs, pervades. People know why they are doing what they do. Performance is an obsession. Processes and services are seamlessly linked, one flowing from the other collaboratively, to maximize synergy. If the process doesn't facilitate services delivery, it's probably counterproductive. Everywhere one goes, everything observed is the realization of the major theme of the whole becoming greater than the sum of its parts.

Communication internally and externally is continuous. An executive director on the job is involved in constant phone coordination, consultation, and regular meetings with purpose. Notice also how planning progresses *through* the process of implementation.[47] Over time, years really, the idea grows from the initial concept to where it's adopted then modified according to the ground truths discovered along the way. When the idea is palatable to stakeholders, it enjoys relative acceptance to the point it can begin to work better and better and become productively routine.

The order of critical action items is not to infer one being more important than another. Building must be sequential. Who contemplates the roof without the foundation? The corresponding effective practices are vital actions that translate the plan to action each in its time. The distinction is that all are well planned before the first client crosses the threshold. They are necessarily tersely stated. Tasking is proven by years of experience across various programs as some of the most productive actions that can be taken. Extra words are extraneous.

Of course, you can add to them, pare them back, refine them as your ground truths dictate, but risk peril if any one of them is omitted. This is not to imply that these are the only salient actions to be taken, because good practices happen daily. But do adopt even the lesser of them, because they mount up to a solid organization. Just make sure they all work together. Leadership is a good place to start.

1. Nurture and Grow Key Leaders Who Know Post-Release Aftercare Services

After observing scores of well-working public sector service projects, I believe *the* determining factor in the success of the idea rests with a local champion. I declare this especially because we're discussing a community-wide role in aftercare reintegration. It would be wonderful if these standard bearers rose fully formed and ready to lead or could be trained in the unique skills of leadership required by this idea. Yes, these champions are messianically inspired but, in reality, they learn by doing. The executive director of LINC began this work part-time and supported himself and his family as a barber! Now he runs a multi-million-dollar enterprise and is changing the face of Wilmington, North Carolina. However, the community must be lucky enough to have one of these people and be humble enough to clear the path for his or her success.

> The executive director is the model staffer. From his or her example, all else flows and grows.

Enough has been written on leadership that it's a matter of what *not* to read than what to read. Still, it's worthwhile to briefly address what these people and the people around them think are the essential character traits, abilities, and skills needed to make a transitional program work.

The executive director is the model staffer. From his or her example, all else flows and grows. That said, the success of this key staffer lies in the leadership body that person assembles, trains, and puts to work. It can be a board of directors or transitional council or post-release team or a reentry roundtable. The logical extension of each leadership group is the key staff and the community. The lead staffer and the leadership body must be potent and work indivisibly from day one. They each have essential and overarching roles.

Simply put, the executive director is the *keeper of the vision,* and the board is judiciously comprised to ensure buy-in and fidelity. They both need to be highly proficient in building relationships as transitional programming succeeds via friendships. Both the executive director and the board "work" the community for support and money. The executive director must be connecting to the community to let them know what the program is doing. The board should also connect with the community, but with the overarching goal of obtaining support—especially money.

While multitudes of effective practices need to be accomplished, identifying these two entities is crucial. Their successful establishment and growth will determine what is done and how it is done. The following discussion will treat how each evolved as evidenced mainly in the working study sites.

Experience demonstrates that the inspired champion rises, usually from an intense experience, to tell the community that something must be done for the formerly incarcerated. For example, the LINC executive director had a brother who needed help and didn't get it. The future LINC director was on his way to the hospital to reconnect with the brother he'd shunned for years because of his poor life choices, only to have his brother die of his addictions before he got there. His regret in not connecting brother to brother was his driving force in creating a national model for reentry. The TROSA director made very bad life choices and knew he had to do something to make amends. He was one of the people he now serves—by the hundreds each year.

With each new endeavor, an inspired few teach us how to go about this business of bringing people home. How these leaders conduct themselves determines the strength of the general staff and the effectiveness of

> **These leaders incrementally master the art of the possible and see everything as an opportunity. They demonstrate a no-obstacles mindset.**

the leadership board. They display 21st-century public leadership. What does that entail?

First, they live with good character, that is with honesty and humility. They constantly work on and epitomize virtue. Thus, they lead collaboratively and by example. Then, they bring those traits to the community, first by putting together networks or matrices of talented individuals to resolve a communal concern. People love to follow these individuals.

Dynamic executive directors understand value by promoting and multiplying the great potential of social capital. That is, they harness the creativity and contributions of those with them and around them. These leaders incrementally master the art of the possible and see everything as an opportunity. They demonstrate a no-obstacles mindset.

The local champion is rare because they embody inspiration, which is multi-dimensional. They intuitively do the right things. This is not to say they never make mistakes, but they certainly learn from them. Their commitment to the vision, mission, staff, community, and especially residents is never in question. When considering character traits, the executive director of the Durham County Justice Services Center mentioned that this person must be willing to compromise. This means they have true empathy for the perspectives, boundaries, and parameters of others. Turfism, if it arises, never takes root.

The cofounder of LINC mentioned that the other man who cofounded LINC is a good storyteller. It was through stories that the vision for LINC bloomed and lessons were driven home. He demonstrated he was "ready to take on the world" and then proceeded to do so. These people are always doing a little more—more for stakeholders, more to develop money, more to make a difference. They're humble, too. I observed they never claim to know all the answers, but they do promise to be open to ideas, confer with staff, and research the best course of action. Then they take that action—but not without introspection.

They understand themselves and are a constant example of continuously evolving, learning, and teaching. In fact, at one site, the executive director was once a resident who had risen from having made dreadful decisions. He knows how it feels to be on the fringes of society, never part of community, with little hope of returning. He now sits atop a national model and helps hundreds of the most hopeless cases every year.

> These leaders are the embodiment of passion. They are enamored with the work and the people of and in transition.

These men are congruent, as they do what they say they will. Thus, they are participant leaders, never asking of staff or stakeholders what they aren't willing to do themselves. They mastered all the classic skills and abilities necessary for transition. They do budgeting, planning, funds development, staff development, community development, organizing, directing sub-projects, setting up communication mechanisms, and learning automation, to mention a few of their skills and endeavors.

Delegating tasks is easy as they personally see to the development of staff and plan for the next progression and even succession. Networking is a skill honed to remarkable acuity. They rarely meet a person they don't convince to do something for the cause. These people are unforgettable—and they're great listeners. I mean they *really* listen and often take notes on which they act. They're informed in detail, they live intensely in the moment, and they plan for an exciting future. Yes, they speak of the ups and downs and the depression of momentary disappointments or even defeats. Still, they're always in action mode, always inching intelligently forward. In other words, these leaders are the embodiment of passion. They are enamored with the work and the people of and in transition.

Sorry to say, this kind of person cannot be completely created, trained, or imported fully formed. However, they do arrive on the scene ready for the challenge, even if they're not yet fully what they will be, formed by experiences. And they never stop learning. The community that has the good fortune to have one of these people in their midst and the insight to recognize the person's potential clears the way for them to lead.

The leader has two initial and simultaneous tasks. One is to put together a core staff, and the other is to organize a leadership body. Oh yes, they also work on and within the community and on developing resources, the vision and mission, performance, process, programming, planning, and a multitude of other necessary details. According to several executive directors, they must get the people thing right immediately. We'll return to key staff because, in keeping with the sequence of process, the guiding body must rise to potency quickly and correctly. This executive board is composed first according to the needs of the returning population and then the need to establish permanency. The former is to determine services, and the latter is to build capacity to deliver them.

I asked each senior executive what he or she would, in retrospect, do first. One of the things they discussed was the philosophy necessary to begin well. Basically, the effort must begin by transforming the stereotype of the person formerly involved in criminality. That view needs to change from seeing people to shun and perhaps fear to one of seeing them as fellow citizens making it past bad decisions and through the hard work of redemption. The larger portion of the formerly incarcerated deeply regrets previous behaviors and decisions and wants to change and contribute. Experienced senior staffers add the disclaimer that the commitment to making a new life is serious, and some people do need the structure of incarceration. Still, "most ex-cons are worthy," staff observe. Thus, LINC senior staff observe, the job of aftercare is one of, "changing the criminal's culture of excuses to a lifestyle of accountability and no excuses."

This is accomplished via an "empowering therapeutic community" where clients of the program learn responsibility mainly by taking responsibility for their fellow program participants and "earning their way up." Using TROSA as an example, the (therapeutic) community is the method whereby *each one teaches one* lays the foundation of structure, accountability, sharing, developing healthy relationships, and eventually learning then earning self-sufficiency. This leads to respectable, productive citizenship. Capacity-built aftercare begins with a few societal castaways and continues over the decades with thousands of good citizens!

Once the board is established, the details of which will be discussed shortly, its purpose is to build buy-in from all pertinent stakeholders. Repeatedly, senior staff observed that their biggest hindrance—more than funding, more than providing services—was overcoming resistance. There's a natural revulsion to convicted criminals, with a drug problem, yet. Public relations are the number one priority as the idea takes shape, observed one executive director. They wished that from the first day they had composed a leadership body that included people who could promote the idea and people in a position to oppose this resistance. Much of this work is misunderstood. Arguments are best answered before they arise, staff say.

Usually, a lean board is better, although the propensity is to go with the idea that more is better—and that even a position or voice in the community is qualification enough for a seat. Not so. Composition must be just right. Inclusiveness means a cumbersome size. A good job of weeding out hopefuls is to have a job description that details the real work of it, not the least of which is attending a lengthy, remote job training course at the University of North Carolina, Chapel Hill. Thereafter, composing the board is done by "selling the viability" of the idea, according to one of the founders of LINC.

The participation and work of the board are the antidotes for obstructionism, members observe. The task of the board is no less than changing the entire community mindset about their responsibility to facilitate reintegration. "Their questions have to be answered before they're asked," noted one executive director.

Major challenges for startups, which are the major charges of leadership, include:

- getting a qualified board and staff in place,
- setting realistic expectations, and
- developing funding streams.

It's easy to get distracted in a chaotic environment where so many "good and necessary" things must be done. The board cannot be freewheeling. Tasking must be specific. Results detailed. Feet held to the fire by self-policing or by the body politic of citizens. Attendance at meetings enforced. This is all to avoid the all-too-frequent management pitfall of managing by crisis.

> The task of the board is no less than changing the entire community mindset about their responsibility to facilitate reintegration.

Like the entire project, the board will face implementation problems.[48] These can be answered by careful recruitment, training, and succession planning. The following difficulties are common and not unsurmountable:

- *Micromanagement* – This can happen by any leader such as the executive director or a board member.

- *Weak composition* – This can result from ineffective nominations and rotations, including removing unproductive members, and either no or little understanding of detailed duties and responsibilities. Being a board member is a lot of work. Be sure to instill that fact before you offer membership.

- *Size too small* – Shoot to be big enough to accommodate the work and committee assignments. Screen with a job description or committee assignment to discuss before offering the job.

- *Weak planning for services delivery* – This may happen if leaders don't thoroughly understand the clientele.

- *No formal board orientation and training*[49] – This is most avoidable as many municipal leadership training programs are available. Select the best by its longevity and opinion of graduates. Also, continue training at retreats, for example.

Therefore, the initial work comes down to *form* the board, *train* the board, and *establish functional working groups* or sub-committees. Now let's begin a more detailed discussion of who needs to be considered according to what they need to do.

Effective Practice
Establish a stable leadership body focused on capacity building and transitional services.

You must determine the composition of your board, counsel, task force, or whatever you choose to name your leadership body by the needs of returnees and the community, and the work of building capacity. Carefully analyze what reintegration requires in *your* community from the perspective of *your* returnee—and *your* capacity to deliver sustained, meaningful impact.

Your board must facilitate this sequence of "musts" by the first day of operations. Planning for present services delivery and program sustainability should be simultaneous. The major work of capacity building is to build friendly, cooperative, and collaborative relationships as the basis of developing resources and political will essential for project survival, then to build permanence. Consider agencies and key people already doing transitions, those that should be doing it, and those that have pertinent expertise and influence.[50] These might include the following.

- *Law enforcement* – Sheriffs and police have a great stake in public safety, an important goal of post-release programming.

- *Community organizations and service providers* – A wealth of largely untapped resources and people need the organization and focus of your reintegration trailblazing. This includes treatment and social service providers and general health and mental health agencies. Subsistence and employment requirements for returnees suggest the need for representatives from housing and workforce development agencies.

> **Family are probably the greatest aftercare supporters.**

- *Victims* – Largely lost in this work are victims. They have a great stake in preventing new crimes and repeated victimization by people in the crime/incarceration/aftercare-reentry cycle.

- *The general public* – People in neighborhoods where these programs will be located are vital to this work. They are most resistant to having criminals anywhere near their neighborhoods. Many will have to be shown, demonstrably, how they will benefit. How and when they are convinced of the viability and especially the value of transitional programs, they are some of the program's greatest advocates. After all, the neighborhood will receive the formerly incarcerated, who tend to return to crime unless they are prepared to become good productive neighbors. Family are probably the greatest aftercare supporters. This programming stops the cycle of criminality for all but a few of the most recalcitrant returnees.

- *The courts* – Judges, for example, are quite interested in how best to transition a court-involved individual because it gives them the flexibility to include residential and therapeutic programs in lieu of incarceration. Judges are reluctant to invoke a sentence if possible. Also consider prosecution and defense representatives. They can't keep up with their dockets and participate in any relief.

- *Jail representatives* – Post-release aftercare success arguably begins with a good relationship with the sheriff, who must welcome service providers to screen inmates for programming and services while incarcerated and after jail. A sheriff can also begin work of decriminalizing the mentally ill, which reduces their recidivating by keeping this population away from infractions of the law. It's amazing how many of this population can avoid jail and its crushing expenses with a proper mental health referral by the responding police officer. (See Capacity Building Vol II: *Decriminalizing Mental Illness*.)

- *Probation and parole officers (POs)* – Corrections officials must understand and contribute to mission accomplishment. They are part of the necessary discipline a program must have. The formerly incarcerated are more likely to amend their ways when their PO is involved.

- *Released inmates and their families* – Only inmates understand inmates. Select a highly successful former inmate for your board. A former inmate's perspective is quite insightful, pertinent, and valuable, born of walking the walk. One of the graduates of LINC is now the chef/owner of a high-end restaurant in Wilmington, North Carolina, which employs a large staff, mostly LINC grads too. He just needed a chance to rebuild. His mere presence in the community testifies to the need for ways to properly assist the population he represents.

- *The faith community* – Many churches include transition as part of their community outreach. Just think how many churches are in even a small township. Make one a partner and others will follow.

- *Elected officials* – Municipal leadership, whether from the town council, the mayor's office, or the county commission, will provide financial and all-important political support. Especially if they are friends and you attend their important gatherings. How about a well-deserved photo op?

- *Appointed public officials* – Local governmental agencies such as mental and public health departments, social services, employment security, and many others have significant resources and intense interest in the success of returnees.

- *Juvenile justice and school officials* – Youth, in comparison, are lost in the fog of assisting adult offenders, yet money spent on salvaging wayward youth is by far most profitable in lifelong returns to the greater good. It may be useful to have a youth member of your board. Youth aftercare programming, which is very effective in stopping the progression to years of adult criminality, crime, and gang involvement, is common sense and arguably the most cost-effective service a local municipality can offer.

- *Private sector officials* – This includes potential employers and businespeople in a position to lend financial and practical support.

The *Transition from Jail to Community Online Learning Toolkit* is most helpful in composing a leadership body for, as the name relates, transition from jail to community.[51]

The leadership body, or board, suggested in this model is composed for and focused on the transition from *community to citizenship*—not just release from the criminal justice system. Notice that in just three words they capture the true meaning and scope of reentry. This one values-laden statement changes everything this organization does for the better.

Essentially, this body focused on aftercare transition is where institutional, criminal justice, and public agency programming *ends*. This body is concerned with what happens long after release, when the client is making decisions and changes in lifestyle to become a good neighbor. The board is structured for cooperation via shared commitment. Its practices are based on evidence that centers on the focal population. It strives to promote an organizational culture of improvement that supports collective and individual growth. While this group is a *buck-stops-here* entity with notable, accomplished individuals, it's the first time these individuals will be assembled for *this* purpose. They need to be trained in their roles, duties, and responsibilities.

Effective Practice
Train your leadership body for effectiveness and efficiency.

Don't assume the board will function well by virtue of the assembled talent. Because they likely have day jobs, board members will have limited time to work on the project, so they must learn quickly. Many proven leaders are asked to serve on a board because they have demonstrated they can get things done. The people chosen for board duty must know how to function as a board (the body) as well as a team member (one of its collaborative parts). They must internalize the duties they are expected to accomplish.

> The board must be a living, dynamic organism with a mantra of "failure is not an option."

Serving on a board requires great compromise for people who are used to having it their way. The grooming of a good board team member begins with your first approach, when you brief them on your vision, mission, and beliefs. Then you explain how those must be performed with respect to your charter, committee assignments, duties, and responsibilities. The board must be a living, dynamic organism with a mantra of "failure is not an option." If one accepts a board position, it is with eyes wide open about the real work beyond attending quarterly meetings and a realization that the commitment can be for a few *years*. It is better to suffer what seems like the loss of a prominent citizen than suffer the strain of a bad fit.

Some key board practices include:[52]

- Continuously recruiting and training members.
- Establishing an executive committee to make decisions.
- Periodically evaluating board and board member performance.
- Establishing committees.

When a position has been accepted, the new board member should have a thorough orientation and be scheduled for board member training. Luckily, many good resident and nonresident training programs for municipal officials are available. The School of Government at the University of North Carolina is such an example.[53] Select a few of your members to attend with the intention of having them train other board members. Plan a facilitated regular retreat, not to exclude board training. It will be evident from the initial training what further training is needed. The board will benefit from continuously upgrading professional and technical knowledge, skills, and abilities, individually and collectively. Working on a board is a dynamic experience that demands its members progress with the evolution of the project.

Effective Practice
Establish a functional committee structure for relationship building, goal accomplishment, and longevity.

The discussion thus far hints at the third major effective practice for the board, to establish sub-committees. Of all the things that occupy a board, its committee designations determine the actual to-do lists that lead to goal accomplishment. This section will dwell only briefly on enhancing the success factors of committee work and suggest some of the more important ones. As always, make them work for you. We remind you to make this implementation checklist your own. Add, delete, modify, make notes as you wish. You will use it again—and please pass it along.

It has been said that there is nothing as settling as a decision. This is another statement about the mindset of the action-oriented program guided by an action-oriented board.

Following are primary determinants of committee success:[54]

- *Written directions* – Each committee should have a written description of purpose and operation to eliminate confusion about the basics of expectations and work.

- *A compelling chair* – The chair must be compelling and competent. He or she must exude character.

- *Able, committed members* – Members should be committed to the effort and able to work as an enthusiastic collaborative part of the committee as a singular, synergistic force.

- *Accountability* – Each committee is best advised to be accountable to the board, staff, the community, and residents for mission and goal accomplishment. It's understood that each member is also accountable to self.

- *Action orientation first and last* – Meetings and general conduct need to be action oriented. Nearly every discussion is best served by resulting in a decision that compels forward movement.

> Committees are only as effective as their strength of interrelationships with the program's internal organization, board and staff, and external stakeholders.

Committees need to be functional regarding the administration of the board and the delivery of services.[55] Each entity has its own charter. Still, the successful ones work synergistically such that duties and responsibilities work together. For example, resources development is deeply intertwined with community relations. The overall goal of the board is to be in sync with stakeholders and their neighbors. This model is all about continuums of functions, processes, stakeholders, and services. Committees are only as effective as their strength of interrelationships with the program's internal organization, board and staff, and external stakeholders. Committee suggestions are made at formal basic board training. Even with suggestions, it would be wise to consider at least the following committees:

- *Executive Committee* – Essentially this body is responsible for the effectiveness of the board. It does this by ensuring the board is staffed, trained, and organized to be nearly maniacally directed toward and by vision, mission, beliefs, and goal accomplishment. It also sets agendas, evaluates the performance of the board, and speaks for the board. It makes sure internal and external communication about the project happens with the purpose and effect of strengthening the idea with real support and capacity.

- *Planning and Policy Development Committee* – The message of this model is one of planning. Inadequate planning can cause implementation to fail. However, endless planning to consider every contingency and keep adding just one more bit of information goes nowhere, according to study interviewees. The board must take deliberate, well-conceived, albeit imperfect actions. There's no such thing as 100 percent surety. Reality will dictate when, where, and how to correct. By making decisions, the board becomes better and better at it.

- *Community and Organizational Development Committee* – This may be the most important committee. Every senior staffer interviewed commented that support from all stakeholders, especially locals, must be carefully nurtured from the first day transitional services are conceptualized.

    This implies that the board via this committee is accountable to each stakeholder, whether it's an individual or group, internal or external. This work is particularly difficult because to win these friends means overcoming generations of stereotyping about the "ex-con." This committee also has arguably the next highest priority—staffing. The best visions of safer and more livable neighborhoods come to naught if qualified and inspired staff are not at their desks or in the field in front of clients. This means every morning, all day, and sometimes into the night, still feeling good about the work at the end of the day, the vision always in sight.

    The task of staffing is doubly difficult as the work is brutal and subject to early burnout, according to the staffers interviewed. Also, their compensation is barely a living wage. The only saving grace is that more than a few see the value and personal reward of this work. I met many of them.

- *Resources Development and Support Committee* – Dual roles are implied for this committee. The board members must develop funding streams, and as stated in these pages, they do this by *earning respect*. Money, money, money is the thorn in the side of these endeavors, according to successful transitional leadership. There's never enough, and it comes in dribbles compared to the need. Thus, this body should be consumed with making the monetary justification for transition services. People and decision makers want proof that their tax or donated dollars are improving quality of life. It takes years of solid cost-effectiveness and great unintended consequences case presentations to develop revenue streams. This work is best served by developing funding streams on the first day the board forms.

These are core committee designations. Each project/program will have others depending on need. For example, there may be committees on services, program performance, case management, jobs development, residential planning, and juvenile issues. A suggested tactic is to form and establish the core committees then add committees according to the assessed need and ability to staff them well.

Another thing: While you should not encourage troubles, have the attitude that the things that go wrong are the things that allow improvement. You learn and progress, learn and progress repeatedly in an upward trajectory. See obstacles not in the way, but as the way, to paraphrase the ancients.

Next, we consider the capacity to deliver on the promise of aftercare.

2. Integrate Capacity Assessment for Project Capacity Building

Capacity assessment relative to this work is not as much science as it is doing relatively simple research. You need just a few measures to understand the community-specific returnee's needs *and* determine the capacity to deliver what you say you will. It's also "selling" what you're delivering. It is paramount.

If you promise to deliver more than is possible, it may mean the end of the endeavor. Early on, aftercare work is about survival to close the services-to-needs gap. Understanding needs juxtaposed with the resources available to satisfy those needs is vital as enthusiastic stakeholders tend to do too much. Again, fewer responsibilities but thoroughly and productively fulfilled is the goal—which only comes from analyzing capacity.

Program leadership and staff must know local needs. A few examples are:

- *Poverty* – The Reentry Policy Council (2005)[56] observed that every county varies in poverty, an indicator of crime. For example, the Council found Buchanan County, Virginia had about 20 percent poverty, whereas Fairfax County, Virginia had about 2 percent (1999).[57]

- *Court supervision* – Court supervision varies, exemplified by the fact that Kentucky released more than 44 percent of prisoners unsupervised, whereas Kansas had less than 7 percent unsupervised at the time of this writing.

- *Revocations* – Then there are revocations. Nearly half of Montana's prison admissions were from parole violations; Oklahoma had about 20 percent (1998).

One community may have hundreds of jail clients who serve only short sentences and have transitional infrastructure ready for them upon release. Another community may receive an inordinate number of prison returnees with long-term criminal histories, perhaps gang involvement, and certainly complicating health and substance abuse problems and relatively few resources in the locale of release. They are the "frequent flyers," a real drain on public expenditures and infrastructure.

Each circumstance requires variations in strategy regarding what programs can best serve the locally defined population. What tactics can be employed? How can specific services be mustered? When should a service be inaugurated? Those in post-release status are likely to have failed at post-release already, gotten little educational and vocational preparation during their incarceration, and served longer sentences.[58] Much work with and by them remains to be done. This profile is further complicated by the fact that they are being released/returned to lower socioeconomic communities where jobs and character-building choices are few.[59] In other words, they return to the circumstances, contacts, and conditions that engendered their criminal behavior in the first place. It's crucial to study and know your returnee and what is realistically available to serve him or her.

Effective Practice
Profile returnee risk and needs factors to determine your mix of services.

Clients for aftercare transitional services will obviously come directly from incarceration and a surprising array of other avenues. They may be channeled from court as perhaps a diversion from incarceration or punishment itself or be referred by service agencies, therapeutic and medical professionals, former clients, family, and friends. What was surprising is that each of the study sites had a fair number of *self*-referrals. It's not uncommon for a prospect to just show up on the doorstep, a walk-in. This becomes more common with program success.

Whatever the source, even if the program has a no-refusal policy, each person must be profiled. (See the *Intake Assessment and Risk/Needs Determination Chart* on page 217.) While the basic needs of returnees are well known, an analysis of the returnee's needs that come to your community is vital to program performance and success. This analysis should answer the following classic questions in terms of the task:[60]

- *Who* is entering and leaving incarceration? There are nuances about each returnee for every community. Learning about needs is usually done by a risk and needs assessment upon beginning a sentence and certainly before acceptance into an aftercare/reentry program.

> The heartening fact proven by the study sites is that these cycles of descent back into crime can be broken.

- *What* policies influence post-release services? Virtually every aspect of transition is governed by a rule or regulation. For example, there are statutes, policies, and practices affecting driver's licenses, food pantries, food stamps, homeless shelters, and Medicaid just to mention a few.[61]

- *Where* do most returnees settle? Each neighborhood has a different personality. You will learn the specific profile of the returnee juxtaposed with the capacity of neighborhood family, friends, church, and services. You will also learn *their* capacity and *their* willingness to add *their* part to the overall aftercare effort—or diminish it. A community in distress, the place that produced your client, is no place for them.

- *Why* does reoffending occur? It is simple to dismiss a revocation or recidivation to a criminal mindset, but that is not the case. Every crime, every return to incarceration is quite complicated. You will find that a return to crime is a combination of lack of choices, desperation, or lack of a process to follow out of bad choices. The heartening fact proven by the study sites is that these cycles of descent back into crime can be broken.

- *How* well are the formerly incarcerated being prepared for release? This varies considerably. Our correctional institutions are not charged, equipped, or predisposed for transition. Their job is to carry out a sentence that our society needs and begin reentry. They do not have the mandate or wherewithal to complete each transition. *Transition begins after release* and can take years. This is the reason that working with the formerly incarcerated is a continuum. The community will need people and processes ready to fulfill the tasks only cursorily begun by jails and prisons.

The Durham County JSC (Justice Services Center) conducts a face-to-face interview behind the jail walls to gain insight into some of the following risk factors, all of which affect success.

- *Type of offense and incarceration experience* – Violent or sex offenders may not be suitable for a day program.

- *Substance abuse problems/history* – While nearly every client that comes to the JSC has or is abusing substances, staff must know if the program can service a particular client's needs. Obviously, a client with a decade's long dependency is, well, complicated.

- *Mental/physical health needs* – Categories of services are commonplace, needs are individual.

- *Antisocial attitudes* – Can the client learn acceptable behavior? Do they really want to reenter the community?

- *Peers* – If peers are gang members, success at transitioning is far more complicated if not impossible. I've spoken to returnees who desperately *want* to quit a gang and just cannot do it.

- *Family* – Is the family supportive? Is poverty intergenerational? Does the family have morals, values, and expectations that will aid the client?

- *Criminal thinking* – Here JSC staff learn some of the criminogenic complexities of the client's involvement in the criminal justice system. For example, how ingrained is it? How can the program help change such criminal or antisocial behavior or both?

Corrections staff are also interviewed as to their impression of suitability to the nonresidential. Even before acceptance, a client's needs determine the specifics of their services—and what can be delivered. This thoroughness (along with years of experience) leads to the true expression of successful transition. According to the JSC executive director, this is accomplished by having an initial job with progression to a career with a living wage. It's being able to exist without drugs and without committing another crime. In other words, it's a return home with a welcome seat at the dinner table.

Only by conducting this analysis can you develop the necessary feel for the target population. This determines how effectively project staff and leadership treat their clients. Staff, especially leadership, commented frequently about how suspicious former inmates have become. Court-involved people are predisposed to detect insincerity then continue to con their way through the day and through your program because it's what they know; it's what they do. Old habits die hard.

Many, they say, never physically turn their backs on anyone as they've been imbued with self-preservation/survival behavior learned in prison. Yet their success is determined by

> **A comprehensive start to aftercare sets the tone for success far into the future. Make sure to get it right.**

trust, and trust comes from staff understanding who comes in the door. From this profile emerges risk factors; from risk factors come an understanding of service needs; from service needs comes a hierarchy of services that begins on the first day after release. This is an important continuum to understand and put in place, because it defines how your program begins the process of individual transition. Many programs focus on the larger service needs, such as getting medical and mental health services, but that's out of sequence. First, a returnee must eat.

- *Survival* – Initially, needs are dire and basic. Many times, people on the first day "this side of the gate" need a meal, a bed, and clothing from the skin out. Each of the study aftercare Reform Movement sites had a clothing closet. So first establish avenues for subsistence, then lay out a plan for a room or housing, medical and mental health care, and substance abuse counseling/treatment, for example. The community has a responsibility to prepare the client for the transitional process. The returnee will need documentation such as identification and services such as prescriptions filled, and transportation for appointments, for example. All this is just *some* of the work of the first meeting between the client and project staff. A comprehensive start to aftercare sets the tone for success far into the future. Make sure to get it right.

- *Employment* – The next level of services will relate to becoming self-sufficient with a first job. Perhaps skills training will be necessary before the job hunt and then connections with employers that have genuine job possibilities. Mentoring and financial services are also recommended.

- *Education* – Education goes hand-in-glove with employment. Programming should consider GED certification plus job, and technical or vocational training. Have you ever seen what an HVAC technician, plumber, or electrician makes? These jobs convey respect.

- *Reintegration* – After all the above and more, the work of reintegration begins. Next come long-term therapies, perhaps in a residential setting. The returnee can begin to unlearn bad behaviors, learn new productive ones, and more than likely come to terms with deeper issues. These might be concerns such as abuse, a handicap, or a decade's-long substance abuse problem, many times combined.

The exercise of understanding the community-specific returnee is vital as it reveals the overall tactics of services delivery to take and the nuances that enhance success. The fact is that resources and programming aren't keeping pace with the demand, yet there are alternatives beyond revocation for many of the formerly incarcerated. Project staff must understand and categorize the community's capacity to satisfy these needs.

Effective Practice
Catalogue local resources according to returnee needs.

Cataloguing your resources is simple but not easy. Why do this at all? Simply, you can't deliver your service alone. You need supporters and partners, true collaborators. They do what you can't or shouldn't. They are the supports that keep you focused on essentials. They provide collective energy necessary for success. And a hidden reason is that they will be there to help you grow your next idea, only smarter and stronger for the association. This is vital.Friends and partners are foundational to developing and making your idea permanent.Friends have a real stake in fostering a community where people can safely live, work, raise their children, and thrive not just survive.

So, ferreting out where services are and what they do, determining if they fit, and if so, how to integrate them requires diligence, time, and the sleuthing of a Sherlock Holmes. Sleuthing is a matter of finding partners who embody your vision and mission and have the will to make a two-way partnership blossom that lasts. This isn't a matter of simply listing what's available from an internet search. Key staff from each possible service connection must be contacted to determine the *details* of what they do, the *applicability* of what they offer, and most importantly, their *desire* to help. With these connections and details, even crises can be solved—and your project improves and grows.

Most important is that, from the first contact you can make a friend. Friends bring a steady stream of hard cash, mutual support, and workable ideas. Besides that, making friends is just plain fun.

Normally the municipality, especially at the county level, will have a list of service providers by category. This would be a good starting point to tailor your resources catalogue according to the needs of your prospective clients. Every time you enfold a partner in your program, you allow for more possibilities. It's the best of both worlds, delivering necessary and important services and freeing leaders and staff to continue mission-critical work. Celebrate your success in making friends when they stay *and* bring others to the fold. Process, again, matters:

- *Assess your community.* – Map resources and identify those with a stake in your idea.

- *Engage potential partners.* – Network. Get out and about. Attend and host meetings. Interview the most promising people.

- *Inventory potential friends.* – Start a database by category of your needs. Keep it relevant and current.

- *Connect with partners and friends.* – Connect via common goals and benefits. Hone a dynamic (continuously improving) and compelling message.

- *Automate.* – Build a website. Research theirs. Judiciously use social media. And don't forget AI. Embrace it. It's here, and it continually gets better and more useful.

- *Evaluate, modify, act, evaluate, repeat.* – You are a learning organization, so learn with analysis. Know how well your partnerships are accomplishing the work and goals of your idea. Celebrate and promote your impact.

- *Build capacity in all its forms.* – Train partner staff in how they are integral to your idea and how they can help.

- *Maintain.* – Stay in regular contact. Attend regular meetings. Ask to visit their boards. Get creative. How about bringing an appropriate, earned award?

Partners are key to a thriving program. Perhaps calls to the major local agencies such as mental health, the department of health, social services, or the employment security commission that will have lists from which to begin compiling a quick-reference resource tailored to transitional services. The Ohio Department of Rehabilitation and Correction has a *Reentry Resource Sheet,* which provides a great example of services by county.⁶² Click on any county in the graphic of the state to be linked to a complete list of local services by category, name, address, phone number, and website. This tool suggests a thorough list of categories that will comprise what is important to your program.

A founding member of LINC mentioned further purposes of understanding services capacity. You will prompt insights critical to the direction of your project through the process of coming to understand your service capacities. One of the most important insights LINC founders realized was that the community needed a much larger residential facility. Local resources just could not serve the needs of the returning former inmates they profiled. Furthermore, the exercise of defining capacity determined the specifics of what they needed.

First, they needed a place, a residential facility, to deliver intense initial services. The neighborhood in which LINC started its work had nothing suitable. Scattered, disconnected services at best offered in a day setting would not work well enough to provide aftercare and reduce recidivism. There's little time to channel former inmates to services they need immediately on release. Going to substance abuse therapy at a clinic is simply not as effective as having it just down the hall from their sleeping quarters.

Secondly, the exercise of understanding their releasees determined that those most likely to recidivate had as their "reentry' plan" to stay at the local homeless shelter and "figure things out." Obviously unacceptable.

> **You will prompt insights critical to the direction of your project through the process of coming to understand your service capacities.**

They saw that substance abuse relapse preceded a return to incarceration, so they monitored that. More than two drug relapses per month resulted in closer monitoring and a ratcheting up of therapy. Targeting the group of people at greatest risk of cycling back to prison led to reductions in recidivism rates—the initial objective of any post-release services program. A precursor to success in overcoming an addiction, for example, was training for permanent employment. LINC staff knew its numbers. Program detractors took notice.

This was a "big attention getter" for stakeholders and skeptics alike, according to the LINC cofounder. Reductions in recidivism saved money, which is politically more palatable than supporting infrastructure for "ex-cons." Furthermore, the real drama of falling recidivism rates and crime told at reentry roundtable community meetings helped persuade citizens near their facility that having LINC as a neighbor was and is a good thing. "Enemies of the program became allies," according to founding LINC staff.

Insights about problems and creative solutions to them come from knowing the juxtaposition of needs to available resources. LINC is just down the road from the University of North Carolina, Wilmington. Staff worked out an arrangement with the university for residents to take noncredit college courses. This gave them a tangible experience with learning *beyond* a GED, which is the basis for a career rather than a job. They aptly called their idea LINC's "Communiversity." This was just one idea that came from their taking time to assess capacity. It's no wonder LINC serves as a national model of a small residential program at the neighborhood level.

So first, you'll want a thorough understanding of prospective clients for your transitional program and the services they will need. Then, you'll need to understand how much—or better yet, how little—can be done well. This brings us to the issue of scope and the Capacity Building guiding mantra of "Less, well done, is more."

3. Determine Project Scope to Focus on the Essentials of Transitional Services

Scope evolves from defining vision, mission, and values, and it determines how much you can realistically accomplish. Understanding how much can be done is vital, because there's a tendency in this business to take on too much, too soon, and too often. A staffer said, "We need less speechifying about impossible things and more doing what we *can* do."

The treatment of this topic will be succinct and only to reinforce the importance of scoping properly. A quick internet search will reveal the entire instructions needed. By the time you go through this critical step, you will have determined the limits of what you can do while continuing to gather buy-in. Be inclusive from the outset. LINC founders observed that it took them eight years to get the mayor and police chief "on board." They were not originally included in LINC implementation. Also in the confusing early days, LINC founders, without understanding their scope and by extension without a vision and mission clearly defined, tried to serve all clients that came in the door. They were quickly overwhelmed and had to downsize to serving a resident population of 12 men. Yes, scoping is determining how little you can do and do well especially initially. Further, and as important, when you know what you are doing, connecting to those who can do it with or, better yet, for you is a process of "capturing hearts and minds," according to one board member. It's also a big part of earning respect, which is so important to success.

This matter of earning support is also a mark of 21st-century governance: First you develop champions via cooperative endeavor. Then you form them into matrix solutions according to defined project tasking, which is an extension of scope. The statements about scoping that follow elucidate how you will organize leadership around practical functions such as staffing, services, and building resources. The process determines whom you will serve and how you will serve them.

The statements below are elements of scope that help define the all-important processes of reaching goals. The ideal Capacity Building process is the epitome of collaboration: It's flexible and should easily flow into a mission statement.[63] Relative to post-release services, the experts interviewed suggested certain characteristics that apply to how they went about determining scope—or wished they had in retrospect.

- *Be inclusive.* – This relates to developing vital connections with people who will determine if your program ever gets off the ground in the first place. Many don't make this connection, but you must start well to end well. This continues the work you will do to put together your leadership. Every executive director interviewed for this model commented in retrospect they wished they would have considered a far wider base of original stakeholders. Dissent, especially after clients are in a program, is doubly hard to temper. Be judicial in choosing participants from service providers, the community, natural supporters, and people who have been incarcerated. Vet them for expertise, ability to collaborate, commitment, and the sincere desire to do something to reintegrate the transitional population.

- *Motivate.* – The scoping process fuels the creativity needed to shape your idea with statements that will guide your project for years. Early on, key stakeholders will be the champions who will shape then define the message via vision, mission, goals/objectives and perhaps a statement of values that direct daily effort to long-term impact and bettering the community.

- *Construct dynamic statements.* – Consider the evolutionary nature of post-release services. For example, if you offer job counseling services, you could begin with how to get a job then address how to keep it. This is how LINC began. Before long, the founding co-executive directors had a small residential facility. Your statements need to be forward looking and revisited regularly. They should evolve.

- *Understand that the process is synergistic.* – Understanding scope is the extension of putting together leadership and understanding capacity. Scope will help define how you evaluate your program, develop resources, add staff and services, and ultimately succeed in meaningful ways.

> **Your story of Capacity Building may be fascinating, but data that show objective results sell your program.**

- *Consider the data.* – The use of data during scoping is a practical insight from stakeholders. "Know what to measure then how to measure it," one senior staffer observed. Don't try to define your project's purpose without grounding it in data. Yes, the numbers contribute to the vision and mission. Since recidivism is the first tangible measure of project success, understand that number at least. "You will have to show payback quickly," according to staff at all the Reform Movement sites. Your discussions will be that much more insightful when you understand that immediate purpose (e.g., reduce recidivism). You need to give stakeholders a way to judge project performance in terms they understand—not what you think they understand. Your story of Capacity Building may be fascinating, but data that show objective results sell your program.

Following is a sample scoping statement,[64] but keep in mind that yours will be unique to your circumstances.

Title: *Adult Reentry Aftercare Program*

Objective: The objective of the Adult Reentry Aftercare Program is to provide comprehensive support and assistance to individuals returning to the community after incarceration, with the aim of reducing recidivism rates, promoting successful reintegration, and enhancing public safety. This program is to collaborate with local resources in a matrix of partnerships.

Scope:

1. Target Population:
   - The program will serve adult individuals (18 years and older) who are returning to the community after serving a period of incarceration in local, state, or federal correctional facilities.

- Priority will be given to individuals identified as at-risk for recidivism due to factors such as previous criminal history, lack of stable housing, substance abuse issues, or limited education and employment opportunities.

2. Program Components:

- Case Management: Each participant will be assigned a dedicated case manager who will conduct comprehensive assessments, develop individualized reentry plans, and coordinate access to services and resources.

- Transitional Housing: The program will provide temporary housing assistance to participants who lack stable housing upon release, with a focus on safe and supportive living environments.

- Employment Services: Participants will receive assistance with job readiness training, resume building, job search assistance, and connections to local employers and vocational training programs.

- Educational Support: The program will offer access to educational opportunities, including GED preparation classes, adult education programs, and enrollment assistance in higher education institutions.

- Counseling and Support Services: Participants will have access to counseling services, substance abuse treatment programs, mental health support, and peer support groups to address underlying issues and promote personal growth and resilience.

- Community Engagement: The program will facilitate connections to community-based organizations, faith-based groups, and other support networks to help participants build positive social connections and engage in pro-social activities.

3. Geographic Scope:

- The program will be implemented within [Name of City/County]'s jurisdiction, serving individuals returning to the community within this geographic area.

- Services will be delivered through partnerships with local government agencies, community organizations, nonprofit groups, and service providers.

4. Duration:

- The program will operate on an ongoing basis, providing support and services to participants for a specified period following their release from incarceration.

- Participants will receive varying levels of support based on individual needs, with the goal of promoting long-term stability and success.

5. Evaluation and Monitoring:

- The program will establish performance metrics and outcome measures to evaluate effectiveness and track participant progress.

- Regular monitoring and evaluation will be conducted to assess program impact, identify areas for improvement, and ensure accountability and transparency in program delivery.

By adhering to the scope outlined above, the Adult Reentry Aftercare Program aims to address the complex needs of individuals transitioning from incarceration to the community, fostering positive outcomes and contributing to safer and healthier communities.

Do you see that scoping is foundational? It has a great effect on everything and everyone involved in your program. Scope helps define, refine, and institutionalize what you are and do. It's essential and must be done right. The time spent is well worth it. Scoping is mission critical.

4. Design the Process Evaluation and Impact Analysis to Justify Reentry Services

You will be warmly surprised at what practitioners, your peers, have determined is necessary for effective analysis and evaluation. It's not much, not complicated, and not impossible. This, too, is essential. However, it's one of the first critical action items to be neglected or not done thoroughly enough. Neglect it at your peril. It may be a new experience or appear complicated, but it's not; just jump in. The executive director at the Durham JSC perceptively states that graduates of their day center for post-release services should:

- Have a path to an acceptable, realistic, decent job.
- Progress through and exit the program equipped for healthy independence from substance abuse.
- Graduate and remain drug and crime free.

These would be considered initial results in the chain of outcomes. The idea is for graduates to progress to being productive and enjoying a place in the neighborhood and perhaps at the family table. Notice all are measurable and can be easily demonstrated in monetary terms; that is in "profit" in dollars saved and reinvested in more or other programming. Residential programs like LINC, Dismas, and TROSA define the above goals more specifically as:

- Having a steady occupation with benefits and career potential.
- Having kicked substance abuse with the ability to manage good health.
- Committing to a crime-free, productive life.

What to Measure

Now the question is, what do you need to measure for your program and how do you do it? Again, less is more. The answer is, ensure your team is adept at data entry at the point of services delivery then at how to analyze it. The best measures can be converted to dollars and cents, profit and loss. If you can't do that, you may not need the measure. The "profit" you make for your partners and the community is essential to your program justification. Finally, know how to tell the story of your successes and needs—with the implications and evidence of what happens if you don't succeed.

A good place to start is with one of the many checklists for reentry, for example the *Jail Administrator's Toolkit for Reentry*[65] or the *Jail to Community: Online Learning Toolkit*[56] have workable sections on data. Local experts would caution that these checklists were written for efforts largely inside the prison gates from the perspective of criminal justice agencies. Local programming is best served to focus on what happens this side of the gates. Community efforts will necessarily be more modest, such as assessing day services programming, which focuses on being a conduit to community-based services. As these checklists are practitioner oriented, they are a good point of departure.

Understanding and, by extension, measuring how to effect a successful transfer from incarceration to true rehabilitation is still evolving and will continue to evolve.[67]

Your program should interpret any measure in a way that's useful to you in determining efficiency (processes) and effectiveness (results). Building your program and its analyses will be very much a result of experimentation and discovery. The implicit message is that what you measure and certainly how you do it is determined by what is meaningful to your circumstances if your program aims to improve the community and efficiently use public funds.[68]

Begin with a measure or two of impact then move to overall measures. These can include: effect on community safety and health; more effective allocation and use of resources; effect on the criminal justice system; and betterment of the target population. You can begin by asking five questions:[69]

- *What data do you need to collect?* – Understand who your clients are. Know their demographic and criminal profiles, education, health and substance abuse issues, and subsistence and job skills needs. From this, it would be helpful to understand and monitor pertinent aspects of recidivism, such as who is recidivating and why. Don't forget the wider needs for "results" from your partners and supporters, especially at budget or fundraising time.

- *How easily can you gather the data?* – Your staff should be responsible for data input, because you will need to source data from the returnee as it is created for the best analysis. Thus, it's helpful if data gathering is as simple as entering a few daily numbers in a communal spreadsheet. One person, hopefully a volunteer, would be responsible for maintaining the database, developing the reports, and assisting dissemination. The main thing is to make all staff participate in gathering data that defines the work they do. They must have a picture of what they are doing and how they are performing, by the numbers.

- *Who should gather the data and who should have access to it?* – Don't assume staff will be able to work with data unless they're trained. Then, as above, make each responsible for their bit of essential data gathering. You can use the data to show how staff are reaching goals and building the program.

> **Your program should interpret any measure in a way that's useful to you in determining efficiency (processes) and effectiveness (results).**

- *How confident are you that the data are accurate, reliable, and useful?* – Theoretical analysts may disagree, but the test of data accuracy and reliability in a *practical application* comes from its usefulness. If your effectiveness and efficiency don't improve, you're probably looking at the wrong things in the wrong ways.

- *What is the best format to collect, analyze, and disseminate data?* – Ask the people who will benefit from the data what's useful to them, then provide it in a format and terms they understand. A busy county commissioner, for example, will want a bottom-line summary, perhaps with one or two telling charts. A granting source may want an explanation of how their money will further their philanthropic goals. Can you make a realistic, meaningful, even exciting report in a one-page brief with one chart? Making one attention-grabbing point matters. Realistically, that's all your audiences can absorb in a meeting. Be prepared with "the rest of the story," if asked.

Your data should help accomplish project goals, contribute to services delivery, translate to monetary benefit, and help build credibility and capacity. Relative to analysis and evaluation, capacity is built in two ways: for program permanence and for analytical, results-meaningful capability.

Program capacity is a theme throughout this model, so data should contribute to justifying program resources for permanency. *Analytical capacity* is the acquisition of automation tools and developing the processes for gathering, "crunching" numbers, and relating how results are progressing. Thus, the goal of this critical feature is to plan and develop software to suit your program and your audiences. It can simply be an Excel spreadsheet. It should, however, be conceived to cover a full range of data for impact and process. Since this discussion is about implementation of a startup, the first data collected must be simple.

Effective Practice
Decide on a few initial impact measures that define results and can be easily gathered, analyzed, and reported.

Program sophistication grows in many ways with the progress and evolution of the work at these successful programs. Data at the Durham JSC is "real time." It's updated at the point of contact by staff and referred to by leadership throughout the day. Upon special request, it's disseminated on the fly at scheduled and impromptu meetings. This is the ultimate expression of how data should serve the idea, not the reverse. Staff resist the temptation to plunder every nook and cranny for numbers. That only paralyzes progress and distracts from everyday work. Yet they are constantly collecting data that justifies the

> **Your data should help accomplish project goals, contribute to services delivery, translate to monetary benefit, and help build credibility and capacity.**

project and streamlines operations with the result that resources flow and they work extremely efficiently. I observed commonalities as to how these experienced community advocates defined how they went about analysis (studying impact) and evaluation (working smarter not harder).

Just about everything at these sites was about maintaining and building credibility one way or another. Staff asked their stakeholders what was important to them and developed those data. Practicality determined what they collected, no matter how difficult it was to assemble.

Another aspect of practicality is that data had to directly affect the mission and operations. Site leadership recognized that their staff were service providers, not analysts. Data collection, analysis, and dissemination had to be simple. This wasn't because staff couldn't develop analytical sophistication, as I saw great analytical capabilities at each site. It was because they recognized that the priority is the client.

Data also must improve things by providing information for action—reflection—action, which is ongoing. The JSC, for example, has a sophisticated spreadsheet that's updated continuously. It's the distillation of five complicated databases that were slashed and meshed into one easy-to-automate tool. It's the epitome of user friendliness, because it was designed with utility in mind. Every staffer contributed input, and all could see individual and collective progress from it. Remarkably, all stakeholders can access it for updates as needed. This is the epitome of *live* data. It's used for daily decision making, to monitor client progress, regular reporting, budgetary presentations to the county commission, and the annual report. Basically, they monitored their clients for:

- *Reduced recidivism* – JSC staff set an initial goal of a 50 percent reduction in recidivism, a goal made more challenging as rates improved. They also keep tabs on recidivism in the general population of the formerly incarcerated compared to the rates from their program participants. Naturally, those in the program did dramatically better.

- *Reduced revocations* – The Durham JSC found that the cognitive aspect of deviant behavior can be altered by a class called *Thinking for a Change*.

So, enrollment and graduation rates in that evidence-based practice were monitored.

- *Reduced drug dependency* – They monitored the successful completion of substance abuse treatment and being drug free during and immediately upon release from the program.

- *Increased employability* – They also monitored the client's work in becoming employable and evidence of getting and maintaining a job. They documented active participation in employment classes and education and if clients were hired during the program. In addition, they documented whether clients increased their employability as evidenced by evaluations during training and upon reaching milestones in the program.

Observe how the JSC staff built the *components of proof*. They could translate reductions in returns to incarceration into money saved. The JSC tracked program effectiveness by monitoring the recidivism of people graduating from their classes and those that did not. Also, they checked several variables that defined recidivism. For example, they tabulated the number of arrests and convictions prior to admission to the program then compared those numbers to the performance one year after program completion. They went one step further and developed a cost-effective statement on the (salary) money saved by posting a 75 percent reduction in recidivism. Reducing recidivism by 75 percent is an extraordinary accomplishment for a local program built with little example for how to do post-release aftercare programming.

> **Reducing recidivism by 75 percent is an extraordinary accomplishment for a local program built with little example for how to do post-release aftercare programming.**

Notice also how the Durham JSC program monitors progress. Overall, they want to improve client employability, which is realistic for their local program. To do that, a client must stay out of trouble and begin to reintegrate. They rightly see it's not realistic to focus on very long-term measures, say the drop in neighborhood crime and improvement in community well-being that a residential program may observe. It's also not reasonable to do a longitudinal follow-up of years with rather complex methodology and a diversion of manpower and money to be able to comment on the ultimate success of clients reintegrating into the community. It would be good to do so, just not practical.

They recognize that keeping their clients from recidivating is a major purpose for their services. Program staff understand their target population and stakeholders, especially those on the county commission. They also understand the operational processes that make these results possible.

Having been in business for several decades, TROSA monitors a diverse set of measures to understand if their processes, services, therapies, and programming are contributing to overall goals, especially that of an effective transition. They monitor:

- Numbers of drivers' licenses obtained by clients.
- Trained drivers.
- Those getting jobs on release.
- GEDs conferred.
- Those who matriculate to trade school and college.
- Dropped jobs.
- Those paying child support.
- Hours spent in various therapies such as Dialectical Behavioral Therapy.
- Those off probation while in TROSA.
- Relapses into diabetes and drugs.
- Those who return to crime and incarceration.
- Dollars saved in jail time by TROSA graduates who do not return to the criminal justice system.

Understanding the efficiency and effectiveness of processes at TROSA is fundamentally important. It's more time-consuming than continually assessing results and impact, because staff at TROSA understand the critical importance of having efficient and effective processes. One must come before the other. All this data and analysis is to educate outsiders on the "bang-for-the-buck" TROSA delivers.

These programs zero in on building capacity with clear results measures. First, they understand how their services are utilized by their target clients. This helps them understand how well matched and accessible their services are to those they serve. They get regular feedback on the quality and effectiveness of their services from those served, including the community. This indicates the level of service expectations and whether a need is being answered. Capacity Building is fundamentally about enhancing well-being. Going home again with dignity is the ultimate expression of accomplishment and well-being. Instead of someone completely dependent on public services, the community has another responsible, productive neighbor.

Each site had a seat-of-the-pants feel to what they did, especially when it came to analysis and evaluation, but each was highly successful at data control, that is, improving how things worked.

> **Going home again with dignity is the ultimate expression of accomplishment and well-being.**

However, mastery over data is not enough. They considered:

- *Progress* – They had policies and procedures for which they gathered data and applied it to monitor progress.

- *A one for all and all for one staff attitude* – Staff were very flexible in how they did this analysis part of their jobs.

- *Staff-centered operations* – Staff managed each client individually, which epitomized keeping things small, simple, and manageable. They worked very hard to understand how they were doing as individual staff members. Their effectiveness was reflected in the progress, or lack thereof, of their clients.

- *Flexibility and dynamism* – Adjustments to services delivery were made continuously, nearly minute-to-minute. Static numbers and charts became dynamic, and thus tasking and goals were accomplished, and their vision was realized.

- *A learning environment* – They functioned dynamically because they established a learning environment. This was partly based on data that allowed them to understand *how* and *how well* clients were being serviced. Every employee knew their effect on the organization.

Their infrastructure of data collection and processes—a critical feature of the Capacity Building model—made a data-driven organization possible, which is foundational to establishing a learning environment.

Effective Practice
Establish a learning environment based on data to evaluate and improve the efficiency of processes.

A learning environment facilitates the action—reflection—action necessary to improve. It includes evaluation focused inward to their organizational stakeholders compared to analysis of impact, which has an outward focus to tell the story of the project to external stakeholders. Yes, understanding your operation begins with data, which can be dry and sterile. However, at these sites the data becomes organic and even exciting in that it paints an accurate picture of process and progress from *moment to momen*t by having nearly instant feedback. This has several advantages. Staff have a vested interest in telling the program story, as they are responsible for data entry and benefit from it. They can see how they're doing as total numbers update automatically. Likewise, people who have oversight responsibility or a stake in transitional services can satisfy any number of questions. So how do these remarkable aftercare Reform Movement sites arrive at this enviable state of evaluation that improves processes? Mainly, they do three things well:

- *They collaborate to learn.* – People are cross-trained, which facilitates idea sharing. They're encouraged to learn one from the other. Various functions, by their nature, collect and organize staff with tasks that require sharing effective practices.

- *Staff are encouraged to learn through education and training.* – Staff are encouraged to attend professional and skill training. Formal education is also promoted.

- *Program philosophy encourages continuous learning.* – Leadership values ongoing personal, skill-based, and professional education and development.

Now let's consider how the attitude of staff betterment reflects in collecting and using information. Basically, each site did two things: They collected essential data and set aside time to ask, "How are we doing?" JSC staff see their day as based on "learning as you go." In the beginning, "No one was good at the data thing," according to a senior staffer. They collected a hodgepodge of information, which became more refined over time. They made sure data was considered a good tool, a friendly thing, focused and focusing attention on necessary essentials. This view is quite contrary to that of some organizations that use numbers to criticize. These learning environments meant that the good and the bad could be discussed without blame and with eagerness to do better. Learning, then continuous improvements, came by:

- *Helpful individual critique of results* – Staff know how their clients are doing, as progress on goals is available on demand. Results here are differentiated from overall program impact. Staff are given information on how they are performing individually and collectively by monitoring, for example, numbers of job interviews, placements, and sustained employment.

> **The model sites placed great emphasis on increasing staff capability, even during dire budgetary times.**

- *Feedback on process* – Regular meetings are held to discuss how different ideas and techniques played out on their client base, overall and for specific staff functions. Originally, functions of rehabilitation and reintegration were assigned to individuals because it's easy to assign tasks. This tradition was constructively challenged by forming a monthly staffing meeting. The meeting became an opportunity for all program staff to meet with clients to collectively see how each client is doing then prescribe action according to the need of the moment. This is a demonstration of the whole being greater than the sum of its parts.

- *Targeting staff development to improve service delivery and capacity* – The model sites placed great emphasis on increasing staff capability, even during dire budgetary times. From understanding process *and* performance, they could see what specific staff training, education, and professional development would expand individual capabilities in line with overall purposes. This approach is patterned after the better parts of the private sector model of staff development.

- *Rewarding creativity, self-development, professional development, and goal accomplishment* – Leadership continually recognized increasing staff capability by celebrating individual and organizational accomplishments. They did this by assigning more mutually agreed upon responsibilities, tailoring duties and responsibilities to each individual staffer, and encouraging experimentation and creativity. People really *wanted* to work at these reform-oriented sites.

- *Critiquing what does not work well* – Staffers had no fear of discussing areas that needed improvement. A problem was seen as an opportunity, not a circumstance to deflect blame or criticize. "No nit pickers are allowed," a staffer commented quietly in passing.

While visiting these sites, I was exposed to example after example of why and how these programs were not merely good, but great. I was invited to one of many meetings to discuss how things were functioning and how things could be improved. But before a typical morning meeting started, the senior executive cooked breakfast for the team! Who does that!? The best of "forward leaning" 21st-century leaders do.

The affair involved a few hot plates, plastic ware, juice, eggs, bacon, and pancakes. With that one gesture, what might normally be a grind or threatening became an event to anticipate with a smile. No, the work didn't change, and yes, it remained intense. Yet, it was fun, with a lot of laughter and concern for one another.

This is just one example of modestly paid public servants loving to do things for others and loving to be at work. They willingly put in overtime and continually did extraordinary work with their clients. In fact, after the breakfast meeting, I asked staff what made the JSC so productive and effective. Staff spontaneously agreed that what makes the JSC a great place to work is that it is family. This sense of family is at the heart of their success at establishing long-term relationships, friends who become mutual and program supporters.

Mission, Vision, Philosophy of Service

Consider your mission first, and your vision will come from that. This is the reverse of a common perspective. Consider *how* you will better the community. What will be your community specific services? Whom will you touch? How will you reach them with your values, public image, and even how you survive?[70] Let it rest for a while then shape it again.

Test scope and all it touches in the real world of daily activity and increasing clarity. Does scope facilitate the processes of daily activity? Does it help make decisions? Does it describe your project in a unique way? Does it *communicate and motivate*?

Imagine some of the most captivating public vision statements. Take for example, the Bill and Melinda Gates Foundation statement on their education philanthropy: *We believe that when all people in the United States have the opportunity to develop their talents, our society thrives.* The Ohio Reentry Resource Center wants *offenders to successfully connect as productive members of society.* Dismas Charities believes in *healing the human spirit.* These vision statements are idealistic, yes, *and* they compel.

Your idea of reentry-aftercare expressed in just a few words and declaring what you want your program to become, will translate well to action.[71] How it manifests in values, what you believe in, helps prioritize effort.[72] The scoping process will help you internally with daily operations and how you interact externally with the community.

It can also influence the preface to your standard operating procedures, which will set the tone for how you expect people to act and behave in the name of your project. The art of this work is that it guides people when they're on their *own*. Even with no watchful eyes, they're steered and motivated to do the right thing the right way. If done properly, scoping will become the conscience of your work.

Among your first decisions, then, is to decide a philosophy of service. One executive director said, "Think big, act small." Doing anything well means your work has a sequential, measurable effect on clients, your neighbors, the neighborhood, and then the municipality in terms or measures meaningful to each interest group. Ask your stakeholder groups what is meaningful to them; don't assume to know.

Reducing recidivism is a good start. Initially, the formerly incarcerated should not recidivate. They should be on their way to a place in the community and at the family table with an occupation that would support a family. The community needs to see a reduction in crime and victimization that translates to public safety and security. Likewise, the municipality will want to see the above plus a "profit" from funds invested. This profit is gained by reducing incarceration rates to reserve jail and prison beds for those who really should be there. It's another way to look at cost effectiveness, the ultimate message for startup support.

Effective Practice
Develop measurable mission and vision statements that focus on the needs of your target returnee.

Each site visited had inspirational and aspirational mission statements or credos simply put. The Durham County JSC believes in *"One at a time."* TROSA lives *"Each one teach one."* LINC focuses on the individual by *"Creating bridges between you* (the resident) *and valuable resources."* This is a universal theme. The message of decades of collective experience is clear: Do only what has the best chance of being done well. Goals will also evolve with the scoping process. One of the founders of LINC stressed that they "need not be lofty, just realistic." The study sites worked on defining who they are by stating what they are doing simply and practically. The grand part of their visions is that changing their communities for the better is done at the micro level, nearly neighborhood by neighborhood. By connecting to resource providers. By winning political and community support. And by serving individual clients. Anything more and post-release services delivery swings out of control, that is, it becomes unmanageable, on the road to stumbling along, failing, and not knowing it.

To summarize the basics of developing guiding statements epitomized by these capacity building experiments, they need to:

- *Inspire and motivate* – A clear vision is a compelling view of what can be achieved. It motivates by being just a bit out of reach—challenging but worthy of individual and collective drive. It motivates all to do the right thing at the right time all the time when no one is watching. In other words, it touches individual inner motivation to accomplish.

- *Define values, beliefs, and purpose* – An inspiring view of the possible is driven by why the organization is there at all. And how the work fits into the betterment of community to be good and do good for the common good.

- *Adapt to the needs of permanency* – Vision and mission must confront uncertainties and difficulties and prosper by their resolution. Growth must endure as most social dysfunction is permanent and must have permanent infrastructure to at least diminish the problem.

- *Be strategic* – Goals must be specific, measurable, and achievable, defined in monetary terms to compel support. The costs of the program consider much more than direct and indirect obligations. A compelling argument for support is best served by stating the hidden costs and unintended consequences of *not* providing the services. Unintended consequences are usually the costliest. For example, according to one senior staffer, the lack of pre-kindergarten or nursery school results later in school dropouts and downstream to a diminished labor pool.

- *Be actionable and proactive* – Action statements compel measurable goal accomplishment. It lets the community know that your program is up to challenges, problems, and permanency.

- *Be innovative and learning* – Be open to new ideas that complement the old. Embrace technology and novel solutions and answers, while seeking outside opinions and assistance. While you learn, also teach. Build an organization where "each one teaches one," as in TROSA.

Capacity Building well done communicates vision and the capability to get there. It compels people to get on board, to be part of something vital, vigorous, and visionary.

While this effective practice recommends that project stakeholders do a formal scoping process, a definition of how much can be done can evolve from the need to get going. Uniquely, the JSC adopted a no-refusal acceptance policy; they had to start somewhere. Intuitively, they were building capacity, but it was much about "by guess and by golly" and a "no failure" attitude. Their beginning was a real bootstrap affair. For example, the new executive director intercepted a newly released client and began immediately to connect him to services. They figured things out as each client passed through the JSC doors because, "Doing nothing was unacceptable." It worked because it had to!

Yes, startups defy this advice to act prudently, the long term firmly in mind. I asked every interviewee what they would have done differently in the beginning of their project development. The TROSA leader replied immediately that he would start big enough, even though he admitted this way of starting is not recommended. He began with the intention of building the infrastructure for a 100-bed residential operation. His justification: "There will be just as much work and hassle as with a small project." These models evolved. Now staff thoroughly understand and qualify whoever comes to them from their jail and prisons. While the no-refusal policy is noble, the scope of it was way too broad.

> **Unintended consequences are usually the costliest. For example, according to one senior staffer, the lack of pre-kindergarten or nursery school results later in school dropouts and downstream to a diminished labor pool.**

At the time of the site visits, after a few years of tough work, a senior staffer from the JSC visited each prospective client while the person was still incarcerated! This was to determine if that individual *wanted* to change her or his life. Was the person willing to submit to a very rigid program with high expectations and consequences for failing certain firm compliance requirements, such as staying off illegal substances. Senior staff also wanted to know if a prospect would benefit from the program and, surprisingly, if the prospect would be hurt or disadvantaged by the offered services. For example, the prospect may already have a job and would not be able to attend classes and therapy. A job is a huge accomplishment.

Every client is well advised to sign on to a highly rigid regimen. In fact, I witnessed a "staffing" meeting of clients and staff/service providers where clients were given extensive group input by JSC staff and transitional services specialists on how they were doing. Then clients would have their activities adjusted according to the need of the moment, their progress or lack of it, and obstacles present and anticipated. Before they began the group experience, held monthly, each client had a urinalysis administered on the spot by the probation officer, the disciplinary arm of the program. One JSC client failed the drug test and was revoked immediately. No ceremony, no mitigating circumstances, no arguments, no excuses. Just a trip back to jail. Dramatic, but demonstrably effective!

The message derived from their scope is clear. JSC staff use extraordinary means to ensure a client's success—unless the client flaunts the rules of conduct. This is why their recidivism rate is respectably very low. It's not surprising that clients or residents of these programs comment that the regimentation and rules of transition are stricter than those behind bars. JSC staff and stakeholders understand their scope.

The Urban Institute lends a good perspective on how to define your vision, mission, and values which underscores the criticality of going through this part of project development. Their toolkit offers summative insights.[73] Everyone invited provides input, though disagreements arise even after statements are written. The goal is buy-in. Physically tie these statements to your processes, policies, procedures, and directives. For example, your standard operating procedures can be prefaced by these statements, which will guide staff in their every endeavor.

Use this scoping process to understand the varied motivations of your stakeholders and make each statement with a view to having it adjusted according to the evolution of your project. The executive director of the Durham County JSC underscored the quintessential reality: "In the end," she commented, "don't get mired in the theoretical. Let reality determine the path—and take it."

Getting your leadership together, understanding your capacity to deliver transitional services tempered by a carefully restricted scope leads into understanding how well your project is functioning. Then, regular evaluation and analysis determines your effectiveness.

5. Nurture Relationships for Resources Development

Developing resources is a major theme that runs throughout this model. Therefore, nothing can be done without an eye toward earning credibility and building relationships that lead to resources.

The mention of only a few insights from the field will suffice to generate ideas for your development strategy. Let's begin with a few notes on the realities of growing reliable streams of sustainable resources. The study sites have cracked this nut, so be encouraged.

Yes, they expressed great frustration at the reluctance of funders, maddening politics, and persistent stereotypes about their clients. They also decried convoluted regulation after onerous regulation that complicated supporting their expensive and complex program. However, they embraced these realities as opportunities and answered them one by one.

> One JSC client failed the drug test and was revoked immediately. No ceremony, no mitigating circumstances, no arguments, no excuses.

They persuaded funders with compelling arguments of cost savings. They smashed stereotypes when program graduates became reliable employees, even business owners and model citizens. They made it politically advantageous to support transitional services. This happened especially when the voting public was helped to understand that their lives were much better when former inmates were assisted. Plus, they became creative, actually very creative, when defining what sustainable support could be. Here are some tips:

- *Know your stakeholders.* – Find, group, and prioritize your potential partners. Make your pursuit long, wide, and frequent. Stakeholders come from the government, the private and private nonprofit sectors, and simply citizens. They don't necessarily need to come attached to money, although that is primary. They can be volunteers or come with in-kind goods and services. And don't forget your residents and graduates, your greatest cheerleaders. Know and be prepared for what answers their best interests.

- *Express your message clearly.* – Get to the point. Even develop a well-honed "elevator speech." Be clear, concise, and confident. Be a regular attendee at critical meetings. You will do well to be on a first-name basis with as many people as you can. Oh yes, and make sure you really *listen, remember, and reflect.* How about this tag line:

    Building Permanent Solutions to Permanent Problems

- *Collaborate when you can.* – Ask to share funding ideas. Maybe ask key people to weigh in on appropriate decisions. Note what is mutual with other businesses, as there's a connection between just about anyone or any organization. Acknowledge effective collaborations.

- *Sing your praises and successes.* – Be ready with a number or two for impact. Share success stories. One aftercare program took graduates to certain meetings. And don't forget to ask for what you need.

- *Network.* – Get face-to-face as much as possible. Look for networking events; host one. Exude how your program contributes to community well-being—the health, development, and vivacity of the community.

Realize that this resource development business can be grueling—*and* it's rewarding, even fun, to make new friends with a common purpose.

Philosophically, model programs understood that credibility and integrity are the keys to earning partners.

Development at these Capacity Building aftercare Reform Movement sites epitomized the philosophy of leaving no resources stone unturned. This broad way of looking at becoming operationally stable encompassed their philosophy of developing reliable streams of funding based on building relationships. Let's see how they went about it, the array of methods they employed, and the sources on which they worked.

Funding streams need to be just that—reliable year after year. That way you can budget services and requests for further resources to fund shortfalls. One program official observed even an annual bake sale can be a reliable source of money—*when* receipts are traced year over year.

Philosophically, model programs understood that credibility and integrity are the keys to earning partners. So they made sure they had impact that spoke to stakeholders and all their dealings were of the highest moral character. Their words were a bond. They said what they would do, and they did it. They also understood that friends make partners, so they became part of the fabric of the community and understood how their neighbors thought and acted. Small is good. No task is too small when it comes to talking up their work. Their problem becomes your problem . . . an opportunity to help in the solution; a gesture that's rarely forgotten.

This also applies to getting big money, for example. The big check more than likely came because the source had been contributing in small ways. It may have been simply that the friend was invited to and attended program meetings—for a long time. Model site staff are very successful at getting support because they are largely not dependent on a single source of funding. An exception is the Durham JSC, which via an agreement with a governmental agency has reliable renewable monies as well as support from the county year after year. Note that government support in this case was not an excuse not to work doubly hard on making friends and developing resources. Developing goodwill by being honest and dependable is a resource also.

Each site had a shotgun approach to developing a variety of funding sources, which stabilized resource streams—the goal of any resource development strategy.[74] Program stakeholders intuitively understood that overdependence on a single source is dangerous, especially if it's in the form of a grant, which can be here today and vanish next year, never to return. They also understood the fairly wide range of choices, such as, but not limited to, the following:

- *Mutual agreements* – Memos of understanding and agreement between governmental and nongovernmental agencies established the specifics of how the burdens of service provision would be shared. These contracts covered simple responsibilities up to and including dedicating extra-agency staff to aftercare.

- *Barter* – People forget that barter works and just about anything can be bartered. Many times, the JSC was in a better position to do screening than other organizations, so they did it for them. In return, those organizations offered various services to the JSC, usually in measures beyond the JSC's gesture of sharing.

- *Federal government partnerships* – Dismas has an arrangement with the Federal Bureau of Prisons (BOP) that exemplifies how well the government can collaborate with a nonprofit. The BOP got services at a cost much below what they could offer them for, while Dismas still made a respectable "profit."

- *Local government funding* – More and more community/county leadership realize they need to have local reentry-aftercare and are willing to budget for it. Naturally, this comes from a program's long-term concerted campaign to court local elected officials with the benefits of support.

- *Sustainable enterprises* – One of the most creative answers to establishing resource streams is sustainable enterprises. When executive director Kevin MacDonald began TROSA in 1994, he knew that a long-term residential program was the real solution for many returnees. These were people who had a record, few skills for a family-sustaining career and community life, *and* serious substance-abuse difficulties.

    He knew he had to be independent to make his model work. So, he began industries such as a moving company, catering, construction services, and a picture framing operation, which would not only employ residents but be very lucrative. You would not believe what people want to give away at moving time.

Every castoff goes to a warehouse, where it is refurbished if need be. Then once a year they have a sale, which attracts countless people from the entire region around the heart of North Carolina.

Each of these businesses operated better than had ever been done before. For example, the moving company is booked months in advance and is the preferred local mover of choice. Based on that success and others, at the time of this writing, LINC is planning similar enterprises plus sustainable aqua and agriculture. Success proliferates success.

- *A grant* – Each site vigorously but cautiously seeks grants. Experience demonstrates that granting is prohibitively competitive, time consuming to manage, and restrictive with regulations. The best grants are large awards and are specifically targeted to program goals. LINC, for example, was able to get a $500,000 federal grant to begin remodeling their new residential facility because it fit the feds needs in detail. Note also that aftercare staff very carefully consider foundations, simply because those grants are small by comparison to, say, federal grants or a line item in the municipal budget.

- *In-kind donations* – This funding stream is limited only by imagination. For example, you can get professional services such as legal, accounting, marketing, and consulting. TROSA looks to Duke university business school for studies. Then there are equipment and supplies such as office equipment and construction materials and equipment. If someone volunteers, their hourly rate, in-kind, for the job done goes toward the requirement for a grant. Also, a volunteer frees up funds for perhaps more critical needs.

- *Gifts and donations* – LINC, for example, has graduated to offering donation opportunities on its website. It allows anyone to become an "Angel" for an affordable $25-$100 or a "Champion" for $2,500+.

- *Fundraisers* – All of the study sites do some sort of fundraisers. LINK has an annual Founder's Gala fundraiser at the local Hilton, which is well attended, as the friends of LINK, who bring their fat checkbooks, grow.

- *Planned giving* – TROSA develops larger gifts via estate planning. They earn bequests from the estates of people who want to participate in TROSA's success.

- *Foundations* – Some foundations prioritize aftercare. They even name specific programs for a bequest donor. No bequests are too small.

The executive director of the Durham JSC provided several insights. They began developing resources by understanding who their potential donors would be, then developing relationships even when they didn't have to. Understand how they went about this—very smart. They "went for the small money," which mounts up handsomely over time. Note that a small donation is only a start. The size of the donation increases also with the willingness to donate. Opportunities are there if you look.

Effective Practice
Map your services to identify resource development opportunities.

When the JSC began with few resources and no idea what services were appropriate. They let their clients tell them their resource needs and then mapped available services with an eye to developing them as supporters, financial or otherwise. Their first purpose in mapping services was to identify partners and gaps in services that could be filled by matrixing agencies for project purpose. Service providers became their first targeted partners. How could struggling local service providers collaborate with anything of significance? Well, not all of them were struggling, nor were they necessarily after money. They were after shared agreements, which proved to be more lucrative than receiving a check.

> Sharing of in-kind resources is doubly beneficial as it frees up money and other resources to do mission-critical tasks.

One of the things JSC did was sign a memo of agreement with the Division of Community Corrections (DCC). This established a dozen points of mutually beneficial collaboration that detailed shared responsibility for the operation of the Durham effort. This statement of responsibilities, expectations, and shared resources established that the DCC would provide the JSC reentry-aftercare program with *four* full-time staff. This was better than money. Besides sharing the essential burden of staffing, the JSC got the commitment of a major state agency that was then vested in JSC. Sharing of in-kind resources is doubly beneficial as it frees up money and other resources to do mission-critical tasks

Dismas Charities has an even more remarkable arrangement with the Bureau of Prisons, in which residents fulfill part of their sentences at Dismas. This is a mutually beneficial arrangement, as Dismas has been successfully doing post-release services since the 1960s. It's also a long-standing demonstration of how a large governmental agency *can* partner with a nonprofit at huge savings of tax dollars.

These memos of agreement are dramatic examples of sharing resources. They not only assure the success of post-release services; they apportion limited resources and funds much more efficiently than institutional responses to post-release services. Many more such arrangements collectively make significant contributions to the success of these programs—and can potentially add greatly to your program capacity. They are there for the asking according to program staff.

A very important aspect of a development strategy is that program staff, especially leadership, were doing development work "even when they didn't have to," according to one program executive director. What she meant was that whenever they had an occasion to see someone, they told the story of their program and how the individual could participate. Senior staff, especially executive directors, had prepared presentations, which usually made one point germane to the audience. At the JSC, for example, they had a very tight electronic presentation filled with pertinent graphics (a picture is worth a thousand words) called *Partners in Crime*. It was given spontaneously by any program staffer and especially a board member. They presented it to their crime cabinet, churches, social organizations, and state agencies. Few events or agencies escape the *Partners in Crime* show.

Senior staff tirelessly went to meetings all the time. Routine meetings were face to face, if possible. For example, the executive director of LINC drove 220 miles round trip for one of the interviews for this project. It could have been done by phone! When they could, staff did little favors and acted on suggestions. On my initial visit to TROSA, they found out about me by researching my bio and had my coffee ready—the way I liked it! Who thinks of such courteous detail? Well, these people do because they know how to build aftercare. It's a small gesture I will never forget and will want to repay. What attention to correct detail! Nothing was left to chance; they knew what they were about.

Staff made real friends because they *worked* at it. Key program people were expected to show up at events and meetings and they didn't disappoint. They learned what was important to people, and people learned how their program was improving the community and how they could help or participate.

The insight into this method of capacity development is that they did *not* overtly ask for support most of the time. They mastered the ultimate soft sell. They simply told their story, plans, and dreams. When they had to solicit real support, they asked an old friend or a close acquaintance. Many times, help was a foregone conclusion; it was just a matter of how much and when. This took years of building character-based goodwill, and it now pays handsomely.

> They mastered the ultimate soft sell. They simply told their story, plans, and dreams.

They knew the importance of starting small with established organizations, according to one executive director. The idea was to construct a solid core of support in people, programs, and an array of resources, wherever they may be found. That way, a post-release services effort could be built on existing programs, which brought with them stability and proven ideas. Furthermore, program planners didn't have to fund the entire aftercare services infrastructure.

Senior staff commented that the idea drives the pursuit of funding. Staff at the JSC knew they had to address the immediate need of releasees. Only after the budget was set did they develop a support fund to buy hygiene products, clothing, and food. Most initial support was not money; the goal of the initial "ask" was to begin a friendship about an idea that was bigger than the sum of the parts. They knew this was the avenue to bigger commitment and money.

How did they get to this lovely state of affairs? The easy answer is because of their action-oriented strategy from the very first days they began their work. Every aspect of this way of resources development is intentional. Plus, one of the most pleasant collateral benefits of working this way is they have *fun* doing it! *Tenacity* is how program staff describe building post-release services.

The next critical feature will discuss some of the nuances of assembling a proper array of services.

6. Develop Performance-Oriented Service Providers as Part of Your Team

This section deals with some of the specifics of post-release services. First, let me review the critical actions you need to take:

- *Recruit leadership* according to their ability to assist or deliver the services of post-release.

- *Determine capacity* from understanding gaps in need and doing an inventory of available services.

- *Decide scope,* or how much you can do well, by understanding the minimum array of services needed to achieve program goals.

- *Analyze the efficiencies* of operational processes and subsequent performance of services.

- *Develop resources* from services providers and extensions of them.

- *Assemble staff* according to the needs of your client base.

This section introduces what successful programs have done and are doing to offer their arrays of transitional services by adding a little more detail and insight to what's already known.

> **Every model site devised a way to test a service for its contribution to overall goal accomplishment.**

The purpose here is not to duplicate the volumes of information about services that are a mouse click away. It's to begin the discussion that defines a service mix to continue the work begun by our major public institutions such as the criminal justice system, social services, mental and medical health, and housing providers.

These successful experiments in post-release-aftercare services have "cracked the nut" of, first, being the conduit to institutional and community-based services and then filling the gaps in those services by providing direct services via their programs. That way they multiply their effort and can stay focused on essentials and sustainability.

Look for how these professionals put together custom matrices of problem solvers to complete service arrays and how they answered the unique and complex needs of this difficult population. Each site has a unique mix of service delivery systems, but all are remarkably successful at helping those who want to return to a place at the family table.

Be sure to make your service offerings performance oriented. Every model site devised a way to test a service for its contribution to overall goal accomplishment. For example, therapies and counseling had to help clients solve their mental, health, and substance abuse difficulties by staying drug free, on prescribed medications, and able to cope by pursuing employment and housing. Site staff took one vital step further in monitoring performance. They are constantly aware of overall recidivism rates, employment numbers, and the rates that clients returned to stable housing, for example.

The lesson here is twofold. First, measurement must be built into the service acquisition. Second, correct measurement should never stop. That way, analysis of any kind is dynamic and paints the current picture of performance. It informs your internal program staff and your external collaborators. This is integral to how the service becomes part of your permanent capacity for transitional services. What you do, what you offer, must perform *by the numbers*.

Remember you are primarily building capacity. The logic is simple: Without the support of service delivery capacity, or infrastructure, a program is vulnerable to collapse. It doesn't matter how good a service is in theory or if it's an evidence-based practice or expands to another location, if the overall idea fails to take root.

Capacity relative to transitional services is the business structure seen in the ten critical features of the project life cycle. These features support your self-sustaining array of community entities and programming that answer the aftercare needs of a client. The difficulty of building an effective post-release program reflects the complex needs of the target population. The study sites demonstrated various ways this can be done. Much of building services capacity, at least initially, is instinctual, reacting to a need and filling it, which was evidenced at all sites. Staffers invented new ways to deliver services.

When staff discovered clients didn't know how to interview, job hunting skills training was added. Employers expect a certain appearance from potential employees, so staff opened a "clothes closet" where decent clothes, actually very good clothes, were available. Clients had a difficult time making appointments, so they began offering transportation or at least bus fares and tickets. These are examples of services' evolution as the need presented; it's necessary and effective seat-of-the-pants problem solving. It worked because *failure was not an option* for these early champions. You may confront some of these issues in your efforts, as the process of building local capacity is largely one of discovery. These early efforts paved the way, and now you can be guided by this Capacity Building model.

Naturally these sites were also more deliberate in developing offerings, especially as they matured. Sites:

> **Notice the process of plan, do, analyze, learn, and do again.**

- *planned* for a service,
- had a *research and data basis for* recommendations,
- established *the service environment,*
- went through a phase of *testing implementation,*
- *measured progress,*
- and usually *improved the service idea and institutionalized it* if it continued to help overall goal accomplishment.

Notice the process of plan, do, analyze, learn, and do again. Whatever works matters, but planning early and well matters more.

What evolved were the following three main types of service models:

- *Community-based* programs, governmental and nongovernmental
- *Day* programs with umbrella services
- *Residential* programs based on income-producing trades

These programs and agencies offered overall transitional services with specific services such as counseling, therapy, medical and mental health treatment, and/or education. Overall services delivery systems are usually guided by a central program such as the Durham JSC day program. This day program also served as the main transitional services agency by providing the umbrella of indirect and direct services.

A residential program is the next level and can be marked by its developing sustainable income-producing enterprises. The residential program exemplified by TROSA is nearly self-contained in that it uses businesses such as landscaping and furniture rebuilding companies to train residents for independence in the community.

These enterprises have the dual function of generating rather reliable streams of money, which facilitate year-by-year programming and planning. This means that spending and programming can be planned into the future—*and* they are the best tools for rehabilitation. They provide residents with a way to learn skills to reenter the social mainstream while they deal with physical and mental health difficulties, such as substance abuse. A job, responsibility, respect, and pride are the best medicine.

Further, these sustainable enterprises, very profitable indeed, are largely therapeutic in that much about life this side of a jail cell or rehab is inculcated. Many times, this involvement is the first time a resident has had purpose in his or her life. These residential programs are stellar examples of how the community can take responsibility for a social need, hold itself accountable, and succeed in collaboration with and usually leading the public, private, and nonprofit sectors.

Effective Practice
Muster your local transitional services and agencies.

Your community is naturally rich in ways to receive former inmates, attend to their immediate needs, and put them on a wholesome path. First, you need to understand the major risk factors of your target group to direct the search for and identify local resources to answer each need. Remember, the services must fit productively into your collaborative matrix of likeminded partners.[75] You should have a fairly good idea of what is in your community by your capacity assessment. If needed services aren't available, you will have to develop them. Following are problems you'll likely need to address:

- *Unemployability* – Work that will sustain an individual and a family is arguably first, as it's key to a return to society. But the first job will more than likely be entry-level labor just to get a few dollars coming in while other services unfold. Some agencies specialize in finding work for people with prison and jail experience. The task is to find employers willing to provide that first job, and more employees are willing when they're given a rational, dollars-and-cents argument for doing so. Officials at these programs have compelling reasons for hiring these returnees, such as reducing crime and victimization, which has a positive impact on the business environment. Furthermore, programs exist to subsidize companies who hire returnees.

- *Marital/family dysfunction* – Families of this population are most times as fractured as they are essential to a successful return home. Staying away from crime and out of incarceration depends largely on familial support. Private and nonprofit agencies specialize in family counseling.

- *Negative peer association* – Noncriminal associates exemplify the benefits of good social skills. Conversely, residents need to steer away from former peers who encourage dysfunctional, asocial, illegal behavior.

- *Substance abuse* – Those returnees with substance abuse need to address their addictions. Many of the residents of TROSA, for example, have grown up with drugs. They want a way out but don't know how to kick the traces, which is a strong reason they make a commitment to the real work prescribed by these programs. Their success will be via a case-managed approach to permanent sobriety. TROSA's program is two years long because experience dictates that conquering drugs and crime and learning new social behaviors is a lengthy, 24-hours-a-day undertaking. Successful reentry is a mental, spiritual, and physical lifestyle reinvention; the whole person has to be rebuilt. Be encouraged, though, because all but a few want to make their "resurrection" happen.

- *Inability to function in the community* – Learning the basic skills of daily living begins upon release. Many *evidence-based* approaches such as Cognitive Behavioral Interventions (CBI) are available to teach these skills.

> **Successful reentry is a mental, spiritual, and physical lifestyle reinvention; the whole person has to be rebuilt.**

- *Personal/emotional dysfunction* – When returnees enter your program, they must learn how to be in control of their daily life, often for the first time. Your clients need to learn how to make good decisions, cope with the ups and downs of life, and maintain good physical and mental health.

- *Improper attitude* – Everyone must learn how to be law abiding. This is made more complex as this group has survived in and out of criminality, They're largely suspicious of people in authority and manipulative according to senior staff. Yet many do learn to have positive views of the world—just not overnight.

Don't duplicate what's being done well. Determine, if need be, that you can build on it frugally, effectively, and permanently.

Searching for service allies according to risk factors also helps shape your service providers to overall program goal accomplishment. Before they become part of the team, you'd best imbue them with your vision and mission, how they specifically fit into the overall scheme, and how they will be measured on their contributions to the program.

Take the Durham JSC as an example of the umbrella program of a day program.[76] This day program functions in two ways. Primarily, it's the conduit to community services as outlined previously. Secondarily, it provides direct services such as individual and group counseling and employment assistance. Note the diverse group of service providers that contribute to the overall purpose of transitional services county wide. They are just waiting to be asked:

- *Community-based Corrections for Adult Offenders* – Here the goal is to reduce recidivism among ex-offenders, thus increasing public safety and reducing incarceration costs.

- *Substance abuse treatment* – Clients are helped to productive, crime- and drug-free lives.

- *Pretrial services* – Pretrial services provide a systematic approach for recommending release as well as community supervision for defendants who don't pose a risk to the community as they await trial.

- *Special programs* – These programs round out service needs by providing a specialized court, anti-gang programming, and vocational training.

- *Screening, assessment, and evaluation services* – This is a collaborative assembly of services for mental health and substance abuse clients.

- *Juvenile Crime Prevention Council (JCPC)* – The name of this umbrella program is its purpose: It galvanizes community leaders, locally and statewide, to reduce and prevent juvenile crime ahead of the criminalization cycle. Stopping crime before it begins is the best sort of recidivism reduction.

This is a case in point of 21st-century governance exemplified by a matrix solution to a local social concern. These programs already existed in Durham but are now unified under the task of first reducing recidivism then returning people home, permanently.

Notice how each one of these service providers individually and collectively exemplify some of the basic philosophies of Capacity Building, which include:

- *The whole is greater than the sum of the parts.* – Have standards and goals to strengthen the parts to strengthen your program. One plus one in this case is much more than two.

- *Obstacles are good.* – This is how we learn to do better.

- Judge the *problem, not the people.*

- Having an *attitude of success is the only option.*

- *Less, well done, is more.* – Thus, bite off only what you can chew and digest. One failed project kills many good ideas. Progress is incremental.

- *Plan/Act/Analyze/Learn/Decide/Act.* – Only action, well considered, matters. This charts an upward trajectory to achieving mission/vision.

Now let's see how they channel specific post-release services to their community.

Effective Practice
Develop a targeted post-release services center.

Once local resources have been identified and enlisted to the cause of returning former inmates home, the task becomes one of developing face-to-face services. You can build service delivery infrastructure with a day program and/or a residential program. Naturally, larger municipal areas would want to continue to develop more sites since their services-to-needs gap will be greater, but the lesson of these programs is to move slowly, deliberately, productively. Get your first programs running productively, which means they are self-sustaining and achieving stated goals. These services are true, unselfish collaborators to your cause. The Durham JSC serves again as an example of the day experiment. Note how the JSC built its array of services already in the community and developed them to its cause. These programs are a construct of the following personal services. They serve as a great example of mustering and managing a services matrix. The JSC doesn't have to fund and staff the following services, only coordinate them:

> Note how the JSC built its array of services already in the community and developed them to its cause.

- *Community-based Corrections for Adult Offenders*

    o *Day Reporting Center (DRC)* – This is an alternative to incarceration and thus provides close supervision and monitoring of program attendees.

    o *Second Chance Program (SCP)* – JSC staff tailor substance abuse treatment for probationers and parolees who don't require the structure and supervision of the DRC.

    o *Reentry Program* – Durham reentry is designed specifically to work with the state prison system. It collaborates with the Durham Police Department, Community Corrections, the Parole Commission, and the Religious Coalition for a Nonviolent Durham to provide support services and supervision. It's also a construct of a separate set of specialized, targeted services:

    - *Mentoring* – The faith community trains support teams for the work of reintegration.

- *Employment* – Clients are assisted in the entire process of going to work. The Department of Correction provides and pays for the Job Developer. (Talk about creative resources development for which the JSC does not have to pay!)

- *Case management* – Tailored case management is another evidence-based practice used by the JSC. Here the case manager's primary duty is to remove barriers to returning home.

- *Transitional housing* – Durham County has purchased a home for short-term housing.

- *Cognitive Behavioral Interventions (CBI)* – *Thinking for a Change*, a 22-lesson evidence-based curriculum, teaches new, productive ways to get through the day.[77]

- *Substance abuse treatment*

    o *Intensive Outpatient Treatment (IOT)* – This focuses on clients with substance abuse dependency diagnosis by providing direct treatment.

    o *Regular Outpatient Treatment (ROT)* – This is also for those with a substance abuse diagnosis and provides them with a continuum of outpatient continuing care.

    o *Aftercare treatment* – This is for referrals from other treatment programs. Here the JSC manages the cases of each referee.

    o *Family program* – Here the family is enlisted to help with recovery; plus, they may participate in their own therapeutic interventions.

- *Pretrial services*

    o *First appearance* – Staff prepare the presiding judge with as much information as possible to enhance the best courses of action for a defendant. This is usually a combination of community-based alternatives to the choices within the criminal justice system.

    o *Pretrial release supervision* – Not every defendant needs jail; many only need supervision when they attend community and in-house services.

- *Substance Abuse Treatment and Recidivism Reduction Program (STARR) –* This is a four-week intensive, in-jail substance abuse and chemical dependency treatment program. It's delivered in cooperation with the Durham County Sheriff's office. STARR Grad is a voluntary extension of treatment for STARR graduates. This part of STARR focuses on relapse prevention, life skills, release planning, and post-release connections to follow-on services. The JSC offers it via an evidence-based practice, Stages of Change, which is a pre-treatment intervention for those awaiting treatment.[78]

- *Special programs*

    o *Drug treatment court –* This involves the court in ensuring treatment recommendations are followed. One of the major contributions of this court is that it seeks alternative, community-based solutions rather than further involvement with (very expensive) public options, especially the criminal justice system.

    o *Comprehensive Anti-Gang Initiative (CAGI) –* CAGI works on reducing recidivism with gang members in the program by offering prevention, intervention, and suppression initiatives.

    o *Project Restore –* This is vocational education.

- *Screening, assessment, and evaluation services*

    o *Court services –* With a court officer request, an offender will be screened for substance abuse, which begins the treatment referral process to the community rather than via jail.

    o *Youth home services –* Durham County JSC also sponsors a youth home for the treatment of those less than 17 years of age. Staff are fully involved in connecting young offenders with what they need to confront substance abuse.

Why this works well is that everything offered and every client is closely monitored for contribution to overall goals and progress through the program. These programs are very much data driven. They're so detailed that slight modifications to how an item in question can be done better is changed "on the fly!" Quick response to a need is evidence of a learning organization that is constantly evolving as it should and must.

Parenthetically, let's observe a remarkable thing. These are extant services, in place, ready to be called. No matter how much they cost in labor, support, and infrastructure, collectively they are a bargain. Compare their costs to say, incarceration alone. The cost-effectiveness of matrix solutions is dramatic. Consider the dramatic effect of extended, even hidden, benefits of a productive citizen contributing to family and community instead of destroying them. The argument for successful Capacity Building is crystal clear.

While the overt purpose of these programs is to keep people out of jail and out of crime, many other reasons exist for building a program. Every one of these study sites provides the judicial system, judges, district attorneys, magistrates, and public defenders other options to incarceration. They keep an offender in the community learning life skills, staying away from crime and substance abuse, and going through the long process of reconnecting. Communities are safer and more secure places to reinvent oneself, raise children, and do well.

> **Consider the dramatic effect of extended, even hidden, benefits of a productive citizen contributing to family and community instead of destroying them.**

The networked matrix solution to the difficulties of released inmates is a model for communities, and it's greatly enhanced by a residential program.

Effective Practice
Begin residential programs based on sustainable enterprises.

A complete discussion of what goes into building a residential program would be a lengthy volume unto itself. Suffice it to say that residential programs thrive, as exemplified by TROSA, LINC, and Dismas Charities at least. Sustainable enterprises, while complex to implement, lessen the work and stress of an initial program from having to fight short-term budget battles with granting (soft, usually terminal money) or governmental entities (except in the instance of Dismas, which has an agreement with the Federal Bureau of Prisons for support). Further, once institutionalized, they provide the capacity plan for the next site. In fact, TROSA planned replication from its inception. They now have a complete TROSA operation in Greensboro, North Carolina. See it, plan for it, do it.

But what does bear mentioning is how these programs become self-renewing. TROSA is the example for enterprises that fit the substance abuse treatment model and generate operating funds. In the case of TROSA, their annual operating budget was about $3 million at the time of this writing, most of which is generated from sustainable enterprises. The budget will probably double with the Greensboro extension. These income-generating, character-building, practical ideas are working in other locations as well. If an idea can make money and rebuild a citizen, it can probably be done. Such income-generating enterprises have wide, near-universal application:

- Lawn care and landscaping
- Carpentry
- Sustainable aqua- and agriculture
- Transportation services
- Car wash and detail shop
- Picture framing
- Secondhand store
- Moving company
- Vehicle maintenance
- Catering

The ingenuity of these jobs is truly intriguing. Take the secondhand store, for example. It opened by offering a garage cleaning service for free. Imagine how much good stuff people just throw away. This dovetails with the moving company, which gets the referrals for the cleaning service. The only cost of the cleaning service is that TROSA gets to keep the best of the take, which is sold throughout the year. As previously mentioned, the remarkable event for this sustainable enterprise is the huge end-of-the-year extravaganza/celebration sale

All these enterprises are tailor-made to the needs of a resident. The related jobs are based on labor but progress into wider skills development for residents. For example, some become lead jobbers, team leaders, supervisors, or managers, and many learn business development, automation, staffing, budgeting, and more. It's no surprise that having a place to go in the morning where one is responsible for work, self, and others supports personal growth. Working hard, giving, and earning respect, having the dignity of a paycheck, engaging in mutual endeavors, and much more are the best of therapies. Through these jobs, every resident is part of something bigger than the sum of the parts—and they *know* it.

Graduates too numerous to count have achieved remarkable life reversals. Many of the senior staff at TROSA are former residents. Some stay for a career. Having a place to go every day lends purpose to life. A resident may begin at the bottom, but he or she sees from the first day on the job that those who persist soon have responsibilities, dignity—a way up and out—a way home.

The next section adds detail on how to mold your post-release services staff into an inspired team.

7. Nurture Reentry Staff by a Process of Human Capacity Development

One of the key features of developing capacity is getting staffing right. Implementation of your (transitional) effort will likely fail unless human capacity supports it.[79] There is a significant difference between human resources and human capacity development.

Human *resources* development focuses on getting work done, where the focus is on skills, knowledge, and abilities—that which gets the job done. It offers employees workplace development and training aimed at competency and strategic job performance, usually following a career path.

Continuously improving human capacity translates to organizational excellence.

Human *capacity* development goes beyond human resources development. It considers the whole person concept of improvement by supporting further education, wholistic health, and employees' contributions to general societal well-being. Continuously improving human capacity translates to organizational excellence. Leaders recognize that well-rounded employees are highly productive and goal and vision directed. Work becomes more than a job. A career is seen as dynamic, ever-changing, and thus it requires lifelong learning—formal, professional, and experiential. Most people, given permission and the opportunity to grow, want to be their best. Out of this development across the board, a true team emerges.

The lesson going forward with Capacity Building? Begin wholistically. Enhance daily successes and the view over the horizon to permanency, where your idea makes a real and lasting difference.

Returning to aftercare, leaders at model aftercare programs further observe that institutionalization of the service idea is a goal on par with effecting successful transitions. It's quite dependent on hard working, inspired leadership, in this case, the executive director and staff whose critical duty is support and guidance of the board. It involves assembling, motivating, training, educating, and directing your project professionals. It's a matter of establishing a positive culture of intrinsic motivation surrounding the belief in the ability of a former inmate to return home as a productive citizen. This culture was evident at each site. Also, contrary to common belief, many of our citizens make amends and return to hearth and home. Keep correctional facilities for the incorrigible.

It involves assembling, motivating, training, educating, and directing your project professionals. It's a matter of establishing a positive culture of intrinsic motivation surrounding the belief in the ability of a former inmate to return home as a productive citizen. This culture was evident at each model site.

Staff were passionate about their work. They knew they mattered. They routinely assumed and accomplished more than they were asked to do. Everyone multitasked. The atmosphere of family was evident, in which everyone's accomplishments and struggles were shared. The executive directors were truly dynamic and especially well qualified leaders who commanded respect as they were usually the hardest working staffers. Overtime and nontraditional hours were accepted, even cheerfully; staff had a plan and a purpose. These people loved what they were doing.

How did this evolve? What were these people doing to be shaped and thusly shape themselves into productive teams? How had they fashioned dynamic, goal-oriented, learning organizations that other operations seek to be and comparatively few attain? This section is not to repeat the lessons of staffing but to lend insight into how the staff at these successful aftercare Reform Movement sites got the employee thing commendably right.

> **The overall purpose of aftercare does not distract from the primacy of developing a learning organization where people can actualize and creativity flourishes.**

First, let us capture the philosophy of staff development that exists in stable transitional operations. The task, according to one executive director is to "create a work environment where people want to learn." The overall purpose of aftercare does not distract from the primacy of developing a learning organization where people can actualize and creativity flourishes.

One executive director asserted that "You get what you pay for." What she meant is that while they needed to recruit and hire talented, motivated, creative people, the real work of shaping staff begins after the contract is signed. In fact, that shaping begins with the job posting. People are best served by knowing what they're getting into. The interview then follows.

This Capacity Building interview is a true conversation about duties, responsibilities, and expectations. It's quite contrary to many job interviews in the public sector, in which the interviewer does much (or all) of the talking. The interviewer recognizes he or she has only minutes to see if there's a mutual fit for a relationship that can last decades! Therefore, the prospect is given the floor for most of the interview.

After the offer is made and accepted, a mentor may be assigned to on-board the new team member. Further, the new hire develops a career progression plan that covers education and professional and personal development. A gifted leader can inspire in many ways beyond a paycheck. Notice, again, the theme of process. A new team member is thoroughly vetted, guided into the fold, given expectations, tutored, mentored, and made part of a family.

The vision- and mission-oriented staff of this dynamic executive director are in a nonstop learning mode, because she and her key people are constantly teaching those around them. Nearly every turn during the day provides a teachable moment. She can be fine-tuning a point while walking a colleague down the hall. She has added the benefit of an enlightened county leadership body that puts a premium on staff training.

Even in genuinely austere times, staff attend conferences, workshops, training, and educational experiences away from the home office, on company time. This sends the distinct message that staff are truly number one, and that's a mantra taken to action, not a platitude. These big and especially little actions are not only good business; they are essential. Providing transitional services is dynamic because it evolves with nearly each person it serves.

Furthermore, "best" practices are routinely proposed. Some work, most do not. A best practice may have worked at one location, but there's no guarantee it will work in any other location. Each location is in many ways its own universe. Thus, Capacity Building deals with "evidence-based" practices, which recognize the uniqueness of every application of a policy, procedure, or idea. Further, they imply a basis of evidence and logic but take constant vigilance to maintain fidelity. Staff must evaluate, implement, and make an idea work, which doesn't happen in a stagnant, dull environment.

The insight here from senior staff is that the work environment must be one in which people can learn and feel compelled to do so by being free to judicially try new ideas. They don't fear failure or the reproach that can come of it. So, staff are "continuously given opportunities to learn new things, refresh the basics, and apply what they've learned," according to one board member. What a great observation of a basic truth.

Effective Practice

*Build an environment in which staff keep skills current
and feel free to apply lessons learned.*

A learning environment helps build a workplace ethos of "*we* not I," according to the founder of the JSC day program. Staff have an equal voice, an equal share of the work—and, yes, an equal share of the disappointments, but also an equal share in real accomplishment. This is team building at its best and another description of a true learning environment.

So, what do these successful professionals do to develop staff? Essentially, *everything* they do is a staff-building, training opportunity. Even before a staffer comes on board, they are vetted for "compatibility." Although they have appropriate education in an appropriate discipline, training in dealing with the returning population and relevant experience, these basic considerations are not paramount. Senior staffers are looking for passion—and they get it. The staff at LINC, for example, are quite young. Each one was attracted to the work by the executive director, who "inspired" them, commented the LINC employment specialist. For example, one staffer passed up a very difficult-to-get law enforcement appointment for a chance to help the community with one of its most demanding callings.

Once at work, the real training and shaping begins. As mentioned, staff are largely on a career path with a combination of training and education. Specific training is unique to each site and a combination of what the organization needs and what the individual wants to pursue. This may include automation training, learning about evidence-based practices, honing therapeutic skills, or learning organizational development, for example. Naturally, they are encouraged to pursue formal education as well. Successful transitional organizations differ from most other public organizations in their relentless push to develop staff as vision-driven professionals. Leadership has the main responsibility to ensure opportunities for education, training, and professional development. However, that just *begins* building staff. It's what they do with what they have at hand for training that's enlightening.

> Successful transitional organizations differ from most other public organizations in their relentless push to develop staff as vision-driven professionals.

Staff teach each other as well. They constantly apply and test what they learn. Lead staff are constantly talking about alternative ways to handle a situation or are discussing how a certain course of action came about. Laterally, staff constantly critique one another on efficiency, effectiveness. and how things can be improved. They grow in that atmosphere. The LINC director promoted staff teaching each other with his observation that "What you see is based on where you sit." Different views bring new insights.

This assumes there's an atmosphere of support for creativity and decision making that may fail. Each one of these organizations accept failure as an opportunity for growth and a reality of progress. People aren't berated for something that goes awry. This is not to say there's carelessness. No. There's an air of competence and necessary caution, but action prevails. Probably one of the most creative, progressive, and effective examples of this is at TROSA. The entire organization runs on the belief that everyone is accountable to their fellow TROSA members, whether they're staff or residents.

Here, successful residents take responsibility for the success of following residents. Residents are a large part of the staff. Who'd think social entrepreneurship could successfully turn to the target population for help in the success of the endeavor? This is a dramatic concept. Residents are given real responsibility with real consequences for their fellow human beings. Residents are seen as a huge staff resource and are trained to the needs at hand. They're expected to assume certain duties and consequently respond to the trust given them by performing at very high levels. This allows the entering residents to see what lies ahead of them as they progress. From the first step in the door at TROSA, they're met, welcomed, and processed by residents. New entrants thus have an impressive example standing before them of the transformation that's possible. They also are immediately informed of the rigors of the program, the high expectations, the fact that it's voluntary, and any violations of rules results in a summary expulsion. Often this is the first time a new resident has been responsible for anything, and subsequent transformations are stunning. On the surface, this idea seems counterintuitive. But it's been years in the making. Duties and responsibilities must be specifically defined for carrying out by residents. For example, all intakes are done by senior residents. Lead staff who are assigned to new residents are responsible for their acclimation to the TROSA way of getting through the day. A hierarchy of leadership, management, and labor is observed. All understand where they fit, what is expected of them to succeed individually, and how to help the organization prosper. It's staff development at its best. Defining the positions to fill is also unique to an aftercare site, especially TROSA.

Effective Practice
Hire and develop staff for your unique returnee and community needs.

Generally, staff job titles follow the needs of a returnee, but the composition of staff skill sets varies by location as observed at the study sites. Internal staff reflect a matrix solution to the locally defined task of aftercare. The JSC and LINC staff structures serve as examples of very different staffing to do the same thing. The common caution from both executive directors is the same advice they offer for each of the critical factors along the project life cycle: Think small when you're figuring things out. Duties and responsibilities for various jobs are, again, unique. A job developer, for example, ostensibly makes connections to employers. But at LINC, the job developer does much more.

First comes developing relationships in the community by telling the story of LINC. The goal is to make five new contacts in the community a day! The job developer is first a "friend raiser." Next, this person serves the varying needs of a resident, which may be helping a client with job readiness. Then there's connecting the resident to a first job. Ultimately, this leads to work with career potential, which means budding sustainability at home and in the community. Also, of course, the job developer is cross-trained in other regular duties and responsibilities. Another site may determine a different way for this position to function.

The JSC is a day program. Notice how lean staffing is for these organizations:

- Pay-rolled JSC staff:
    - Executive director
    - Probation officer
    - Program manager
    - Case manager
    - Substance abuse counselor
    - Counselor – Treatment Alternatives for a Safer Community (TASC)

- Non-pay-rolled external staff – Positions based in the community and part of the team
    - Housing coordinator
    - Mentoring coordinator
    - Faith community representative
    - Mental health providers

LINC staff are also lean, considering it is (or was at the time of this writing) a residential model of 12 beds.

- Executive director
- Program director
- Social worker
- Resident manager
- Job developer
- Administrative assistant
- Facilities manager
- Staff for youth services
    - Case manager
    - Youth specialist (two positions)

> **If there's a staff hierarchy, it's bottom-up as witnessed through leadership by example and participation.**

A telling fact emanating from discussions on staffing was that executive directors always began by describing what staffers do, starting with the least of their employees. They recognize that these people are their most important because they have the most interface with clients. Only last did they discuss their own jobs, and then somewhat reluctantly. If there's a staff hierarchy, it's bottom-up as witnessed through leadership by example and participation. This speaks volumes about the palpable importance of team members.

When the team is assembled, and members feel they are truly a priority, there's a sense the job will get done no matter what. It sort of goes on "autopilot," according to one staffer, as all team members learn what they need to do and do it with little prompting. Initiative is evident. On one of my visits to LINC, I had an occasion to sit for a minute waiting for the first interview—but not for long. One staffer saw my idle moment, approached, and offered to begin an interview.

Associated with this eagerness for the job is delegation of duties. The executive director must delegate work as soon as other staff demonstrate competence or be overwhelmed with the work of the day. There are two ways to delegate. The obvious way is to assemble essential staff and cross-train them and delegate as circumstances demand. Good people rise to the occasion. Cross-training is also a survival mechanism for a startup. Secondly, as quickly as possible, hire an assistant director to focus on internal operations and free the executive director to focus on external matters and relationship building, meaning resources development.

The issue of cross-training came up at every site. However, I encountered no consensus about whether to do it or not. One executive director said emphatically that there's no time to learn other duties. Another has his team develop a functional awareness of other core duties, including that of the executive director. Whether or not cross-training is adopted is probably a function of the maturity of the service effort. While the project is in the startup mode, a few people will have to assume the full range of essential tasks. These are largely determined by what they see needs to be done and by the phone ringing. Transitional services tend to begin in somewhat of a state of chaos. Early on, cross-training may be a necessity, but later it's a choice. Learning how other jobs function is also a definition of succession planning. This is a concern as the organization matures and especially as senior staff move on and founding members consider retirement. It's also a consideration when expansion is planned. Their unique perspective is that cross-training is one of the best ways to continue the work and services when they have the inevitable staff turnover or the work ebbs and flows.

The lesson from these aftercare Reform Movement sites concerning staffing is that it's a genuine priority, if not *the* priority, as evidenced by the continuous emphasis on staff development. LINC leadership, for example, sees that the entire staff is trained in leadership at the local university *off-site* twice each year. These enlightened leaders see that time developing their staff is not time away from production; it's a way to multiply staff productivity. Yes, there's concern about the critical work of capacity building, but at the core of each criticality are staff. The LINC director said it best: "*[Staff development] is about empowering people to empower people.*" When staff development is done right, work becomes a pleasure. Every line-level staffer interviewed wanted to come to work in the morning.

Summing Up Planning for Your Reentry Aftercare Program

Think about planning with respect to the long-term nature of capacity building. Understand that the task is not about reentry as defined by the criminal justice system; rather it's about post-release services aftercare that leads to successful community reintegration. Consider each critical phase so far: Leadership, such as a board of directors, must be a functional, working body with the main purpose of building relationships. Capacity and project scope should be defined according to returnee needs. Only one major and a few subsequent measures are all that are necessary to determine your progress toward results. Evaluation data on process should help nurture a learning environment. Map resources to identify opportunities to make friends. Muster available local resources to augment program services. Make staff your number one priority by adopting a philosophy of human *capacity* development, not the more prescriptive human *resources* development. Remember that post-release service delivery and coordination should be established with permanency in mind.

When planning your transitional services delivery systems, take the long view. First measure improvements in your clients' initial abilities soon after release (see Reentry Skills, page 221). Then ultimately, if possible, measure improvements in community well-being evidenced by the contributions of increasing numbers of returnees going home as good citizens. Consider the following.

What would successful reentry aftercare look like? In the short term, it might mean that inmates leave jail with necessary medications in hand, identification papers in pocket, a roof over their heads at least the first night out, and someone in the community—be it a sponsor, a family member, or a treatment provider—ready for their return. A few years down the road, you might set your aim higher to continuously reducing recidivism; having fewer and fewer relapses and fewer and fewer returns to hospitals and shelters; and increasing stability and productivity among the returning population. More broadly, we would expect to see less crime, fewer victimizations, improved public health, and stronger, safer, healthier communities.[80] Not to mention much less public expenditure as a direct savings. What more if an individual is resurrected to a good family, sustaining job, and a true member of the community.

The best advice comes from experience. I asked several executive directors to reflect on their planning experiences. Their comments were simple, insightful, practical, realistic, and imperative, such as:

"Don't develop anything in a vacuum."

In other words, don't dream up a plan from your office. Consider your agency to be the hub of community transitional services. Get out and about. Participate in therapies with clients. Look for any opportunity to spread the good word about your program. Know what your partners, internal and external, want and give it to them. Get buy-in as soon and as solidly as possible.

"Be realistic about the budget."

Getting dollars goes two ways. The director of the JSC cautions not to just dream about funds coming; relentlessly pursue them. Once the dollars start arriving, don't pad budgets; the people in charge of your funding need only to see this done one time to become skeptical. Credibility is everything. "Make sure you have enough money to keep the lights on," observes the LINC founder.

"Staff your project with subject matter experts."

As you assemble staff, look for subject matter experts who can make practical applications. A good manager knows what people are interested in and allows them to participate. Most folks like to plan and do something new. Let them do it. As the LINC executive director says, "Make sure your staff want to show up." Everyone must see and understand the vision. Demonstrate that this work is not a job, "it's a lifestyle."

"You can't be all things to all people."

Know your target population and zero in on them. Understand your capacity; only do what you can do well. It's much better, even easier, to put a few souls on the right track than to fail at many more.

"Institutionalize."

Build things so that when staff come and go, the program remains. Do this by being a faithful partner. *Do what you say you will do* is the voice of experience from LINC, TROSA, Dismas, and the JSC. Look for weaknesses or threats to your purpose and address them immediately. Be inclusionary from the beginning. Gather stakeholders early and "Keep them near and dear." Always explore possibilities. In the long run, the process matters. It's how results are manifest.

"Live honesty."

Although this is self-explanatory, the LINC director provides the insight that this "just happens with good and motivated people." Thus, we again see the importance of vetting staff. Honesty is credibility. Make sure you have a good name in the community.

This chapter covered the essentials of planning and implementation based on the experiences of successful aftercare sites. Consider all this advice carefully before you get into operation and stabilization, the topic of Chapter 4—although planning and operation are, of course, intertwined.

Chapter 4

PHASE II OF THE PROGRAM'S LIFE CYCLE – OPERATE AND STABILIZE

Chapter 4

PHASE II OF THE PROGRAM'S LIFE CYCLE – OPERATE AND STABILIZE

Details make perfection, and perfection is not a detail.
– Leonardo Da Vinci

Documenting planning and operations necessitates discussing them separately. This allows a thorough treatment of essentials. Many programs can separate the phases and tasks of project development. However, the nature of public sector projects is such that they're intertwined in a somewhat chaotic fashion, which hinders accomplishing the essentials. When talking about delivering post-release services, project staff relate that planning and implementation began simultaneously from the inception of their aftercare efforts. Each executive director had stories of coming to work in the early days to find a returning former inmate in need. Naturally, they got right to work helping him or her with their immediate needs.

From this grew their impressive programs. This is certainly not to say that good planning should be neglected. Again, each site has done, is doing, and will continue to do extensive planning. That's how they continuously grow to meet demand. They caution to be aware that planning has a different focus from that of operations. You need to separate the functions of each for thoroughness

> **The operations stage is an opportunity to reflect on how and how well things are being done.**

as it's easy to dismiss planning in the confusion of getting through the day. However, neglect good planning and rigorous implementation and you'll court failure.

Site practitioners observe that progress is made by paying attention to the right details. It also helps to remember perennial priorities as you carry out operations:

- *Continue to build relationships.* – Gather your friends to your cause. This is arguably your first priority. Your program will rise or fall depending on the support you garner and keep.

- *Continuously build capacity.* – Nearly every activity in which you're involved should be done with permanency in mind. Your primary functional goal should be to construct a self-sustaining operation. This functional goal is differentiated from the overall goal to effect transitions. The former is internal, the latter is external, and one builds on the other. Capacity building is mentioned as the first priority because a program must first sustain itself before any long-term goals can be accomplished.

- *Continuously support staff.* – Never take for granted those who are doing the job. Training at the sites is a daily occurrence.

- *Continually build services.* – Services are not set; they are always in flux. The effectiveness and validity of services should be examined regularly.

- *Never lose sight of the ultimate goal.* – Your goal is to successfully reintroduce to the community former inmates capable of contributing to community well-being. This drives all else.

The operations stage is an opportunity to reflect on how and how well things are being done. It's time to test the plan against reality and make modifications in a calculated virtuous cycle of action-reflection-action. Each program observed is constantly in flux and expanding as means and opportunity dictate. Therefore, this discussion of operations considers how these aftercare reform-minded sites interpreted the work of building toward self-renewing permanency.

8. Operationalize Your Reentry-Aftercare Plan

A parole officer offered this observation: "*Nothing* can prepare a former offender for return to the community." He meant that personal relationships will be different; the returnee will have the stigma of being a former criminal (in many cases a felon); employment will be hard fought and low end; and the world will have changed during a prison sentence. Program staffers observed further that some people began incarceration "before ATMs, cell phones, and Google." Parolees are often "lost." They also pointed out that, against some of the stiffest odds, "These guys make it." They have seen a murderer get a job in one week. They note that, "Older guys make it." Their program provides accountability and the realization that there are no excuses. This drives home the point that the community must be aware of the realities of this aftercare work. It's complex, difficult, necessary, worthwhile, and rewarding.

We begin the discussion of operations with the first critical feature, leadership, and how it needs to evolve from what it is in the planning stage. Planned, calculated action matters—so act you must.

Leadership

Obviously, leadership is multi-layered, especially in the bureaucracy of a successful post-release services enterprise. Leaders that influence a post-release effort are found in the courts, corrections, and law enforcement. They are the senior staff of local governmental and nongovernmental departments and service agencies—and they are the middle managers of the project itself. Most leaders in this constellation can be considered partners, but the most relevant are the executive director and the board. It's helpful to understand some of the fine points about how they conduct business.

The executive director continues to be a singular element in the success of local service projects. In all the model sites except Dismas, the executive directors were also the primary founding individual. Dismas traces its roots to a priest in the 1960s, who saw the need and potential of former inmates. It's the vision and diligence of the directors that makes the programs possible. Many projects flounder and perhaps fail because the senior staffer confuses multiple roles. He or she is the keeper of the mission, the guardian of the goals, the protector of project respect, and the primary technician. He or she has internal and external duties and responsibilities. The pitfall for this leader is that it's often expeditious to attend to the urgencies of daily business at the expense of developing and maintaining essential relationships in the community. The crisis of the moment rules. On top of it all, is the keeping, planning, and guiding of the vision of the way forward.

Leadership in the planning section discussed some of the unique aspects of internal management, and there's a wealth of information on operating an organization, which needn't be duplicated. Thus, this section will hew to some of the nuances of the director's role, especially concerning externalities. The senior staffer must shift gears from the crush of internal daily business without losing control to concentrate on relevant externalities that serve to build and preserve the program.

Effective Practice
Ensure that the executive director emphasizes building external relationships.

The astute executive director will find a balance between internal and external duties and responsibilities. As quickly as possible, he or she needs to hire and train an assistant director, if the project funds allow such a position, and appropriate functional managers, then *learn how to delegate.* Every executive director interviewed agreed that preserving the image of the program in the local community is important and consumes time. The art of it is to also keep a careful watch on daily work. These key people go two ways; either they focus on the cacophony of daily work that demands their specific attention, or they find it easier to be somewhat of an absentee manager while attending to business away from the office. Each executive director defined and conducted external duties with nuance. They were ever present, on site, conducting business *and* remained connected to wider interests. Easy to say, tough to navigate. They never lost focus of their purpose, which was to serve their clients. Most participated in delivering services and counseling clients and still found time to grow the business in a dramatic fashion. Their electronic communication media were constantly in use. Texting was the primary mode of real-time communication. The following examples serve to demonstrate how they understood there's a difference between internalities and externalities, yet successfully combined and masterfully accomplished the two.

- *Front-line presence* – One middle manager commented that her executive director was "so far into the community that (their agency) was the first in line for any services that come to town." The director constantly looked for ways that "everyone could fit into the program." This individual attended numerous meetings, celebrations, and formal and informal gatherings in the community. She made it a point to attend the county commissioner's meetings and relevant meetings of court, correction, and law enforcement agencies, for example. She became a fixture and soon was expected to be in attendance. She "seemed to be everywhere." She was available to tell the story of her growing service. She also did many favors herself, had her staff help when appropriate, and traded services. In other words, she made a lot of friends and built a remarkable bank account of goodwill. For example, when the Department of Correction sent a job developer to town, the first person contacted was this executive director to see how she wanted to utilize the services of the specialist. Correction officials knew by experience this would be the best partnering of their resources. This assuming of services goes both ways. The director always looked for ways to barter. She had a "willingness to give more than [we] have to," mentioned the manager.

- *In the weeds* – A program case manager sat on a case review board where many community professionals were involved in working with high-needs clients. The case manager assisted materially by providing services and making referrals. No, this was not the program case manager's job. However, this put their program right in the middle of high visibility community decision making to which they could contribute. There was much give and take and sharing.

  Generous sharing is essential for relationship building at its best.

  On one occasion, this mutual support kept a critical partner from bolting and, in fact, preserved the post-release services program from possibly dissolving when it was in its fragile infancy. Early critical stakeholders wanted to pull out. They had every excuse—no time, no money, and no payback in helping an "ex-con." The executive director was already participating in a sister agency's quarterly "notification" process, helping coordinate housing and providing case management and therapy for needy clients at *no cost* to the sister department. The dissenting department found it better to stay with the coalition as there was long-term mutual benefit. With this and many other gestures, the coalition stayed intact. This kind of generous sharing is essential for relationship building at its best.

- *Clear obstacles* – Now for a brief look at how board members treated their role during operations. According to a LINC board member, their focus changed to the complementary roles of assisting staff, enhancing the credibility of the project, and anticipating the future. They "established policy and saw it was carried out but with a careful and gentle hand." The overall purpose of the operational board was to let the project blossom and "clear the way" for the executive director and staff to do the job. Each site became a model for how to blend leadership oversight and line-level production. It could be best described as a mutually beneficial relationship of communication, contemplation, and action.

  Individuals understood their duties, how they fit with teammates, and how they contributed to stated goals. Essentially, this body became an encouraging, sometimes strict yet kind avuncular figure and frequent cheerleader. They worked very hard to avoid an "us versus them situation." This meant helping move bureaucratic obstacles that would inevitably be encountered from agencies, elected bodies, rules and regulations, and the hidebound nature of bureaucracy. They continued to cement old relationships and make new ones. They trained themselves for their duties of oversight and the next stage of planning for their going concern. They anticipated growth, which included planning for infrastructure, expanded services in number and capability, and staffing to begin to close the services-to-needs gap. They focused on the data that related how much they could realistically continue to do, the health of the project in terms of how well they were doing and their march to goal accomplishments. The board self-ensured they were ready for the job as it evolved.

  Being present, in the weeds of delivering services and removing obstacles, is integral to the methods, manner, and meticulous work done by 21st-century leaders. They assume correct responsibilities and understand the role of oversight as the project matures. What they do is different in the planning stage than during operations. Planning is laying out what and how things will be done. Implementation and stabilization are more hands-off for leaders, but they still work to anticipate headwinds and prevent them as much as possible. The program is now very much self-directed.

Effective Practice
Have the board assume responsibility for organizing and training themselves for the progression of roles from planning to oversight and preparation for the future.

The most experienced board member at LINC commented that the program evolved to a philosophy of service to the community. They felt responsible "for and to the community" and for the credibility of LINC. The model, though nascent, made transitioning the formerly incarcerated possible; so, in turn, returnees became emissaries of the program that showed them the way to respect and productivity. It was not uncommon to have a former resident on the board. People who have "made it" are flesh-and-blood proof that they can win respect and productivity.

The board at LINC redefined or altered its purposes and solidified the partnership with the executive director and staff. For example, board members would spend a day each with a staffer and mentoring a resident. This is unheard of with most public boards. Many board members see their roles as visionaries and are hands off. Not so in these models. Spending time with staffers is an important gesture exemplifying a shared purpose in this tough, tough work. It allowed for the "candid and open [exchange] of ideas, an avenue to develop mutual respect, and a format for arriving at mutual decisions," according to the LINC senior board member. They knew that LINC must, and more importantly *could,* expand. Stability became paramount. This meant the board had to strengthen current operations, look to expand, and tell the story of LINC to anyone who wanted or needed to know it.

One of the many intelligent things they did was to commission a strategic plan from the local university, which mapped the plan to expand from 12 to 60 total beds. This allowed them a view of how to run and sustain a large, state-of-the art full-service coeducational residential facility. They could see and *feel* the future, which energized all concerned and made clearer what needed to be done.

One of the first things they did was to reorganize themselves in subcommittees, slightly altered from the suggestions for board committee composition during planning:

- *Development* – They rightly saw that board members had to be the primary engine of bringing in support and money.

- *Marketing* – Early successes gave them the ammunition to "sell" LINC, which each member took as a primary duty.

- *Recruiting and training* – They continually courted new board members and saw to their own professional and technical training as individuals and collectively as a body of one mind.

- *Infrastructure* – They intuitively saw the importance of building capacity and dreamed of goals that were just out of reach, uncomfortable and challenging. Who would have thought they would have a state-of-the-art residential facility? The next dream was a gated community for the formerly incarcerated.

- *Succession* – The spark that ignited LINK was the executive director. Inevitably, he would move on, and that moment needed preparation.

- *Grant writing* – This board saw the need to focus on developing soft money, even with its vagaries and constrictions. Thus, they formed a committee to pursue a granting strategy that dovetailed with their other funding and resource streams.

They worked to be a capable, diverse group composed of varied ethnic backgrounds, genders, talents, and skills. Recruiting like-minded talent never stops. So, their membership included attorneys, academics, a banker, and electronic and media-savvy technical professionals, with more to come as talent and work needs arose.

There were many creative ways they became stronger and better board members. For example, they sought out people who were serving on other boards and asked them to be mentors, a request which was enthusiastically accepted. Besides a professional strategic plan, the board reconstituted itself and members enrolled themselves in a program sponsored by the local university—Quality Enhancement for Nonprofit Organizations (QENO).[81] One of the many advantages of this type of advanced and pertinent schooling is that it further developed the intangibles of the board, that is, their character, even ethics, as a team. They got a chance to probe their duties as workers, not merely as idea people with ideas that others should do. They rightly saw that coming up with ideas is the easy part. They furthered their collective and individual commitment to LINC and experienced the excitement of energy generated as a body that's greater than the sum of its parts, according to this board member. The only regret expressed by board members is they wished they would have begun doing these things earlier. Part of this refocusing meant a thorough understanding of how much they could handle as a program. They understood to the core the virtue of doing only that which could be done thoroughly. For this, they needed to assess capacity.

Capacity Assessment

How to construct the criticalities of one of these programs varies, depending on the nature of the client population. Yes, returnees have similar categories of needs, but there are differences in clients between sites. Dismas treats former federal prisoners. TROSA assists people with severe substance abuse and other difficulties. LINC has programming for adults and youth. The JSC has nonresidential day clients. Attending to each client group is nuanced. Project staff independently explained it as the translation of theory to practical application.

When considering capacity, the Dismas executive director applies a business logic model for the program rationale. It's based on an intimate understanding of the target population, which is the basis of determining the capacity to deliver services. In the business vernacular, his *product* is changing lives. His product *consumer* is the community. The program *customer* is the Federal Bureau of Prisons, BOP, which is the primary funder of Dismas. He defines his residents with respect to risk categories of low, medium, and high. Risk determines which and what amounts of services to deliver. From that, a Statement of Work, SOW, is developed. This is essentially the scope of services expected of a contractor. The contractor then would present an idea of what could be done, which would be considered an evidence-based theory until proven to be an evidence-based practice. The practical execution of service ideas will become the evidence-based program according to the Dismas executive director.

When thinking this way, the next logical progression is to expect a profit. The resident can expect his work and commitment will lead to a place in the community. The community will profit by having better safety and security, great savings in avoided criminal justice system costs, and in the very long term, the productivity of a new community member. The BOP saves federal dollars by collaborating with an established company that efficiently and effectively treats inmates and former inmates at greatly reduced costs from federal alternatives. Sentencing a federal prisoner to Dismas also frees up BOP resources for inmates who need them.

> **How to construct the criticalities of one of these programs varies, depending on the nature of the client population.**

Effective Practice
Continually assess your clientele—especially their risk factors—to monitor and adjust your services delivery and mix.

This business model is a good point of departure, but some examples of how the sites understood and adjusted capacity are in order.

LINC did it using an external analyst. The LINC board and founding member went into the capacity assessment thinking they were delivering only initial transitional services such as shelter, subsistence, and a lead to the first job. They came out of it knowing they needed to do core initial transitional work *plus* provide educational, health, and medical services. With that in mind, they set about organizing local community resources to satisfy the redefined needs. They looked to the North Carolina Department of Education to train ex-offenders. And they successfully sought funding for and hired a health and wellness coordinator. In this case, capacity assessment redefined LINC, according to the founder. LINC also used benchmarks to determine production. Many data points were collected, but one serves as an example. Staff knew by experience and a history of documenting hiring experiences, that if a client needed to get a job in six months, he needed to see 25 employers and ensure that at least 10 of those prospects had the power to hire.

The JSC learned that clients were more focused on that first job no matter what it may be than training for one with a little more potential. JSC staff assumed, theorized that is, that former inmates wanted work training, but not so. Staff were looking through their own life prism, not that of their charges. Most want a job *without* training, and in fact couldn't be forced to go. Therefore, less money was put into training and more into job hunting skills and preparation for the interview and offer. It was enough for an ex-murderer to get a job in a restaurant washing pots and pans. It became a priority to get clients a decent suit of clothes. And it worked.

In another example, staff monitored caseloads for their clientele from the courts and from the Department of Correction. They realized dealing with these clients instead of walk-ins is different work. Staff were pressured to combine various clients for each case manager because it seemed more efficient, but it was not. Actually, the numbers and experience showed that case managers specializing in one category of clientele and taking fewer cases was the way to more successful transitions. Notice what continually assessing your target clients turns up. Theory is constantly tested at these sites, especially during operations. While data helps, in the end, experience enables a practitioner to make the correct decision for the most productive course of action.

Here are a few summative thoughts on operational capacity assessment from those interviewed. A senior manager at the JSC cautioned that data, while important to all criticalities including capacity assessment, is a primary "driver of results." However, it doesn't hurt to think beyond the limits of data. The TROSA operations officer dreamed of a day when a client sentenced to TROSA for five years has the goal of becoming whole again and earning a two-year degree from the local technical college. This work is full of hope.

Now let's consider the adjunct to capacity—scope.

Scope

Practicality shaped by reality and backed by a little data is the watchword of operation. Scoping done during the action of operations is likewise driven by practical considerations. Nearly every staffer constantly considers how much more they can efficiently and effectively do without burning out. The program manager for the JSC went so far as to say, "Scope is determined by experience and the realities of doing the service or programming idea." Scoping seems to be done on the fly. It's not.

How much they do is indeed an experiential decision, *and* it is backed by data—in that order.

Staff at each site would agree, generally. But upon closer examination of how the various sites tackle the question of how much, their answer is that how much they do is indeed an experiential decision, *and* it is backed by data—in that order. Each site has a way to track those measures directly related to improving processes and determining progress. They keep numbers on every key service (outlined in Phase I). Take employment, for example. Each site has at their fingertips a variety of the number of employers they have registered, those contacted, how many contacts and interviews each client has had, job placements, time on the job, and so forth. This data builds profiles of employers most likely to hire this specialized clientele, what the job seeker must do to conduct a successful search, and especially, how the staff can best facilitate the process. TROSA is somewhat different as much of their employment is via their in-house enterprises. Still, TROSA has a sophisticated data gathering, analysis, and application process woven throughout its operations.

Even with experience, the lessons of evolving reality, and progressive sophistication with data, scoping is a "best guess at readiness" to take the next action. Practitioners are not paralyzed by needing more data or the usual cautiousness seen in public agencies. How did they get to this progressive way of moving their organizations forward? Simply, they worked extensively to understand all aspects of their business.

Effective Practice
Use performance data to support experiential decisions on how much can be done effectively.

The JSC, to continue the comments made by its program manager, has a "just say yes" manner of determining how much to do. They tend to agree to assume a responsibility even if it's an additional client load or a semi-permanent task to assist a sister agency *then* figure out how to go about it. Now for a quick disclaimer: While this seems to fly in the face of the calculated way more responsibilities are assumed, the staff at the Durham JSC has years of experience concerning what can and cannot be done. On one occasion, the JSC began a program with existing staff then determined the need for and requested additional staff. Another example of reality and experience informing scope is what the program manager called the "let 'em fail" way of doing business. Their faith community partners tended to want to help all returnees, including violent and sex offenders. Though they wished it, churches could not be "all things to all people;" and they had to fail to learn their limits. They had to be overwhelmed before they learned the true scope of their abilities, which trumped their desire to serve. Failure is another practical way of testing and teaching limits, the limits already learned by the JSC to serve only a certain class of post-release clients. So here we have the contrast of practical application observed at every site and just saying yes then learning by failure—or success. Yet, my observation and interviews determined there's much more than meets the eye.

Failure is another practical way of testing and teaching limits.

These seemingly erratic decisions are made by very experienced professionals at the JSC who have decades in the business, years on the job, and are serving in the flagship day program in North Carolina. No decision is as cavalier as it seems. Also, data is pervasive at the JSC. As mentioned earlier, they have a database that's the distillation of five databases honed over a decade of use. They know what's happening just about minute-to-minute. Each staffer not only makes real-time entries, but they can refer to them momentarily. Likewise, that data is available to internal and external stakeholders. So yes, they may seem to shoot first on an experiential decision to assume more, but not without being rooted in analysis. Here, information gives confidence to the seemingly quick move.

The discussion of scope gives pause to consider the practitioner use of theory. Senior staff discussed the juxtaposition of theory and reality-based practicality. Simply, they did not dwell in the theoretical. This is a lesson on getting the job done and minimizing distractions. Of course, they knew the difference and learned quickly from theory—then moved on to getting the job done.

Consider readiness. Practically speaking, the readiness to do something assumes meaning beyond the theory of it. Many changes happen based on externalities, such as the economy or the whims of elected bodies, and theory can't accurately anticipate reality; that's why it is called reality. The LINC executive director gave an example. In his municipality, at this writing, he has no way of determining exactly how many ex-offenders will be returning to his community. He knows limits must be imposed, so he employs limits such as only taking certain levels of offenders and only those who have a sincere desire to "make it on the outside." Case load efficiencies and effectiveness are monitored and adjusted, which is a form of determining how much can be done by a staffer. With that knowledge, they recruit and employ external service agencies to help with demand.

Staff and board members at LINC always knew the demand exceeded what they could satisfy and that a larger residential facility would be the answer. How to make that happen had escaped them for years. But when they found an abandoned county facility they could rent for $1 a year and renovate and retrofit for post-release services, they were ready. It had taken them a decade, but they knew the time had come. This evokes the philosophy of scoping expressed by the Dismas senior official who said Dismas seeks to "change the world by changing a world of individuals." In other words, there seems to always be, "room for one more," at these aftercare Reform Movement sites. This philosophy is not held without knowing how, understanding process efficiencies, and knowing how well they are doing, which are the topics of the next section.

Process Evaluation and Impact Analysis

Your data should now be telling the singular story of your program with the synergistic themes of efficient processes and effective services. Data should continuously eke out little efficiencies that overall have a large impact on getting the daily job done and help staff and critical stakeholders know the program is succeeding. A primary project goal is credibility due to a program that works well and arrives at mutually beneficial consequences. This section will continue to relate the experiences that program staff have evaluating processes and analyzing impact. Operation is "where you face reality and change—or succumb to it," according to the program manager at the JSC.

> They changed their programming from just getting a job to having the skills to reintegrate into the community.

Reality will change subtle nuances of your measurement systems that make all the difference. These insights will not become evident unless processes for data collection, analysis, and use are in place. Use is the most important part of the data issue; it is the reflection-action-reflection cycle of progress. Consider the JSC: Staff monitor the data points outlined in Phase I. Employment serves as an example of data in action. Initially, the numbers surrounding getting a job were tabulated. Something was wrong. They were not getting the success rates of job attainment they knew were possible. They had the proverbial reality check that a certain number of clients will still end up hustling a living and remain on public assistance. The insight was that the clients they were choosing were less and less employable on average. By contemplating and working with the numbers from day to day, they discovered that employment was not the goal, employ*ability* was. So, they changed their programming from just getting a job to having the skills to reintegrate into the community. Therefore, they included more testing to determine the employability of each individual and then the skills, like better decision making, that each client needed the most. Tracking then changed from just following the number of job placements to include, for example, completion of *Thinking for a Change*. This was their cognitive behavioral evidence-based program, which is especially effective with the high-risk clients they wanted to address. This is data in action that supports a learning environment.

Data also serves to reallocate resources to enhance effectiveness. Again, consider the employment data point. When the goal became employability instead of employment, more JSC clients were subsequently placed in substance abuse counseling and fewer in employment counseling, so resources were taken from the former and devoted to the latter. Data worked because JSC staff set aside time to reflect on what data told them.

LINC also monitored the length of stay in their program and noted that the average stay was three months in a nine-month program. On examination, they found they were serving low-risk clients when their goal was to serve the moderate- to high-risk resident. They retargeted their client base to get back on track to stated goals. Data is the avenue to the reflection and action of forward movement.

Effective Practice
Reflect on what the data are telling you and adjust resources allocation for effectiveness and keep processes flexible for efficiency.

These successful sites are truly client-based. The first client base is the people in their program, and the second is stakeholders of it. They used data to "understand (and identify with) the client and act programmatically to focus more on holistic[82] case management," according to the JSC program manager. They expanded mental health services, the housing mix, and outreach (home visits) for noncompliant clients. If they couldn't do a home visit, they made sure they made phone contact. No surprise to them, recidivism rates declined! An important outcome was realized because LINC staff monitored resident contacts. Originally, they thought *any* contact, whether it was in person, by phone, or by email was acceptable. They noticed that the more personal face-to-face meetings elicited the best responses and behavioral outcomes. Naturally, they emphasized the personal touch. This *reduced* staff workload, which is contrary to the first blush logic that more (electronic) contacts were better. In fact, the calling and emailing was more demanding because the electronic methods of contact needed constant repetition and had marginal results. The program director at the JSC said it best by remarking that staff are "neck deep" with a client. By focusing on data and reflection-action "personalities were taken out of decisions; let the results tell the truth," according to the LINC executive director.

While the discussions on process and results *seem* the same, each feeds off the other, noted a senior staffer about process. The reason to understand process is to notice "entrenchment." This is another (better) word for inertia, which denies the need for flexible ways of doing business. She put it this way, "Entrenchment is a lack of common sense." This happens when processes are too "systematic" and people are "invested in their own agendas and looking out for their own." The client management plan written by the service case manager serves as an example. This intake plan became immutable. Once written, it had to be strictly followed even if an exception arose, which happened regularly. The logic for being so regimented was that, after all, these are difficult people to serve. If a client didn't need the prescribed counseling, the plan "fell apart." Staff questioned this process and decided to have an external process evaluation for all processes, with the primary purpose of building flexibility into how they were doing business. Essentially, they established a policy of "show me" that an item in question works. This is another definition of efficiency. The efficient-effective project is the best sales tool to appeal to people you hope will become friends of the project and be your major supporters, especially for resources development.

Resources Development

This section will be necessarily brief because resources development is woven throughout the processes of putting together the life cycle of project growth. When one criticality, aspect, or task works well, everything works better. It's a way of thinking and acting that's a virtuous cycle. It begins with paying attention to details, which establishes credibility, which leads to sharing goals and gaining mutual support. Then comes a return to paying attention to a new set of details. Its essence is the virtuous cycle of capability/honesty/credibility/capability. As the program manager from the JSC observed, developing resources is simply a matter of making and maintaining a contact based on this virtuous cycle.

Effective Practice

Give partners ideas about ways to collaborate.

Savvy practitioners give partners ideas for collaboration. The community development planner for Wilmington, North Carolina and funds coordinator for LINC observed that elected and appointed officials and public career professionals were looking for ways to connect with good ideas. So, "give them a reason to come on board. The city is eager to work with a partner who knows how to solve the city's problems." As the representative of the city, she saw and helped weld the mechanism for the municipality to partner with LINC. Together, they could help find housing for the homeless, reduce crime and victimization, enhance community safety and security, and reduce jail overcrowding. The art of this "deal" was that the executive director had been meeting with community officials, attending city council and county commission meetings, and had been generally available. He helped the city officials see that connecting with LINC was a very smart thing to do.

> **It begins with paying attention to details, which establishes credibility, which leads to sharing goals and gaining mutual support.**

This community need is the opportunity, justification, and purpose for your development strategy. Give supporters a way to come together so they feel part of something important and help them realize that, together, they can be bigger and better than they had imagined.

Effective Practice
Train and develop your board and staff to network for and maintain essential resources.

The interviewees then turned the conversation about operational resource development to maintaining their supporters. LINC, for example, sought advice and material help from their local university, the University of North Carolina, Wilmington. The Quality Enhancement for Nonprofit Organizations department (QENO), mentioned previously, provides university-level professional consulting. The consultants help build nonprofit capacity and increase philanthropy statewide. For LINC, they designed a program of consulting, board development, on-site workshops, assessments, and connections to the community. They conducted monthly roundtable discussions with the board and devoted considerable attention to developing and maintaining resources. Note again, resources extend way beyond money to political and agency support. They trained board members on appropriate topics such as establishing board policy in general and specifically how to assemble essential support. QENO is solidly connected to the community by being seated at a major university and by being charged with developing nonprofits and philanthropy. Their evaluation aligned LINC with city goals such as addressing homelessness with LINC's transitional housing, providing job training and employment, enhancing public safety, and improving neighborhood quality of life. In turn, the city provided money from the general fund and a large $550,000 grant to make expansion possible because it made great political and business sense. QENO staff were also able to network for LINC and thereby recruited partners and potential board members.

The insight here is that LINC understood and catered to the needs of two significant partners: QENO needed healthy nonprofits to develop, and the city needed a proven idea to make progress on solving some of its most difficult problems. This was a brilliant connection made by a resourceful executive director.

The community development planner made a significant observation: As city coffers shrink and they have to right-size staff, elected officials must increasingly look to nonprofits as efficient and effective multipliers of limited funds. She also said that spending is evaluated on a point basis. By being involved and aware of municipal needs and the fact that funding was done by ranking projects, the executive director and board set out to partner and score well as various essential local needs are vetted and funded. Yet another organization was inspired by LINC vision and mission and a very involved staff and executive director who gave them the idea working together would be highly productive.

The funds coordinator for Wilmington offered this advice for connecting with a local municipality:

- *Sell social entrepreneurship.* – The city of Wilmington wanted to see self-sufficiency in its partners, who can make a return on the investment of limited public funds.

- *Diversify resources.* – This is a theme of capacity development. Diverse funding streams are the way to becoming self-sustaining. Funding agencies see this strength and feel better about lending a hand, if not compelled to do so. Potential funders see others participating in success and want to be part of it.

- *Stay focused on the mission.* – Don't get distracted by money, nor should the mission be changed to fit a source of funding, especially a grant. Don't go for easy money; go for money that contributes to mission accomplishment, growth, and sustainability.

- *Guard against burnout.* – Here she was commenting on LINC staff who are inspired by their work and the ongoing construction of their new facility. She could see the danger in having one key person handle too much. Her suggestion was to develop all staff to "do *and* lead" to share the burdens and the rewards.

- *Focus on the long term.* – Again, practitioners at these sites were not only focused on the important daily details of running an organization but had a plan or vision that recognized that this work is one of decades.

One of the bases for the productivity regarding this connection between a municipality and a nonprofit is services that work.

Services

Operation is where your planned service array is uniquely shaped to your environment. Practitioners in the trenches say, "It's tough, because so many agencies are trying to do reentry, and all have different ideas on how to provide their services." Each has an opinion for how others should do this work. Most have a narrow view that the task is reentry rather than the necessary view that it's about post-release *aftercare*. Their faith-based partners, for example, believe in "grace," which means "endless forgiveness." While this is noble, it excuses very poor choices and doesn't hold offenders accountable or responsible for doing the work of their return home. Employers may be more concerned about a prospective employee's background than qualifications for the job. Housing officials would like the post-release services probation officer to visit their housing to keep it safe. An assigned probation officer may not believe in treatment, which is critical to reintegration, and may be all too quick to revoke. All these helpers are going in different, albeit closed, directions. All clamor for limited funds. The multiplicity of opinions on how transitions should be affected hints at the task of the umbrella agency to keep partners focused and part of broader goals. These goals may vary from their purposes and especially their view of how things should be done. There seems to be no unifying vision until one of these model aftercare programs takes root.

> There seems to be no unifying vision until one of these model aftercare programs takes root.

Effective Practice
Court and shape service partners early.

It's necessary to have shared responsibility for goal attainment. It takes a long time for calculated measures to turn "I want" into "we need." In other words, there "have to be plenty of opportunities for team building," according to the JSC program manager. The case manager at the Durham JSC essentially advises to begin courting and shaping services partners early:

- *Develop working relationships.* – Set expectations from day one. Have honest and frequent communication. Ask direct questions such as, "Do you do drug screening, and can we get results as you will be getting results from us?" And keep resource providers informed on the progress—the good and the not so good—of clients. This intimately involves service partners in the success of programming and continuously reinforces their awareness of how they fit in and contribute to overall goals.

- *Develop the agency culture of experimentation.* – The JSC executive director steeps her program in new ideas. This gives staff and partners the freedom to innovate and try new ways of doing business. This is essential to effecting successful reintroductions, which have a dynamic nature and need to constantly evolve. What worked a little while ago may need some tweaking or more.

- *Actively recruit service providers.* – Recruiting service providers also flows from the culture of experimentation. The JSC staff, especially the executive director, are "always collecting business cards." Now here's what makes a so-so program into a model: The executive director always follows up on the contact or assigns staff to do so with the express purpose of exploring possibilities.

- *Remember THE stakeholder.* – Every site made sure clients had input to services. The JSC has an ex-felon advising on what is needed.

- *Write it down.* – Memos of agreement/understanding are the formal way of setting expectations. It may be agonizing to thrash one out, but it's essential to deliver an overarching, mutual service, and the buy-in is vital. This gets the turf issues out of the way early to set the groundwork for the team mentality to emerge. The successful program has written agreements with nearly all partners. (See the Memorandum of Understanding on page 223.)

- *Stress accountability from the offender.* – Ultimately the client is responsible for making it home successfully. It's easy to lose sight of this as each partner is held to certain expectations. The danger is to assume responsibilities and accountabilities that rightly belong to the returnee.

- *Make service partner responsibilities plain.* – A partner is well advised to deliver a service that's realistic, detailed, and especially agreed upon mutually. Also discuss the fact that extended nonperformance may result in the partner being asked to leave the partnership. Service providers like this simplicity of knowing where they stand.

The mutual shaping of program staff and service partners needs time to evolve. Senior staff at these sites see a major operational duty is to remove barriers and "not just focus on the numbers." Daily work with a partner is mostly relational, according to the JSC case manager. This means that core program staff should have a good feel for how the partner deals with a client. When there's a positive drug test, for example, do they ignore it or do they take program-appropriate action. Or worse yet, the partner may not disclose a positive test just to give the client another 30 days to work on the problem in defiance of program policy, which may be to "fire" the client. Does the partner have regular, frequent, and appropriately productive contact with clients? Does the partner keep other team members informed? Does the partner have the expertise they claim to have? Are they measurably successful? The JSC manner of working ensures plenty of face-to-face time with every stakeholder to resolve that which might hinder progress and a good working environment.

There's been much discussion about service mixes that materially guide a client to independence and away from crime and bad choices. It would be helpful to understand how the umbrella organization musters the locally defined service mix. The JSC has the simplest design. It determines each client's needs and fixes the services around them first to afford them the best chance of graduation. Then it extends the offer of services to *any time* after program completion. All the former client has to do is stop in and ask for a little help and have a willingness to make a new start. The plan has two action-oriented entities:

- *The case manager* – The case manager completely profiles the incoming participant and recommends a plan of action. Much is standard, but some individualization of the services mix is necessary.

- *The "staffing"* – On a monthly basis, each client meets with appropriate staff, service providers, and a probation officer. This combines several named programs: Second Chance, the Day Reporting Center, and Reentry, which function as conduits to services. Clients are seen one at a time. A drug test is administered on the spot. If the client fails it, there's a very brief discussion then consequences—revocation—swift, with no extenuating circumstances for a reprieve. If the client passes the drug test, the assembled group checks progress on therapies, training, education, job hunting, social connections, and anything germane, all with a surplus of earned encouragement. They make suggestions for the plan, and the client returns to the path of staying out of incarceration.

Structure allows everyone to focus on the process. This takes some of the negative aspects of personality out of interactions. It also allows everyone, especially leadership, to be problem solvers, according to senior staff. Each participant is aware of differences but is not materially distracted by them because they're focused on something bigger than self-interests.

Interviewees revisited an essential point. Nothing much matters until the client fully dedicates him- or herself to staying out of jail or prison and becoming a productive neighbor.

> **Core program staff should have a good feel for how the partner deals with a client.**

And the client "knows when [the program] is serious about helping," the job development specialist at LINC noted. Consequently, there's an element of tough love counterbalanced with strengths-based programming in all these programs. Rules and expectations are set and agreed to. Staff recognize manipulation by these master manipulators and will not tolerate it. Any transgression is met head on, even harshly. A smuggled mobile phone at Dismas is punishable—possibly with dismissal. Every service partner must understand and enforce this.

This enforcement is strictest with TROSA, where senior residents are made responsible for junior residents, and as previously mentioned, a client can self-eliminate from the program. I personally witnessed a TROSA resident sit in the place in the cafeteria that begins an end to the journey—albeit with much heartfelt dissuasion. Some cannot stand the rigors of TROSA and prefer a return to the cell. Client opinion matters. Residents see that one failure is a failure for all, and consequently, the system is largely self-regulating. Few have to leave. Each site sought input from former inmates. The JSC has a former felon on their board, and many of the staff at TROSA are successful graduates who want to give back. Only a former offender can know what it's like to leave society at 19 and return a decade later to a whole new confusing world. One commented that he went in a boy and came out a man and had never used a cell phone! Each of these programs has staff who stay in contact with people who complete the program. At JSC, for example, the "doors are never closed to graduates." It's a very special staff that make all this work.

Key Staff

Each of the study sites has a singular spirit: The professionals I met believe! They are capable, energized, engaged, and productive and know they can do this work. Their backgrounds and origins don't seem unusual. Yet put into these environments collectively and over time, they are turning around former inmates by the thousands.

How are they molded into a single-minded body that returns hapless and often hopeless people to the community? To be succinct, staff are truly valued by organizational officials, each other, and their sphere within the community.

How does this value manifest? First consider the mechanical things. Yes, they are well selected for their education, experience, and technical and social-behavioral skills. Beyond that, however, they were selected for their spirit. They *wanted* to do this work. When on the job, they never stop learning. They go to professional meetings, conferences, and seminars. They are cross-trained. And succession is considered. Still, these things are routine in a forward-thinking organization. Good personnel practices don't explain how they gel into a force that improves the community.

Effective Practice
Develop a common sense of purpose immediately

What these sites did with their human capital is beyond team building as we may learn of it in a workshop. They built a sense of shared purpose that guides and motivates team members as a whole. Staff are constantly challenged to apply new ideas. Supervisors are constantly taking advantage of teachable situations. Staff self-impose extremely high standards and expectations. The planning director for the JSC relates that they are constantly challenged to "figure it out." Much of their development is on the job, experiential. Leadership is "constantly looking at who is doing what and matching talent to needs and needs to talent." Because staff believe in the underlying goodness and potential of their charges and believe their program can bring out those qualities, they see that potential manifest time after time.

Summing Up Operations for Your Reentry Aftercare Program

Senior executives comment that operation is "all about the basics." It's about simplifying the complex. "There are no shortcuts," the executive director of Dismas commented. The lead staffer, usually the executive director, must concentrate on developing external relationships. At the same time, the director must stay involved in daily business so as not to lose control and be aware of the nuances of the business.

The board must be cautious not to manage too closely but understand the "heartbeat" of what they are helping create. They do this by perhaps spending a day delivering services or attending a group session or making a presentation to a potential partner. When the program is functioning and delivering services, board tasks change from planning to helping develop relationships that translate into political support and operating resources. The board must also plan to sustain the project as the first step to incrementally expanding with the aim of closing the services-to-needs gap. This is when real impact defined by improving lives and communities begins to happen.

Client risk factors determine who your service partners need to be and, by extension, your capacity to deliver those services. You can easily be overwhelmed by deserving returnees. While it's noble to want to help all who should be helped, your duty is to succeed with everyone accepted for services. Each success determines program success, which you can "sell" to anyone and everyone. Even a little failure can hurt the overall effort.

Data are vital to your effort. Every service must have measurable contributions to community wellness and monetary return on investment. Thus, data are the mechanism of success. Data are key to seeing how, when, and where you need to modify what you do. What works one day may not work the next. Data help you build in flexibility by alerting you to difficulties, which allows you to respond to the dynamic nature of post-release services. "Nothing is constant," observe practitioners. The key to developing resources is to give your partners, especially your service partners, opportunities to collaborate. Everyone on your team should be expected to conduct business honestly, to build credibility by doing what is promised, and by being capable while demonstrating it.

According to practitioners who are succeeding, if there is one factor that will determine your success, it's your staff. Nurture staff to have a common sense of purpose from the beginning. Instill this by making sure they are trained, professionally developed, intrinsically motivated, and *challenged*. People who do this work are not well paid but are inspired by it. Foster this basic human drive.

When you've overcome the difficulties of implementation, when your program is operating smoothly, when you have dependable resource streams, when you're demonstrating impact in the community, when you have general trust and confidence in your partners, *then* you may consider expanding. Arriving at the time when growth is warranted, which is what you've been working toward, is when you can *begin* to make a truly notable difference. The next chapter discusses the sustainability and expansion phase of your program.

Chapter 5

PHASE III OF THE PROGRAM'S LIFE CYCLE – SUSTAIN AND EXPAND

Chapter 5

PHASE III OF THE PROGRAM'S LIFE CYCLE – SUSTAIN AND EXPAND

Nothing in this world can take the place of persistence. Talent will not: nothing is more common than unsuccessful men with talent. Genius will not; unrewarded genius is almost a proverb. Education will not: the world is full of educated derelicts. Persistence and determination alone are omnipotent.
– Calvin Coolidge

Neither the public sector nor the private sector alone can provide services expected or needed for the community, especially regarding post-release services and aftercare for the long term. Only by combining the two can the services-to-needs gap be improved.

Each sector has weaknesses and strengths, so the task is to minimize weaknesses and employ strengths. The sites in this model and many other successful local projects visited by this writer for over 20 years employ some variation of a strengths-based approach. Essentially, harmony and inclusiveness are necessary. This has been a priority of the Reform Movement sites that shared their ideas and experiences.

They've found a way to be a conduit for the considerable resources of our public agencies *and* our neighborhoods, magnify their strengths, and focus those strengths with dramatic results on a specific problem.

This phase in which you will gain permanency and the ability to expand is critical to the survival of your idea. More than that, it's critical to figuring out how our most difficult social problems can be solved.

Staff and knowledgeable practitioners explained how they went about stabilizing and expanding. What they teach is no less than how to build a third sector—a public and private alliance.[83] According to senior staff, it's smart to have certain things in place currently in the evolution of your idea. You need to close service gaps in your program and at the community and state levels. At the program level, you will constantly adjust staff and the mix of services. The community always has deficits in services that must be filled to comprehensively treat a returnee. Even at the state level, gaps in services and certainly in needed support will be evident, according to senior JSC staff. The criminal justice system and our social, health, and mental services always struggle against the demand. Practitioners observe that both formal and informal ways to close gaps are available.

9. Sustain Operations

The Urban Institute has a long relationship with what jail officials are doing after an inmate's sentence is finished.[84] Their discussion of the key to sustaining a jail-based reentry program is applicable yet tempered by what senior transitional staff are discovering *this side of the prison gate.*

First, the service idea must survive implementation. Be inclusive so people learn from one another and assimilate varying views by sharing ideas and communicating freely. This learning implies that team members take time to teach one another while being facilitated by the constant stream of teachable moments. Adopt the philosophy that "My (collaborator's) success is my success." *Any* dealing should have a mutually beneficial result. Repeatedly, staff retell stories of doing favors that came back to them manyfold and in unsuspecting even delightful ways. Look forward to collective problem solving, constant improvement, and shaping the continually evolving and progressing effort. Design your work for flexibility and permanence. Empathize by building mutual respect based on being personally congruent: Say what you will do, then do it. The idea is to create synergy, a smooth process of working together for a common goal beyond agency or personal goals.

The summative nature of this new way of working together is to *enable the possible*. It differs from agency thinking, which is often characterized by bureaucracy and rules. By intention and intuition these model reform sites are enablers of constructive collaboration. The ones who assume this task come to the neighborhood ready to work; constant "visioning" does *not* work. The result has implications for our new reality as a society changed forever by globalization, information, and austerity. The one constant is that we will always need well-educated, productive neighbors, even if some of them have had a brush with the underbelly of life.

A caveat: The suggestions that follow are the collective wisdom of many practitioners in four unique circumstances. While they describe a path to success, it would be difficult to do every idea mentioned. You may choose which of these ideas to make your own, dictated by how your program has evolved, how you choose to address transitioning/aftercare and permanence, and especially the stakeholders you have when you consider scaling. Remember that each of these aftercare Reform Movement sites are an experiment in replication and scaling, and thus they present concrete evidence it can be done. TROSA has its roots in the Delancey Street Foundation in San Francisco. LINC has its roots in TROSA. Local post-release transitional projects have models for success and are ready to go to scale—to begin to close the service-to-needs gap.

Each senior executive commiserated about going to scale. One put it plainly by citing the chicken or the egg conundrum. What must be first—operating funds or staff and infrastructure? The answer was emphatically money. These aftercare Reform Movement sites were able to grow because they planned for funding, worked for funding, and thus had funding. In fact, the entire exercise of building your idea is a struggle of increasing your capability to more effectively serve and close the services-to-needs gap. While the gap is a constant specter, it would be helpful to engage the question of funding in earnest when you do the work of stabilizing. Unfortunately, this problem of reassimilating those who pass through our criminal justice system and our social services will only worsen. "There will never be enough facilities to treat those coming out of jail," according to a senior practitioner. You can begin the work by assessing your organizational structure.

> **By intention and intuition these model reform sites are enablers of constructive collaboration.**

Effective Practice
Reassess, reform, and refocus agency functions for scaling up and out.

Will your work last? Scaling is about contemplating succession, the future, and how you keep the project going. This includes leadership succession, staff succession, funding succession, and the succession of what works. Here we focus on leadership. These conundrums drive senior transitional practitioners to distraction. They know they must move on, must face retirement. So, how *do* they transfer years of expertise and learning? They begin by discussing how the organization transitions to permanency by adjusting or refocusing how it is organized and how it functions. Following are their suggestions:

- *Management teams* – Reassess how your systems are reforming and refocus your management teams for scaling. You probably would not consider where to go next without some sort of team system in place. The difference here is that scaling up adds another dimension of complexity to each of the critical functions in the life cycle of your project. Running a successful day program is quite different from considering expanding services with a residential facility, for example. LINC formed a transition team to design, find a site for, plan, build and operate their new facility. TROSA took a similar route as they now operate a fully functioning satellite in a neighboring city.

- *Board of directors* – Reassess how your systems are reforming and refocus the board of directors. The board must have as its priority the task of making the project permanent then scaling it. This is decidedly nuanced because of the population served. Board members will be tough to recruit and retain because delivering post-release services, especially for the startup, is "not pretty" board members say. The people who have talent and energy are already overwhelmed and many just do not want to be associated with ex-prisoners. Yet, expansion is the stage of development when continued effort by talented people is arguably most needed. LINC turned to a superb organization, the Quality Enhancement for Nonprofit Organizations (QENO), for general and board-specific training and guidance.

    Hopefully you have been working toward this day when leadership sees the value of intense and long-term participation and has a history of many successful program graduates who are walking proof that an "ex-con" has a productive place in the community.

- *Financial Team* – Reassess how your systems are reforming and refocus your financial team. Now financial soundness in the form of permanent funding streams is paramount. TROSA, for example, is contemplating planned giving and establishing an endowment to perpetuate key positions.

- *Agency functions* – Reassess how your systems are reforming and refocus essential agency functions for scaling. It's interesting that the mature post-release transitional program can and should be organized by functional agency, which is why this form of organization was built into the program very early during planning. Functionality allows for targeted interventions, continuous self-evaluation and analysis and the uninterrupted pursuit of stability. Each agency provides essential services and allows for more effective budgeting. It also is the mechanism for the continual recruitment of services, both state sponsored and private, to these fundamental functions.

    o *Transitional services* – This is when the return to the community will be realized. Initially, the client would find food, shelter, and clothing. Then there would ideally be an initial job, recovery from addiction, long-term rebuilding, and progression to a life-sustaining career, then productivity and earned respect.

    o *Health and medical services* – This would be for substance abuse—medical and mental health treatment at a minimum. It could also provide HIV/AIDS treatment and a gym membership to focus on wellness, for example. In fact, TROSA has a splendid gym, including full-court basketball.

    o *Educational services* – This would be comprehensive such as, for example, job readiness including resume writing, GED education, computer skills and basic technology literacy training, even college preparation.

- *Staff* – Reassess how your systems are reforming and refocus staff. It always comes back to staff. Don't be afraid to plant the seed with graduates that they can have a place on the staff. Naturally, the best staff composition is a mix of former and nonoffenders or "straights. The goal at the expansion stage, according to staff, is to have "equality." This means residents are taught by staff how to get out of "inferior thinking" in which the ex-offenders see themselves as "screw-ups." Staff partner with clients by teaching them how to be accountable.

When you have it right, as these sites do, you'll have a certain energy of possibilities where everyone wants to be at work.

Effective Practice
Build the therapeutic community.

There seems to be confusion about applying an evidence-based idea. They are discussed as if they're a complete program for effecting a transition, but they're not. They are part of a complex array of services supported by public and private business delivery systems, which are the critical functions discussed in this book. Evidence-based therapies are only part of what a client needs, which extends from having the proper ID to satisfying survival needs upon release to various medical and mental health services. Most important is how the evidence-based practice is applied. A therapeutic community is based on the statement, "What can this person be?" Social entrepreneurship, the process of identifying and developing value in an individual, is the other entrepreneurship, besides the business enterprises that can comprise a residential facility. A community of modalities should be tailored to each client. TROSA, for example, has a few of the following in its array of services:

- *Seeking Safety* – Therapy for trauma, substance abuse, and/or post-traumatic stress disorder (PTSD).[85]

- *Women in Recovery* – A sober setting for women recovering from alcoholism and/or drug abuse.[86]

- *Dialectical Behavior Therapy* – Balancing the contradictory states of change with acceptance for clients with acute psychological difficulties. It focuses on skills training for both healthy internal and interpersonal processes.

- *Anger Management* – Proven techniques and tools to help individuals reduce and control anger.

- *Relapse Prevention* – A behavioral self-control program that teaches individuals with substance addiction how to anticipate and cope with the potential for relapse.[87]

Each site was creative with how therapies were selected, contracted, or delivered. For example, TROSA, in the happy circumstance of being a neighbor of Duke University, worked out an arrangement with the psychiatric department for pro bono therapists.

Staff encourage anyone thinking about or doing this work to remember to dream. LINC staff, for example, see that upscale residential community for post-release services and program graduates mentioned previously. With the opening of the new 40-bed facility and when sustainable enterprises become established, they see procuring land and building houses in an impoverished part of town as the next expansion of LINC. This is less star gazing than one might think. Some thought the next 40 beds were impossible. It's part of an unfolding plan they can visualize to help encourage its manifestation.

10. Plot the Long-Range Strategy and Tactics for Expansion to Scale

Those who are doing the work of helping others return home offer comments on the struggle—especially the strain of going to scale. It's complex, with few examples of how to proceed. Hence you need to begin building permanency from the beginning. That is, document everything— procedures, processes, policies, and plans—and never pass up a moment to make friends and allies. Recognize you're in a complex environment of bureaucracies and behaviors, aftercare practitioners caution. Thus develop a philosophy

> **Document everything—procedures, processes, policies, and plans—and never pass up a moment to make friends and allies.**

that persistence wins with bureaucracies and impossible people. A TROSA executive summarized the aftercare environment as being "unruly." Officials at agencies and municipalities and those you serve, "just don't have discipline." Thus, "accountability has to be built into your systems."

Gaining support for what you do is a constant struggle. Little public sector money is available compared to need. Public agencies largely have a different mandate than local municipalities and programs that facilitate assimilation. The point is well made that the systems of incarceration are built as an arm of the criminal justice system and do those associated duties well but, "They set former prisoners up to fail" after their sentences, observe practitioners at every site. The simplest example of this is that upon release, returnees usually don't have their basics, such as an ID, a Social Security card, health insurance information, housing documentation, legal documents, and financial resources. These documentations are crucial for successful reentry into society, as they enable individuals to access essential services, secure housing and employment, and navigate legal and administrative processes. Without them, former inmates may face additional barriers to rebuilding their lives and reintegrating into their communities. Efforts to provide support in obtaining these documents can significantly improve the reentry process and increase the likelihood of successful rehabilitation.

Unfortunately, upon release many are left to fend for themselves after completing a reentry program. Even program clients often have a sense of resignation that the work of recovery and rebuilding is not worth the effort. A common thought among returnees, according to local officials, goes something like, "Who wants a grueling two-year or more program right after a stint behind bars?" The informal selection process for potential program attendees is: "They have to want it by proving it."

Next, staffing is bedeviling. How should these most critical "assets" be recruited, trained, and retained when they're underpaid and overworked? And yet, these successful practitioners do just that.

Many unintended consequences of developing permanency arise in this arena of work. Each site mentors other sites and local services in the cause of transitioning. It "strengthens the consortium," according to the executive director at LINC.

People will want to be part of what you are doing. Resources, while tough to come by, sometimes "appear at your doorstep." TROSA staff know they only need to entice someone to the grounds for a tour to get a convert. This happened with local judges, who are now some of their staunchest supporters and salespeople.

Effective Practice
Refocus leadership as an Expansion Task Force.

This task force aims to discover what is needed versus what is available—knowledge that comes only from boots on the ground. Develop a "resource center without walls." If your leadership team has been evolving with scalability in mind, they will have done their homework to learn the business of transition. The executive director from LINC, who is an integral part of the board, began learning this business by participating in transitional services "from the view of the world as an ex-con." He first talked extensively to the people returning from incarceration to "feel and absorb" how to transition. Then, he went about building his network of leadership and providers from the perspective of the target population. This is an extension of other transitional programs, such as TROSA, where key staff were former criminals or substance abusers or both who had reformed and felt compelled to return the many kindnesses of their new success.

Then, after a good grounding, the LINC director went about assembling 15 key leadership players, who meet regularly and have done so for over a decade (at the time of this writing). He recruited talent with funds development experience, a banker, a corrections representative, a person with housing experience, and generally looked for people with "influence." He commented that he began with complete faith that it (transitional services) would work and continuous personal experience with residents to keep himself grounded in what is essential. His lesson to the board: Embrace enabling strengths.

Effective Practice
Have a project development strategy.

Senior staff at LINC defined project development relative to stabilization and expansion as the "management of influence," differentiated from developing resources. This was an insightful way of looking at what development really is. Most times, it's a term mistakenly used merely to refer to securing the next grant. Oh yes, these practitioners were also concerned with money, but it was influence, another term for building relationships, that made funding streams possible. Managing influence means staying in touch with those who can act as producers of a product, whether it's hard money, a building, a contact list, sweat equity, or a political connection. Again, the LINC executive director used the example of his expansion from a 12-bed facility to 40 beds. Connections with elected and appointed officials and business leaders resulted in an expansion package of grants, gifts, a condemned old jail, and contractors to build a state-of-the-art full-service transitional hub for men and women. It took *11 years* to put everything and everyone together. *That* is faith in an idea. The city will even cut the grass for free at a significant savings. It's already a model for a transitional facility with national implications. This strategy is and has to be based on a plan.

A *working* strategic plan, or one like the TROSA business model, is one that holds its drafters accountable, according to the LINC executive director. It holds the

> **Residential services are proving to be the mechanism that reduces recidivism to very low rates.**

service idea accountable to the community for its betterment by being responsible for performing well and with results. It forces the organization (read, the board) to a productive path by legitimizing it. The strategic expansion plan serves as a neutral, objective "party," which tells stakeholders how to be successful. It's the tool that facilitates stakeholder relationships, especially the unique ties between staff, in particular the executive director and the board. Simply put, this strategic plan is a potent to-do list.

As a program fights for survival in its early days, assuming more to do is very much a "seat-of-the-pants feeling," senior staff observe. As projects mature, "more and more, analysis plays a big part." Again, LINC turned to QENO for guidance and step-by-step assistance. TROSA turned to the business school at Duke University for theirs. Budgets are thoroughly analyzed for expansion dollars. More specialized staff are hired, such as an IT specialist and COO for TROSA. The only regret voiced by senior staff is that writing a formal business plan should have been done first, no matter how difficult it was.

Effective Practice
Consider the residential option with socially conscious enterprises.

If your work with post-release services began as a day program, consider augmenting it with a residential option, because it's the preferred platform for essential services and the long-term nature of their delivery. Without housing, LINC founding staff were overwhelmed with "pushing services." At first, it was quantity not quality. The LINC director suggested being creative, such as approaching a church that may already have rooms or can convert a few rooms to be the kernel of the critical mass of clients to sustain full transitional services. It's also a good way to learn the business by going small and doable *and* doing business with one client at a time.

Residential services are proving to be the mechanism that reduces recidivism to very low rates. To underscore this, LINC had 29 residents for the 2010-11 year with *no* rearrests; they predicted a return to incarceration rate of only 2 percent! These rates are stunning by the way. Residency is where core competencies are delivered.

Lives begin to stabilize. "Capturing" the audience can "stop life in the streets from getting in the way of the work [of returning]."

> **Just about all work on money is about acquiring it; experience dictates that using what you have well is the first consideration**

TROSA and LINC prove that post-release services can be self-sustaining in most creative fashions. As mentioned previously, LINC leadership hosts enterprises that are socially conscious, including sustainable agriculture from which come the nutrients for aquaculture. LINC's hydroponically grown vegetables can be ordered over the internet and delivered fresh to locally contracted restaurants. The restaurants, in turn, donate their garbage to return to the gardens and armies of specially bred earthworms that convert organic matter into compost. Oh yes, and the worms can be sold also. Naturally, any idea will be adapted from working models. The goal was to have jobs with a living wage for half of the residents and self-generated income streams for the project. This is the definition of being self-sustaining with the capacity to incrementally scale up. The business plan based on these ideas outlined that the construction loan for their 40-bed residential facility would be paid in full within five years! By then, they will be in a virtuous cycle of reinvestment and expansion. Residents will pay for their *own* return to the community at little or no public cost.

Effective Practice
Formalize resources development with a development officer.

A development officer and indeed the entire staff must be concerned with much more than the amount of money coming in. Just about all work on money is about acquiring it; experience dictates that using what you have well is the first consideration. Interestingly and insightfully, one conversation about funds development at TROSA began with conservation. "Pay-go" is the watchword for each of these aftercare Reform Movement sites. They obsess about not being over obligated and working smartly with available resources.

The biggest gains in conservation come from the smallest of ideas to run daily operations more frugally. Again, we turn to TROSA for an example: snacks. When hundreds of residents are usually doing heavy manual labor, several snacks a day are more than a luxury. Snacks for this large residential business are at the time of this writing calculated to cost at least $10,000 a month! But every sticky bun is donated, thus the cost equals zero. A very used truck from the state salvage yard immediately broke down, which made the purchase a bad decision, but it led to acquiring the next truck from military surplus, which worked out.

One of TROSA's first businesses was potato peeling! This was to support the catering business. Yes, the potato peeler was a used machine which they learned to maintain. Local large businesses are always down- or right-sizing, which means hard goods become available. Much first-rate furniture came from GlaxoSmithKline (GSK) and IBM. The route to these gifts was paved long before they became available because these companies were made aware of TROSA and what the program was about. The executives at these companies could see a handsome afterlife for their cast-offs. These companies were ready to donate; the call merely set the date. It's not entirely a factor of how much you bring in, but how its effect is multiplied.

The lesson is to always look for an alternative, a donation, a bargain, a deal, and use everything to its fullest. TROSA also has the In-Kind division comprised of a bank of residents each pulling an eight-hour day filling orders for any needed item from angel food cake mix to windows for the next residence. Any request is entertained, and the work-order requests stream in. As their function implies, most orders are filled gratis.

Funds are also generated by ideas brought about by opportunity. A tree trimming business grew from voluntarily helping clean up after hurricane Fran. These aftercare Reform Movement sites never give up experimenting and borrowing good ideas. Very few things pass the TROSA gates that are not a bargain, used to their fullest, repaired, reused, and recycled.

Cash, in-kind goods, barter, goodwill gestures, donations, sustainable enterprises, residents working within the program, granting, planned giving, endowing positions, using a truck for multiple purposes, volunteer help, recycling, repair, conservation, pay-go; *all* of these are resources development, way beyond the dollars. In their totality, these ideas beyond money are the reason a reentry/aftercare idea can take hold and survive. Ideas are borrowed from wherever they are working. Many seem bright with potential until they are tried and don't live up to expectations—and so it is with resources. Many, many ideas have been tried and discarded, such as a dog kennel: too much liability. They tried to start a cleaning service for Duke University dormitories, but University policy wouldn't allow former felons near students.

Many of these pages have been devoted to building the flow of sustainable resources. The expansion stage of operation is more than likely when it's advantageous to formalize development by hiring or appointing a development officer. Development is experimentation. There are the usual sources such as grants and a giving/donation campaign, but your mix of streams will be uniquely defined by your circumstances.

The development officer with TROSA focuses her attention on the following sources in ascending order of productivity:

- *Government* – While government support has the greatest potential, it's not practical. This is a threefold problem. First, government funds are very sparse, competitive, and complex and thus expensive with which to comply. Still, program officials judiciously apply for grants without sacrificing time and effort on more productive activities. The potential for this source is when an agreement can be reached for criminal justice funds, e.g., state-level correction monies, to be directed to these programs. They are more stable. One-time grants are fraught, as they have a whimsical, unpredictable nature—here today, gone tomorrow. Try them, but don't depend on them. The solution lies in legislation to construct a partnership whereby both residents and dollars can be diverted from the criminal justice system, for example, to these programs. This can be done at great savings in tax dollars, as Dismas does with the Federal Bureau of Prisons.

- *Corporate* – These funds are also difficult to pursue as private giving is usually "focused," which means funding projects are strictly defined.

- *Foundations* – Foundations are like corporate donors, as they have well defined purposes that complicate collaborations to work with the formerly incarcerated. TROSA, however, has come up with a creative solution. Let's mention again that they approached the Duke University Psychiatric department for assistance doing the program counseling and now have an arrangement for free services. Still, programs get general operating support, which makes the pursuit worth the time. The Mary Duke Biddle Foundation, for example, has a mission to support arts and education. A fit was found to pay tuition at the local Community College for art classes. Another foundation contributed to TROSA Scholars to help repay tuition loans.

- *Individual* – Surprisingly, this is a very good source. TROSA, for example, has established ways for individuals of any means to participate. *Friends,* at $75, can get discounted services and early access to yard sales. *Allies,* at $500, get value-added services. And the most productive level, a *Partner,* at $1,000, is invited to a holiday dinner and gets a Christmas wreath.

- *Etcetera* – This is a great category. Ideas abound! But they are not taken without painful analysis, planning, and experimentation—again, "one at a time." Many experiments have failed. Following are a few that have worked out or are showing promise:
    - *Christmas tree sales* – An original experiment at TROSA with a load of trees has now expanded to six sites, one of which is in an adjoining city. I'm told it's highly successful. The unintended and priceless consequence of this is that thousands of neighbors get to meet residents and have a wholesome interaction that's mutually fulfilling. This has created incalculable goodwill, according to the development officer.
    - *THE aforementioned "Yard sale"* – This event is the "mother of all yard sales." The moving company, while loading up the family kit and caboodle, offers to clean the garage and dispose of clutter. Most goes to the dump, but some is repurposed. A "king's ransom of good, good stuff" is repaired, refurbished, and restored for the annual sale, which has turned into a "happening." Thousands come from the entire region to scoop up bargains.
    - *Estate/Planned giving* – Even when some of these projects were a one-person entity, these early champions knew that estate planning is a viable component and not the singular purview of large universities. They suspect that families of successful graduates will be compelled to demonstrate their gratitude and will be ready to assist them with their gifting. Donations are tax deductible, and if put in a Donor Advised Fund, invested in conservative stocks, rising in value tax free.

The development officer at TROSA is a mix of qualifications and enthusiasm. First, she's a first-rate technologist. She employs all the latest information-sharing tools for communication. What stands out, besides her enthusiasm, is her ability to connect with supporters.

This strategy outlined by the above sources is a theme with mature and forward-thinking local service agencies. Reputation brings expanded funding opportunities at this stage of the project life cycle. At the time of this writing, TROSA is convening a meeting of foundation and private people just to explore possibilities for going to scale. They dream of a TROSA academy to train the next generation of TROSA staff and champions. They have already begun that endowment. These practitioners are ever so cautious about every responsibility yet fearless about taking next steps when it's "right"—and much is going right with this reentry aftercare program.

Summing Up Your Program Sustainability and Expansion

Expansion is perhaps the least understood part of local programming, with its struggles, failures, and disappointments, yet it's supported with the power of an idea and the rewards of a reclaimed life. Just how do you expand to begin to close your needs gap? Expansion is "supporting the basics of survival," according to the TROSA founder. Which comes first, the chicken or the egg? Do you somehow focus on building revenue streams or hire and develop staff first? Let's mention again, experience demands that money comes first. Two keys to expansion, especially in a residential setting, are enabling residents and producing funding streams. Predictable streams justify budgets and spending planning. Both are based on training. Residents, or clients, must be trained for their reintroduction to the community and to give back to the program as a resident employee or as an example of success. Staff, resident, and nonresident must be continually trained for current duties, additional duties, and the inevitable turnover. That broken-down, first-salvaged truck of TROSA's became a well-used fleet of 100 vehicles of all makes and models that are maintained by only two residents. However, they will move on just as they become well-paid master mechanics. In fact, TROSA resident "staff" turn over every two years, and all that program expertise must be replaced or the program crumbles.

Getting to an effective transition is also about the effect of all this work on the community. Yes, an individual, a family, the neighborhood, the community are much better off with a productive citizen. Crime and victimization are greatly reduced. Public funds and resources are much better spent and allocated. Beyond that, the community as a whole is made better by acts of goodwill. For example, TROSA helps Duke University with fundraising. The local Latino community has an annual festival and fundraising event, and TROSA helps with the gargantuan cleanup. TROSA residents also help the Junior League with their annual meeting, and the meals they cater for local events are first

> **Staff, resident, and nonresident must be continually trained for current duties, additional duties, and the inevitable turnover.**

class. TROSA grounds and facilities are orderly and immaculate. Facilities are rebuilt, remodeled, or new and lift the appearance of the entire campus. In fact, the main facility at TROSA was an abandoned dairy, which is now a showplace. It's flanked by brand new dormitories, manicured grass, and lovely landscaping, done by their landscaping enterprise crew, of course. Tours are a regular occurrence, and the executive director is continually on speaking engagements.

How will you know you are succeeding at this? The LINC executive director began getting awards such as the Coastal Entrepreneur of the Year for Nonprofits. Phone traffic increases; strangers call for information, to volunteer, and to offer spontaneous compliments. The police department reported a decrease in crime rate and associated it with LINC. Customer satisfaction increases. The program receives numerous calls from judges and law enforcement and corrections officials wanting information and inquiring about services availability for people in their systems. The numbers, such as those for program graduation (which go up) and recidivism rates (which go down) improve. Practically speaking, a successful program is in a perpetual state of expansion.

Now let's look at some of the lessons learned by our model aftercare programs that they've so generously shared for those wanting to help in this way. In addition, as more grist for the preparation mill, you have further questions to contemplate for your readiness.

Chapter 6

CONCLUSION

Chapter 6

CONCLUSION

How long are you going to wait before you demand the best for yourself?
– Epictetus

What you are doing by transitioning the formerly incarcerated is reinventing how a neighborhood, a community, a township needs to take care of itself. You and your fellow practitioners in this work need to assume a leadership role for public and private entities. This is a complete reversal of how things are normally done, as it's bottom-up then top-down and around again in a virtuous cycle. And with each cycle, the idea, or program, becomes stronger and more permanent by building the capabilities to improve the community. It's the essence of synergy—teaching and learning from one another while becoming more than the sum of the parts. It's the definition of modern, 21st-century govern*ance* that harkens back to the pioneering spirit of self-reliance and neighbor helping neighbor.

> It's the essence of synergy—teaching and learning from one another while becoming more than the sum of the parts.

Lessons Learned

Throughout the lengthy process of learning from the remarkable people cited throughout these pages, the following themes or lessons are a few that emerged:

- *The new returnee is not "old school."* – The new inmate is much more complicated than the returnee of a few decades ago. Today, according to practitioners, your client or resident likely "is younger, mentally ill, traumatized, and without a work ethic; has a substance problem and no practical life experience; and may be inextricably gang affiliated."

- *Transition begins after release.* – Most information about planning reentry and providing post-release services is normally from the perspective of criminal justice agencies. From the model Reform Movement perspective, the bulk of the work effecting a life without crime depends on how the community rallies around returnees and provides support for them.

- *Plan on expansion from your first days.* – Assemble initial leadership—the executive director and guiding board—with expansion as a major purpose. Though it may seem a luxury, write business and strategic plans. Get professional advice and help if you can. Be inclusive and assume the leadership role for community efforts.

- *Ask for resources for this work.* – Focus the gaze of your community, public and private, on post-release services. Never pass up an opportunity to make friends, as they will lead you to the money, people, and things you need to progress. When working on acquiring resources, credibility is everything. Tell people what you will do, then deliver. The goodwill of resources development comes in a thousand acts of kindness.

- *When considering operations and scope, be sure to consider your values.* – People internal and external to your organization need to know where you stand. Let them know your commitment to:
    - A community-centered approach.
    - Collaborative partnerships.
    - Accountability and responsibility.
    - Empowerment and self-sufficiency.
    - Continuous improvement.
    - Community well-being.

Your fellow practitioners need a compass to help them with the minute-to-minute decisions that, in turn, need to connect to overall goals. You also want those who look at your program to be able to clearly identify your values.

- *Process remains more important than impact.* – If your daily processes are goal directed and working well, you will have noticeable and significant results.

> **Expansion is a feeling, an attitude.**

- *Services are a continuum.* – Services are defined by the returnee's needs, beginning with basic survival needs and developed in concert with their progress toward a productive life. You need to deliver services as a seamless process, one feeding into the next, collaboratively gathering strength from one another to support the individual to independence.

- *Plan for succession.* – Hire with succession in mind. Essential staff move on, resident staff graduate, and leaders retire. Write formal job descriptions as they evolve. Document processes, procedures, and policies. Formalize agreements between partners. Be in a perpetual state of training.

- *The primary task of operations is to build capacity that builds permanency.* – The tendency of any startup is to focus on the crisis of the moment and on services, in particular an evidence-based practice (EBP). That's easy to do as it's what you're delivering. However, it distracts from the essentials of capacity building. How well an EBP is delivered doesn't matter if the program dwindles or never starts with strength.

You aren't held to a "timeline" for expansion. The point has been made that expansion is a feeling, an attitude. The deputy director of the JSC explained it was a matter of *determination* and *inspiration*. First, leaders and staff had a level of conviction that "we can make it happen," which progressed to realizing, "Oh my God, we *can* make it happen!" Their scaling efforts went from one idea at a time, incrementally, to being able to bring several ideas to life. However, the work of supporting those who've been through the criminal justice system and are finished with bad choices and circumstances has just begun. The potential is limitless.

ABOUT THE AUTHORS

JAMES KLOPOVIC, Major, USAF, retired, holds a Doctor of Public Policy (DPP) from Charles Sturt University, Sydney, Australia, with concentration on service program capacity building at the organizational and community levels.

James is helping cultivate the next generation of leaders via character-based education and development. He promotes the understanding of how to build teams that accomplish more than the sum of the parts and combines this passion with developing better ways to deliver municipal public services with collaborative Capacity Building.

After retiring from the United States Air Force, James continued providing leadership at federal, state, and local levels for a total of 45 years. He served as a senior staffer for 25 years on the North Carolina Governor's Crime Commission, where his responsibilities encompassed strategic planning, municipal governance, financial development, federal granting, and community and organizational development, implementation, and evaluation. Now he writes, publishes, and consults.

One of the numerous programs he created detailed the processes and procedures for School Resource Officers, which resulted in continuously improving learning environments statewide while making schools safer. Those programs continue today.

As the principal investigator/program director on a series of research programs, he analyzed and proposed model local programs leading to grant proposals for dozens of municipal and state initiatives. He has broad experience in logistics, training, and education. His expertise in program design, implementation, and management includes ensuring program and organizational permanency. His technical support to numerous local government entities created and enhanced service ideas such as delinquency prevention, reentry, and decriminalizing people living with mental illness.

James is cofounder of The Nicole and James Klopovic Family Charitable Foundation, which lends support to local social programs with funding and knowledge of Capacity Building to encourage *Permanent Solutions to Permanent Problems.*

He has authored numerous publications regarding community policing, community development, and effective/efficient delivery of public services as well as books for fun. In descending order of date, they include the following:

The Good Life: My Legacy for You. A memoir. (Morrisville, N.C.: Affinitas Publishing, 2023) Available through Amazon and *http://www.affinitaspublishing.org*.

Volume I, Capacity Building Series: *Building Capacity from the Bottom Up: The Key to Sustaining Local Services.* (Morrisville, N.C.: Affinitas Publishing, 2024) Available through Amazon and *http://www.affinitaspublishing.org*.

Volume II, Capacity Building Series: *Decriminalizing Mental Illness: A Practical Guide for Building Sustainable Crisis Intervention Teams.* (Morrisville, N.C.: Affinitas Publishing, Second Edition 2024) Available through Amazon and *http://www.affinitaspublishing.org*.

Volume III, Capacity Building Series: *Accelerating Juvenile Reentry: A Practical Capacity Building Model for Sustaining Aftercare.* (Morrisville, N.C.: Affinitas Publishing, 2024) Available through Amazon and *http://www.affinitaspublishing.org*.

Volume IV, Capacity Building Series: *Accelerating Adult Reentry: A Practical Capacity Building Model for Sustaining Post-Release Transitional Services.* (Morrisville, N.C.: Affinitas Publishing, 2024) Available through Amazon and *http://www.affinitaspublishing.org*.

Becoming a New Wave Leader: Principles and Practices to Live and Lead Well. (Morrisville, N.C.: Affinitas Publishing, 2021) Available through Amazon and *http://www.affinitaspublishing.org*.

Your Moral Compass: A Practical Guide for New Wave Leaders. (2020) Available through Amazon and *http://www.affinitaspublishing.org*.

Little Stories: A Legacy of Living, Laughing and Loving. (Morrisville, N.C.: Affinitas Publishing, 2019) Available through Amazon and *http://www.affinitaspublishing.org*.

The Honest Backpacker: A Practical Guide for the Rookie Adventurer over 50. (Morrisville, N.C.: Affinitas Publishing, 2017) Available through Amazon and *http://www.affinitaspublishing.org*.

Effective Program Practices for At-Risk Youth: A Continuum of Community Based Programs. (Kingston, N.J.: Civic Research Institute, Inc., 2003). Available through Amazon and *https://civicresearchinstitute.com/index.html.*

Contact: *jklopovic@gmail.com*

NICOLE KLOPOVIC is the daughter of James Klopovic. She holds a Doctor of Medical Science and is a certified Physician Associate (PA-C), practicing in the areas of Emergency Medicine, Urgent Care, Aesthetics, Weight Management, and Primary Care. In addition, she is a captain in the U.S. Air Force Reserve Medical Corps and is pursuing her Air Force career concurrently with her career as a PA-C.

She stays active with dance instructing, weightlifting, hiking, and cycling and enjoys cooking and traveling, striving to embrace the motto *carpe diem* while maintaining her passion to mentor, help, and teach others.

Nicole is cofounder and CEO of The Nicole and James Klopovic Family Charitable Foundation, which lends support to local social programs with funding and knowledge of Capacity Building to encourage *Permanent Solutions to Permanent Problems.*

APPENDIX

GLOSSARY

21st-century governance

The emphasis in 21st-century gove*rnance,* not govern*ment,* is the importance of collaboration, innovation, and inclusivity in addressing social challenges and delivering effective public services. Govern*ment* is what is done. Govern*ance* is *how* it is done for the betterment of the community and thus society. By fostering partnerships, leveraging resources, and engaging stakeholders across sectors, local public service entities can create more equitable, resilient, and responsive systems that empower individuals and strengthen communities.

Capacity Building

Capacity Building in this model of local project development refers to building the infrastructure and resources to resolve a locally defined social concern. The primary purpose of this systemic, wholistic approach is to build, support, and sustain local service ideas that promote community well-being. Its vision is to: *Build Permanent Solutions to Permanent Problems.*

This infrastructure is a matrix of those resources and services specifically chosen for their long-term commitment and capabilities of resolving the local problem addressed. These supports are both internal (organizational) and external (private, community, state, and federal). They include a combination of:

- *Political will* – The collective means and determination to see the project through to sustainability.

- *Human capacity* – Staff developed for their wholistic contribution to building the service idea.

- *Leadership* – An executive director and board chosen for the will to succeed by long-term collaboration.

- *Dedicated matrices of local services* – A team of local entities chosen for their applicability and dedication to the program.

- *Facilities* – Including equipment and supplies, with funds for replenishment, operation, and measured expansions.

- *Capability* – Operational capability, such as financial management and training.

- *Funding* – Separate reliable streams/sources of financial support for program development, maintenance, and expansion.

- *Processes* – A measurably effective means of service delivery; the efficient and effective daily work of the project. For the purposes of Capacity Building, a process is continuous versus a project, which is terminal. The former focuses on vision; the latter aims at getting a task done.

- *Measured effectiveness* – A means of analysis in place to measure the effectiveness of improving the target population and developing the "picture" of success for program justification. This is the *how* of understanding a well-working entity. Analysis of efficiency is also necessary. This measures if the correct activity is done efficiently.

- *Measured efficiency* – This is a means to measure and ensure that processes are doing what they were meant to do. This is the *what* of actions in a process.

The overall goal of Capacity Building is to close the services-to-needs gap.

Criminogenic factors

Criminogenic factors are personal factors, internal or external, that lead to criminal behavior and possibly involvement in/dependence on public services. The Ohio Department of Rehabilitation and Correction discusses the major categories of criminogenic factors.[88] These include anti-social personality, anti-social attitudes and values, anti-social associates, family dysfunction, poor self-control, poor problem-solving skills, substance abuse, and lack of employment skills and employability. These are like risk factors but differ in that much of the attention of services during incarceration and certainly post-release from the criminal justice system are devoted to developing strengths and behaviors to overcome these factors. The greatest initial focus of post-release services is preparation for and maintaining gainful employment. This is one of the leading factors in overcoming criminogenic factors and successfully returning to society and away from crime. Not insignificant is developing pride in place and self after overcoming difficulties to become self-sustaining and respected.

Evidence-based practice (EBP)

An EBP is the careful use of the best evidence in making decisions or taking action.[89] Its research basis determines that, under certain conditions, the practice can have a measurable, positive result or results—usually a favorable change in behavior of a target population. More important, the way an EBP is conducted is heavily data dependent. Data is collected, analyzed, and used in some cases on an hourly basis. However, stating a practice is evidence based is only the beginning of making such a practice work from location to location.

Pennsylvania's Juvenile Justice System Enhancement Strategy says it best:

'Evidence-based practice' simply means applying what we know in terms of research to what we do in our work with youth, their families, and communities in which we live. It is the progressive, organizational use of direct, current scientific evidence to guide and inform the (delivery of) efficient and effective services.[90]

Relative to capacity building to deliver local public services, sometimes the term "evidence-based practice" is mistaken for the entire task of building capacity or the program itself. However, an EBP is a relatively small part of capacity building. It's usually a service or procedure within the wider work of building the supporting infrastructure for that service or procedure. So, for capacity building, an evidence-based practice is a service within a program, such as a therapeutic modality with a scientific basis for a positive, measurable effect that contributes to goal accomplishment.

Caution: An EBP in one location is no guarantee it will work in another.

An EBP is well and good if it is guided by the goal of Capacity Building with sustainability in mind. Even an exciting EBP can be misguided, which is a tragic misdirection of resources. Program staff may be "sure" they're making progress but are not. In the worst case, funding and political will fade; then too does the project.

Life cycle concept of post-release services

Everyone understands a life cycle. A car has a life cycle to be sourced, manufactured, distributed, sold, operated, and salvaged for materials. A life cycle is easy to communicate, teach, and act upon. In this case, it unravels the complexities of Capacity Building for a local reentry strategy. Thus, the program's life cycle has three phases: I. Plan and Implement; II. Operate and Stabilize; and III. Sustain and Expand, leading to Realization.

The critical elements of Capacity Building are Action Items and Effective Practices for each phase of the life cycle.

Recidivism

"Recidivism," according to the Bureau of Justice Statistics, "is measured by criminal acts that result in the re-arrest, reconviction, or return to prison with or without a new sentence during a three-year period following the prisoner's release."[91]

A problem with this definition is that recidivism is usually only measured while an inmate is still under court supervision or in a reentry program when measurement is easier to gather and manipulate. What about, for example measuring revocation back to a cell? It's that much more remarkable that aftercare reduces recidivism at far greater rates than criminal justice system-sponsored reentry programs.

Recidivism, therefore, doesn't reflect the true performance of the aftercare programming necessary to complete the inmate's transition to home and community. Still, the recidivism rate is used as a primary measure of institutional or agency program reentry "success." The term, thus the measure, can mean many things. Is it a return to injurious behavior, for example, a relapse to substance abuse? Is it a re-arrest or a reconviction? Or is it simply a return to criminal activity? It is all these, so clarity is needed.

Recidivism should be measured in yearly increments after all programming is completed, but this is quite expensive and difficult to do. A simple definition elucidates what the result of a criminal justice-oriented project versus a local aftercare service program should realistically be. A return to criminal behavior signifies a return to social dysfunction and unproductivity, a probable return to dependency on expensive social and private support networks, more victimization, and the loss of a potentially productive citizen.

The term recidivism needs to be reconsidered because, as it's now used, it only measures reincarceration for the short term. It doesn't reflect the reality that the work of reentry is only done to prepare for the long-term work of successful post-release aftercare. It's aftercare that completes the individual's transition to the community and away from bad behaviors and crime to productivity. To accurately reflect the effect of reentry/aftercare programming, recidivism must have a long-term reference. It should refer to a return to criminal behavior, usually several years after a sanction or rehabilitation program, whether there's a re-arrest, a reconviction, or a return to incarceration. Recidivism defined this way is better suited to measure the effect of a good aftercare program, the aim of an overall local reentry strategy.

Reentry

This is a bit of a misnomer, as the term connotes that a person is equipped with the skills to function in the community. However, reentry programs only begin to address the work of transition. The term *post-release services* better describes programs that prepare people formerly involved with the criminal justice system for a successful return home.

Scope

Relative to Capacity Building, determining scope means determining how to do just enough and do it well—not to attempt too much and risk failure. The scope of capacity building for a local reentry/aftercare strategy encompasses a comprehensive range of activities and initiatives aimed at enhancing the capability of local agencies, organizations, and stakeholders to effectively support individuals transitioning from incarceration back into the community. Scope enables community leadership and staff to do just what is needed to support individuals in successfully reintegrating into society, thus reduce recidivism, and promote safer, healthier communities for all residents.

Transformational capacity building

This approach emphasizes innovation, efficiency, and citizen-centric services to address local challenges and improve the overall quality of life for residents. Here are some key characteristics of a capacity-built transformational local public service:[92]

- *Innovation and creativity* – Capacity building is a new way to think about delivering public services to permanently address persistent and difficult social dysfunction. It's marked by reimagining capacity building and creative problem solving marked by evidence. Evidence justifies expansion. Problems are seen as opportunities to improve, grow, and make a difference. Calculated experimentation determines what works and how it does so.

- *Citizen-centric focus* – Matrix solutions assemble specific talents and organizational resources to attack the social dysfunction at hand. Everyone is seen as a possible partner and encouraged to apply their specific contribution, be it funding, expertise, or political will. Thus, communication is completely transparent. Virtue—character and well-being—are both expected and demonstrated.

- *Efficiency and effectiveness* – It's all about the data. Data drives everything from decisions, actions, and budget justification to expansion. Processes are continually optimized for the correct production. Red tape is headed off or at least minimized. Any public effort must show a monetized "profit" as public dollars are dear. Data is reduced to a dollar-and-cents argument as that's the compelling justification for further support, project continuation, and funding. Efficient work must lead to effective goal accomplishment meaningful to those served.

- *Collaboration and partnerships* – A capacity-focused project attracts partners to multiply effort and resources in a collaborative effort that results in the whole being greater than the sum of its parts. This generates new funding streams and compounds expertise and vital collective enthusiasm for the program.

- *Matrix solutions* – Combining single-agency services delivery, commonly called silo (or stovepipe) services, into a matrix of a service targeted to a single purpose where the whole is greater than the sum of its parts. These stovepipes are less than effective and a misallocation of resources because they duplicate services and add to bureaucracy. Matrix solutions compel viewing the project from the wholistic perspective of well-being, versus a limited view of problem solving.

- *Service accessibility and inclusivity* – Capacity includes built-in, ever-increasing orbits of service based on supporting data to do so. This most effectively serves the defined target population regardless of social condition.

- *Continuous learning and improvement* – Staff are imbued with the need for self-development and the pursuit of integrity and character. They are encouraged to continuously learn and improve themselves with a wholistic approach to life and contribution to communal effort. This makes for continuing and self-fulfilling esprit de corps, and a continually growing core of staff and stakeholders as a team targeted to goals by inspiration.

- *Long-term vision* – The foundation of Capacity Building is to sustain service ideas that continuously attempt to close the service-to-needs gap. Most social dysfunction is intergenerational, endemic, and embedded in the community. The community is where the problems are and where the answers must be. Such a public endeavor learns by serving this generation so it can serve future generations. Thus, strategic planning is intergenerational.

A transformational local public service organization is proactive, responsive, and dedicated to making a meaningful difference in the lives of its target population and community. Once the Capacity Building model is employed successfully, other ideas become quite realistic to achieve. These successful, productive, impactful programs then prove as examples for municipal, state, and federal government. Capacity Building adapts to challenges, embraces change, and continuously strives for excellence in serving the community.

REFERENCES

Bravin, J., White, B., "Top Court Sets State for Felons to Go Free," *The Wall Street Journal*, Tuesday, May 24, 2011.

Bureau of Justice Assistance, "Justice Reinvestment Initiative," 2006. Viewed 18 May 2024: *https://bja.gov/program/justice-reinvestment-initiative/overview*.

Bush, J., Glick, B., Taymans, J., *Thinking for a Change: Integrated Cognitive Change Behavior Program*, National Institute of Correction, Wash., D.C, 1997, revised 2/02. Viewed 24 May 2024: *https://nicic.gov/resources/resources-topics-and-roles/topics/thinking-change*.

Carmody, J., "Effective County Practices in Jail to Community Transition Planning for Offenders with Mental Health and Substance Abuse Disorders," National Association of Counties, Wash., D.C., 2006.

Conservative Case for Reform, "Right on Crime." Washington, D.C.: Viewed 18 May 2024: *http://www.rightoncrime.com*.

Crayton, A., Ressler, L., Mukamal, D., et al, *Partnering with Jails to Improve Reentry: A Guidebook for Community-Based Organizations.* Washington, D.C.: The Urban Institute and the John Jay College of Criminal Justice, 2010. Viewed 24 May 2024: *https://www.urban.org/research/publication/partnering-jails-improve-reentry-guidebook-community-based-organizations*.

Durham County, North Carolina, Justice Services Center, Viewed 23 May 2024: *https://www.dconc.gov/county-departments/departments-f-z/justice-services/*.

Economist, The, "Tackling Recidivism: They All Come Home – Effective Re-Entry Programmes Can Keep Ex-Prisoners out of Jail," 2011. Viewed 18 May 2024: *http://www.economist.com/node/18587528?story_id=18587528*.

Esteves, J., Pastor, J., "Analysis of Critical Success Factors Relevance Along SAP Implementation Phases," Seventh Americas Conference on Information Systems, 2011.

Federal Advisory Committee on Juvenile Justice, Annual Report 2010. Viewed 25 May 2024: *https://facjj.ojp.gov/sites/g/files/xyckuh291/files/media/document/2010-facjj-annual-report.pdf.*

Greenwood, P., "Preventing and Reducing Youth Crime and Violence: Using Evidence-Based Practices," 2010, Governor's Office of Gang and Youth Policy, Sacramento, CA.

Hagan, J., Dinovitzer, R., "Collateral Consequences of Imprisonment of Children, Communities, and Prisoners," *Crime and Justice,* 1999, vol. 26, Prisons.

Hecht, F., "Reentry Programs and Rural Jails," Jail Reentry Roundtable Initiative, The Urban Institute, Wash., D.C., 2006.

Jannetta, J., Dodd, H., & Elderbroom, B., *The Elected Official's Toolkit for Jail Reentry.* Washington, D.C.: Urban Institute, 2006. Viewed 22 May 2024: *http://www.urban.org/research/publication/elected-officials-toolkit-jail-reentry.*

Klopovic, J., Vasu, M., Yearwood, D., *Effective Program Practices for At-Risk Youth: A Continuum of Community-Based Practices.* New York: Civic Research Institute, Inc., 2003.

Kolat, K., Grosshans, B., Margolies, R., Dipko, J., Loftus, A., "Statutes, Policies, and Practices Affecting Prisoner Reentry in Wisconsin," 2011. Viewed 24 May 2024: *https://evidence2impact.psu.edu/wp-content/uploads/2023/05/s_wifis26c.*

Lyman, M. "Whys and Hows of Measuring Jail Recidivism." Washington, D.C.: Urban Institute, 2006.

Lynch, J., Sabol, W., *Prisoner Reentry in Perspective.* Washington, D.C.: Urban Institute Justice Policy Center, Crime Policy Report, v 3, Sept. 2001.

Martinelli, F., *Building an Effective Board of Directors,* 2011. Viewed 23 May 2024: *https://www.naco.org/sites/default/files/documents/EncouragingVisionaryBoardLeadership_NCCAE_Oct%202012.pdf.*

McGinty, T., Radnofsky, L., "More Are Ensnared by Criminal Laws," New York: *The Wall Street Journal,* July 23-24, 2011.

Mellow, J., Mukamal, D., Lobuglio, S., Solomon, A., Osborne, J., *The Jail Administrator's Toolkit for Reentry.* Wash., D.C.: The Urban Institute, May 2008.

Mellow, J., Christiensen, G., Warwick, K, Willson, J, *Transition from Jail to Community: Online Learning Toolkit*. Wash., D.C.: The Urban Institute, revised May 2011.

Najavits, L. M., *Seeking Safety: Treatment Innovations*. Viewed 24 May 2024: *https://www.treatment-innovations.org/seeking-safety.html*. Also: *https://www.samhsa.gov/resource/dbhis/seeking-safety*.

National Reentry Resource Center. Viewed 18 May 2024. *http://www.nationalreentryresourcecenter.org/what*.

Nelson, M., Tarlow, M. "Jail Reentry and Community Linkages: Adding Value on Both Sides of the Gate," Jail Reentry Roundtable Initiative, Wash., D.C.: The Urban Institute, 2006.

Ohio Department of Rehabilitation and Corrections. Viewed 24 May 2024: *https://drc.ohio.gov/web/reentry_resource.htm*.

Periman, D., "Prisoner Reentry and the Uniform Collateral Consequences of Conviction Act," *Alaska Justice Forum,* vol. 27, No 4, University of Alaska, Anchorage, 2011.

Pinto, J., Sleven, D., "Critical Success Factors Across the Project Life Cycle," *Project Management Journal,* v 19, iss 3, 1988, pp. 67-75.

Prisoner Reentry Institute. Viewed 25 May 2024: *https://cjii.org/focus-areas/diversion-and-reentry-support-2/prisoner-reentry-institute/*.

Re-entry Policy Council 2005, *Report of the Re-entry Policy Council: Charting the Safe and Successful Return of Prisoners to the Community*. New York: Council of State Governments, January 2005. Viewed 24 May 2024: *https://csgjusticecenter.org/publications/report-of-the-re-entry-policy-council*.

Reintegration, Center for Justice Innovation. Viewed 18 May 2024: *www.courtinnovation.org*.

Rhine, E., "The Ohio Plan for Productive Offender Reentry and Recidivism Reduction." Columbus, Ohio: The Ohio Department of Rehabilitation and Correction, 2002. Viewed 24 May 2024: *https://drc.ohio.gov/systems-and-services/2-reentry-services/reentry-programming/reentry-programming*.

Rivers, J., "Improving Criminal Justice and Reducing Recidivism Through Justice Reinvestment," Bureau of Justice Assistance, Office of Justice Programs, Fact Sheet 000336, 2010.

Robinson, M., White, G., *The Role of Civic Organizations in the Provision of Social Services: Toward Synergy.* Helsinki, Finland: UNU World Institute for Development Economics Research, 1997.

Roman, J., Chalfin, A., "Does It Pay to Invest in Reentry Programs for Jail Inmates?" Justice Policy Center. Wash., D.C.: The Urban Institute, 2006.

Sabol, W., Lynch, J., "Did Getting Tough on Crime Pay?" Wash., D.C.: The Urban Institute.

Sackett, D. L., Rosenberg, W. M., Gray, J.A., et al, "Evidence Based Medicine: What It Is and What It Isn't, 1996. Viewed 25 May 2024: *https://pubmed.ncbi.nlm.nih.gov/8555924/.*

Second Chance Act of 2007, PUBLIC LAW 110-199, Apr. 9, 2008. Viewed 4 May 2011. Second Chance Act authorizes federal grants to government agencies and nonprofit organizations to provide employment assistance, substance abuse treatment, housing, family programming, mentoring, victims support, and other services that can help reduce recidivism. Viewed 24 May 2024: *http://www.nationalreentryresourcecenter.org/.*

Solomon, A., Osborne, J. W. L., LoBuglio, S. F., Mellow, J., Mukamal, D., "Life after Lockup: Improving Reentry from Jail to the Community," 2008. Viewed 28 May 2024. *https://www.ojp.gov/ncjrs/virtual-library/abstracts/life-after-lockup-improving-reentry-jail-community.*

Somers, T., Nelson, K., *The Impact of Critical Success Factors Across the Stages of Enterprise Resource Planning Implementations.* Proceedings of the 34th Hawaii International Conference on System Sciences, 2001.

Urahn, S., *State of Recidivism: The Revolving Door of America's Prisons.* Washington, D.C.: The PEW Center on The States, 2011.

Urban Institute, "Returning Home Study: Understanding the Challenges of Prisoner Reentry." Viewed 25 May 2024: *https://www.urban.org/policy-centers/justice-policy-center/projects/returning-home-study-understanding-challenges-prisoner-reentry.*

Urban Institute, *Transition from Jail to Community Online Learning Toolkit*, 2010. Viewed 24 May 2024: *https://apps.urban.org/features/tjctoolkit*.

Webb, J., "Why We Must Fix Our Prisons," *Parade,* 30 March 2009.

Wolf, R., "Reentry Courts: Looking Ahead – A Conversation about Strategies for Offender," U.S. Department of Justice, Office of Justice Programs, 2011. Viewed 18 May 2024. *https://www.ojp.gov/ncjrs/virtual-library/ abstracts/ reentry-courts-looking-ahead-conversation-about-strategies-offender.*

Zimmerman, G., Olsen, C., Bosworth, M., "A 'Stages of Change' Approach to Helping Patients Change Behavior," *American Family Physician,* 1 March 2000. Viewed 18 May 2024. *http://www.aafp.org/afp/2000/0301/p1409.html.*

A CHECKLIST FOR YOUR ADULT REENTRY-AFTERCARE PROGRAM

The collection of Effective Practices makes a respectable checklist for implementation based on proven experience and successes in the field. They demonstrate that taking your reentry-aftercare idea to a point at which it's permanent and making a difference flows from one action item to the next. While these actions are synergistic, they're by no means in lockstep. That is, each phase needs attention from the first day the idea is considered, and you'll need to work on many simultaneously. The point is that all these major phases do have to occur, and you'll need to consider all the effective practices. Certainly, you don't have to do them in sequence, but you'll need to do them to have the best chance at success. Eliminate one at peril, but you can add to this checklist as you see fit and as experience informs all concerned.

This ensures your success as much as possible. Because a failure reverberates for years at the expense of good and worthy ideas that are never even contemplated because "it failed before."

Also, seeing the flow of your project's development graphically makes several points. This is long-term work that depends on services delivery capacity. While it's a lengthy process of years, with persistence, the work will result in a program that's both permanent and makes a difference.

This checklist first appeared in Chapter 1 under How to Get the Most Out of This Book. Having read from there to here, you will have a better understanding of the whys and wherefores of this outlined procedure. Most importantly, this checklist is only the beginning. It's advisable to edit and add items as your journey dictates. The checklist can also be used to strengthen an existing program. You will likely use the process again with another idea or at another site or in helping a colleague get started. Use and amend it according to what works for you. This checklist is yours. It should aid your progress considerably.

Figure 1-B. Capacity Building Checklist for Reentry-Aftercare Practitioners – Phases I-III, with Key Action Items and Effective Practices
Phase I of the Project Life Cycle: Plan and Implement – *Design and implement essential local reentry-aftercare operations.*
1. Nurture and grow key leadership familiar with post-release aftercare services.
Establish a stable leadership body focused on capacity building and transitional services.
Train your leadership body for effectiveness and efficiency.
Establish a functional committee structure for relationship building, goal accomplishment, and longevity.
2. Integrate capacity assessment for reentry project capacity building.
Profile returnee risk and needs factors to determine your mix of services.
Catalog local resources according to returnee needs.
3. Determine project scope to focus on the essentials of transitional services.
Develop measurable mission and vision statements that focus on the needs of your target returnee.
4. Design the process evaluation and impact analysis to justify reentry services.
Decide on a few initial impact measures that define results and can be easily gathered, analyzed, and reported.
Establish a learning environment based on data to evaluate and improve the efficiency of processes.
5. Nurture relationships for resources development.
Map your services to identify resource development opportunities.
6. Develop performance-oriented service providers as part of the local reentry team.
Muster your local transitional services and agencies.
Develop a targeted post-release services center.
Begin residential programs based on sustainable enterprises.
7. Nurture reentry staff by a process of human capacity development.
Build an environment in which staff keep skills current and feel free to apply lessons learned.
Hire and develop staff for your unique returnee and community needs.

Phase II of the Project Life Cycle: Operate and Stabilize – *Establish your idea to expand.*
8. Operationalize your reentry-aftercare plan.
Leadership
Ensure that the executive director emphasizes building external relationships.
Have the board assume responsibility for organizing and training themselves for the progression of roles from planning to oversight and preparation for the future.
Capacity assessment
Continually assess your clientele—especially their risk factors—to monitor and adjust your services delivery and mix.
Scope
Use performance data to support experiential decisions on how much can be done effectively.
Process evaluation and impact analysis
Reflect on what the data are telling you and adjust resources allocation for effectiveness and keep processes flexible for efficiency.
Resources development
Give partners ideas about ways to collaborate.
Train and develop your board and staff to network for and maintain essential resources.
Services
Court and shape service partners early.
Key staff
Develop a common sense of purpose immediately.
Phase III of the Project Life Cycle: Sustain and Expand – *Realize Reentry-Aftercare.*
9. Sustain operations.
Reassess, reform, and refocus agency functions for scaling up and out.
Build the therapeutic community.
10. Plot the long-range strategy and tactics for expansion to scale.
Refocus leadership as an Expansion Task Force.
Have a project development strategy.
Consider the residential option with socially conscious enterprises.
Formalize resources development with a development officer.

INTAKE ASSESSMENT AND RISK/NEEDS DETERMINATION CHART

This chart is directed toward assessing the needs of people *entering corrections,* but it can be modified to assess the risk and needs of the individuals beginning reintegration into a specific community. For example, you may want to add sections on job skills and training needs. As the Report of the Reentry Policy Council Charting the Safe and Successful Return of Prisoners to the Community, observes: "Though these categories are critical to thoroughly assessing the risks and needs of individuals entering a correctional facility, this table should not be considered a checklist. Some individuals or populations may require additional or alternate assessments, and some assessments may cover multiple categories at once."[93]

Therefore, this chart is a point of departure. You need to modify it and make it your tool, relevant to your returnees.[94]

Figure 2. Intake Assessment and Risk/Needs Determination Chart			
** person to identify or assess *** information source (in addition to self-report)			
	24-72 hours	**2 weeks**	**Ongoing**
Security Level/Risk	• immediate risk to staff or other clients • security group or individual threats gang involvement, enemies, etc.) ** trained intake worker ***pre-sentence report, criminal history, prior institutional history	• housing unit placement • presumptive scheduled movement plans to lower security based on criminal record and performance in program ** trained intake worker ***review of previous criminal case and institutional history, outstanding issues	• review of program behavior and programming to determine eligibility for lower security setting • review of risk/needs/strength-based programming needs

Accelerating Adult Reentry

Figure 2. Intake Assessment and Risk/Needs Determination Chart

** person to identify or assess
*** information source (in addition to self-report)

	24-72 hours	2 weeks	Ongoing
Mental Health	• suicide risk • medication needs • clients in need of further assessment ** trained intake worker ***justice system medical record	• detailed mental health assessment • identify–contact with previous mental health provider ** mental health clinician ***community-based medical record	• individual or group counseling/ assessments • medication review **clinician
Substance Abuse	• assessment of drug usage at intake/ drug screening • detoxification needs • identify inmates in need of further assessment ** trained intake worker	• detailed substance abuse assessment ** substance abuse/ addiction specialist	• regular testing • measure effectiveness of programming in changing – attitudes, behavior ** program staff or substance abuse/ addiction specialist
Physical Health	• identify inmates in need of further assessment • medication/ treatment needs • screening for infectious diseases HIV/STD testing availability ** trained intake worker ***justice system medical record	• detailed assessment/ physical examination • medical/treatment history ** clinician ***community-based medical record	• inmate education • in-reach possibilities with prior provider • subsequent check-ups ** clinician ***regularly-updated medical record

Figure 2. Intake Assessment and Risk/Needs Determination Chart

** person to identify or assess
*** information source (in addition to self-report)

	24-72 hours	2 weeks	Ongoing
Educational/ vocational history/ learning style/ learning abilities		• employment and wage history • education level/ credentials • math and reading skills • vocational interests/ aptitudes/goals – learning styles • strengths/interests ** trained intake worker ***professional licenses, educational records	• appropriateness of educational/ vocational programming • appropriateness of in-prison work assignment • appropriateness of work-release assignment ** program staff or workforce specialist ***certificates or program records/ evaluation, school transcripts
Housing		• lease or rent obligations • type of housing (potential for loss) ** trained intake worker ***local PHA or homelessness services case file	• appropriateness of housing • availability of alternate housing for release ** housing specialist
Family data/ relationships/ social services involvement	• dependent care responsibilities • victim/offender history • community aftercare/safety planning (for brief jail detainees)	• visitation plan • genogram of family members • agency involvement and planning • child support obligations ** trained intake worker ***family consultation	• changes in family/ expectations • effectiveness of visitation or connectedness plan, communication • child support modification needs ** family services specialist

Figure 2. Intake Assessment and Risk/Needs Determination Chart			
** person to identify or assess *** information source (in addition to self-report)			
	24-72 hours	**2 weeks**	**Ongoing**
Family data/ relationships/ social services involvement	** trained intake worker ***family or children's services case file		
Financial assessment		• personal debts • court fines and fees • restitution • support obligations including child support • benefit enrollments (including enrollment of family members) • financial obligations that may accumulate ** trained intake worker ***court documents, public welfare case file	• ability to engage in in-prison work towards financial obligations • service and entitlement linkages for families, inmates upon release ** benefits consultant

REENTRY SKILLS

Figure 3. Reentry Skills	
Reentry Skills	**Demonstration in the Institution & Community**
Daily Living • Financial management • Food management • Personal hygiene/sanitation • Transportation • Identification • Housing • Residential Reentry Center placement • Family care	Displays independent living skills commensurate with institution or community opportunities. These skills include: maintenance of a clean residence, a responsible budget to include a savings account, meal preparation, appropriate personal hygiene and appearance, and proper etiquette. Obtains, maintains, and/or contributes financially to a legal residence and any necessary transportation. Obeys institutional rules and regulations and local, state, community resources for basic needs.
Mental Health • Substance abuse management • Mental illness management • Transitional plan • Appropriate sexual behavior	Maintains sound mental health through avoidance of substance abuse/dependence and other self-destructive behaviors and use of effective coping techniques. Participates in appropriate medication and/or treatment regimen to address any acute or chronic mental health issues.
Wellness • Health promotion • Disease prevention • Disease/illness management • Transitional plan • Communication	Maintains physical well-being through promotion and disease prevention strategies such as a healthy lifestyle and habits, routine medical care, regular exercise, and appropriate diet. Participates in appropriate medication and/or treatment regimen as necessary to address any acute or chronic medical conditions.
Interpersonal • Relationships • Family ties/support system • Parental responsibility • Communication	Relates appropriately and effectively with staff, peers, visitors, family, co-workers, neighbors, and members of the community by observing basic social conventions and rules. Displays the ability to develop and maintain healthy relationships to include the avoidance of co-dependency. Avoids negative interpersonal influences.

Figure 3. Reentry Skills	
Reentry Skills	**Demonstration in the Institution & Community**
Academic • Intellectual function • Literacy • Language • Computer skills	Participates and progresses in educational activities commensurate with ability and occupation to serve as foundational skills for other reentry skills. Reads writes, and utilizes basic arithmetic at a level necessary to function in a correctional environment and in society.
Cognitive • General behavior • Criminal history • Domestic Violence/Abuse • Criminal behavior	Engages in accurate self-appraisal by acknowledging and correcting irrational thinking patterns. Is cognizant of the importance of goal setting. Solves problems effectively, maintains self-control, and and displays prosocial values. Acknowledges and appropriately corrects criminal thinking patterns and behaviors.
Vocational/Career • Employment history • Career development • Institution work history • Post-incarceration employment	Acquires and maintains employment to become self-sufficient and fulfill financial obligations. Engages in purposeful activity, develops abilities useful in the acquisition and maintenance of post-release employment and pursuit of career goals.
Leisure Time • Use of leisure time	Engages in meaningful recreational activities and hobbies, making positive and effective use of free time and facilitating stress management and favorable peer affiliations.
Character • Personal character • Personal responsibility	Maintains a sense of accountability to self and others through attention to the potential impact (short and long term) of actions. Seeks to engage in behaviors that reflect prosocial values, thus creating a positive impact in their life and the lives of others. Displays a healthy tolerance for delayed gratification. Displays the capacity for self-reflection and consideration of meaning in life in relation to a particular faith or personal philosophy.

MEMORANDUM OF UNDERSTANDING

(Agency)
Memorandum of Understanding[95]
With
(Agency)

Purpose of Agreement: The purpose of this agreement is to provide referral resources with general information concerning the _____ program, to establish a relationship of mutual cooperation, and to outline general referral procedures.

Mission Statement: The mission of the _____ program is to provide care management services to drug-involved and mentally ill offenders. The _____ program combines the influence of legal sanctions with recommended treatment modalities. Through treatment matching and closely supervised community reintegrating, the _____ program seeks to permanently interrupt the vicious cycle of addiction, arrest, conviction, incarceration, release, criminality, and re-arrest.

Description of Services: The _____ program functions as the bridge between the criminal justice system and the treatment system by identifying drug-involved and mentally ill offenders who demonstrate the likelihood for rehabilitation based on program criteria. The _____ program assists the judiciary in making decisions about sentencing options, implements court orders to treatment and monitors individual treatment progress for judicial and correctional systems.

The _____ program provides an array of services dictated by person-centered service plans developed with each offender. These services include: assessment, referral to various treatment programs, care management, education programs, monitored urine screening, and monthly written reports to the referral source concerning client progress.

Eligibility Requirements: The criminal justice system (CJS) maintains primary responsibility for referral to the _____ program for assessment. Election of treatment by an offender or a referral for the _____ program services by the CJS is contingent upon meeting program eligibility requirements.

The _____ program's service populations are represented by the following criteria where the individual:
- is involved in the adult criminal justice system, and
- voluntarily consents to participate, and
- indicates evidence of a history or potential substance abuse problem or mental health problem, or
- is charged with a drug offense.

Exceptions can be made to accept a referral with justification and written supervisory approval.

Responsibilities and Expectations between (first) program and the (second) program:
1. The (first) program will provide the (second) program with copies of the _____ program assessment, judgments, and release forms prior to client's intake appointment.
2. The _____ program will provide care management services such as follow-up, monitoring, and reporting compliance for all _____ program clients referred to the (second) program.
3. Utilize the _____ program automation system to track client progress and make a report as needed; monthly is recommended.
4. Establish and maintain a portal of entry process for clients transitioning from the criminal justice network.
5. Facilitate and access process for (first and second) program clients needing higher levels of treatment such as inpatient and detoxification services.
6. In compliance with state regulations, the (first) program care managers will attend (the second) program client staffing meetings for the Day Reporting Center, Second Chance, and Reentry Programs.
7. The (first) program will attend (the second) program Advisory Board meetings to provide input, support, and feedback regarding services and service gaps.
8. The (second) program will participate in joint planning sessions that involve the development of mechanisms to enhance community agency collaboration.

_____   _____
Director   Director
(first program)   (second program)

_____   _____
Date   Date

ADULT POST-RELEASE AFTERCARE RESOURCES AND KEY CONTACTS

In this section, you will find resources for funding, contacts and information for the model programs, and contacts and information for organizations, as well as reports and publications, data and analysis, and internet resources.

Foundations

The Nicole and James Klopovic Family Charitable Foundation funds local capacity-built projects for sustainable public services resulting in *Permanent Solutions to Permanent Problems*. It uses the four-volume series on Capacity Building by these authors as a guide to the process. The series tackles a municipality-wide strategy for reentry/aftercare that includes prevention, decriminalizing mental illness, and juvenile and adult reentry/aftercare. It promotes spending limited funds wisely for continuous returns to community well-being in which families can be safe and thrive. Contact: *jklopovic@gmail.com*

Funding

One of the biggest challenges faced by reentry programs is how to establish funding. Depending on the services offered by your organization, various funding sources could be available. The trick is finding them. The following are a few resources on how to discover the latest information about available funding for criminal justice initiatives, courtesy of The Urban Institute:

The National Reentry Resource Center collects and presents information about funding opportunities for reentry. The mission of the Center is to advance the reentry field through knowledge transfer and dissemination and to promote evidence-based best practices. The Center is a project of the Council of State Governments Justice Center, with these key project partners: the Urban Institute, Association of State Correctional Administrators, and the American Probation and Parole Association. The Center is also guided by Advisory Committees, which help coordinate support and services for Second Chance Act grantees and the reentry field. Their objectives are to:

- Provide a one-stop, interactive source of current, user-friendly *reentry information.*
- Identify, document, and promote *evidence-based practices.*

- Deliver individualized, targeted *technical assistance* to the Second Chance Act grantees.
- Advance the reentry field through *training, distance learning, and knowledge development.*

www.nationalreentryresourcecenter.org/ (Viewed 25 May 2024.)

The Report of the Reentry Policy Council is a good source for tips on funding strategies for reentry efforts. The report includes a chapter on securing funding streams for reentry initiatives with comprehensive information and suggestions. The Reentry Policy Council (RPC) was established in 2001 to assist state government officials grappling with the increasing number of people leaving prisons and jails to return to the communities they left behind. The RPC was formed with two specific goals in mind:

- To develop bipartisan *policies and principles* for elected officials and other policymakers to consider as they evaluate reentry issues in their jurisdictions.
- To facilitate *coordination and information-sharing* among organizations implementing reentry initiatives, researching trends, communicating about related issues, or funding projects.

https://csgjusticecenter.org/publications/ (Viewed 25 May 2024.)

Candid, formerly The Foundation Center, offers a directory of U.S. private foundations. (Information was current at the time of this writing.) It's supported by close to 550 foundations and is the leading source of information about philanthropy worldwide. Through data, analysis, and training, it connects people who want to change the world to the resources they need to succeed. Candid maintains the most comprehensive database on U.S. and, increasingly, global grant-makers and their grants—a robust, accessible knowledge bank for the sector. It also operates research, education, and training programs designed to advance knowledge of philanthropy at every level. Thousands of people visit Candid's website each day and are served in its five regional library/learning centers and its network of 450 funding information centers located in public libraries, community foundations, and educational institutions nationwide and beyond.
https://candid.org/?fcref=lr (Viewed 25 May 2024.)

Grants.gov provides public access to comprehensive information on new federal funding opportunities. This site allows users to register for daily email updates. Grants.gov is your source to find and apply for federal grants.
www.grants.gov (Viewed 25 May 2024.)

Model Programs

Much can be learned through studying the structures of successful programs. The first group are examples of jail and court-based programs, which are a necessary precursor to the community effort to complete successful transitions from incarceration to the community.

The Allegheny County Jail Collaborative (Pennsylvania) consists of the Department of Human Services, the Allegheny County Jail (ACJ), and the Allegheny County Health Department. It was created in 2000 because county leadership observed that not enough was being done for former inmates to support their reentry into the community. Since that time, the Jail Collaborative has met monthly to address two primary goals: increase public safety and reduce recidivism. To achieve these goals, the Collaborative joins forces with government agencies, court officials, service providers, ex-offenders, faith-based community organizations, families, and the community at large.
http://www.alleghenycounty.us/dhs/jail.aspx (Viewed 25 May 2024.)

The Auglaize County Transition (ACT) Program (Ohio) is one of the nation's first jail reentry programs. The goal of the program is to reduce recidivism of jail inmates once they reenter the community, and thus the program addresses the numerous problems faced by inmates during reentry, such as medical and mental health issues, job placement, or drug and alcohol addiction. The ACT Program relies on case managers, who link inmates to resources that can appropriately deal with these issues, both in the community and in jail.
http://www.crimesolutions.gov/ProgramDetails.aspx?ID=130
(Viewed 25 May 2024.)

Dismas, Inc. has the mission to provide quality, cost-effective, community-based supervision and treatment services to individuals within the criminal justice system. Founded in 1964, Dismas is considered a leader in providing effective

community-based reentry programs for offenders. Understanding that crime is a community problem, Dismas involves families, faith-based institutions, employers, experienced staff, volunteers, and other service organizations to create a structure and environment that supports successful reintegration. Dismas programs are cost-effective. Community-based supervision costs taxpayers less than prison and jail confinements. In addition, community-based supervision allows offenders to work full time and pay child support, taxes, fines, and restitution or to provide valued community service work.
htttps://dismas.com (Viewed 25 May 2024.)

Dual Diagnosis & Mental Health Jail Reduction Programs (Macomb County, Michigan). This is a **Cognitive Reflective Program (CRP),** which is designed to provide court-ordered offenders alternatives to their self-destructive patterns of substance abuse and/or criminal behaviors. CRP is a problem-solving program that incorporates cognitive restructuring and social skill techniques. The goal is to replace self-destructive patterns with prosocial thinking, beliefs, attitudes, and values. Offenders are to practice techniques that produce these prosocial changes. The curriculum is comprised of 16 sessions with lessons on understanding self-destructive thinking patterns and how they control how we act, finding alternatives, and how to appropriately interact with others and utilize new techniques to problem solve difficult situations.
https://www.macombgov.org/departments/office-county-executive/its-more-jail (Viewed 25 May 2024.)

Durham County Justice Services Center, formerly known as the Criminal Justice Resource Center, has a mission to provide a wide array of services to criminal justice stakeholders, as well as adult and juvenile offenders. Service delivery builds upon and is provided in cooperation with various agencies within Durham County, such as the juvenile and adult detention center, The Durham Center, the judicial system, other human services organizations, DJJDP (Division of Juvenile Justice and Delinquency Prevention), Durham Public Schools and the North Carolina Department of Corrections. The department's functions focus on three goals:

- Delivery of quality services so offenders and at-risk youth can become productive, successful citizens.

- Supervision and monitoring of high-risk offenders residing in Durham County to increase public safety.
- Collation and dissemination of information, including criminal and treatment histories.

https://www.dconc.gov/county-departments/departments-f-z/justice-services (Viewed 25 May 2024.)

Leading Into New Communities, Inc. (LINC) is focused on empowering individuals with criminal histories or youth who are at risk to becoming serious offenders of the justice system to make positive life choices, enabling them to become productive members of the community. LINC provides services that meet the immediate needs of ex-offenders, such as shelter, food, clothing, and employment. The organization also refers clients to other social service agencies that provide services to further facilitate their reintegration into the community. *http://www.lincnc.org* (Viewed 25 May 2024.)

Pre-Release and Reentry Services Division (Montgomery County, Maryland). This Division provides residential and nonresidential reentry services to convicted and sentenced individuals who are within 12 months of release and who have been incarcerated in the county's correctional system. Additionally, the Division is contracted by the Maryland State Division of Correction and the Federal Bureau of Prisons to serve prisoners in state and federal custody who are within six months of release and who are returning to Montgomery County and the Greater Washington Metropolitan area. The program carefully screens and accepts only those individuals that it assesses can be safely managed in a community setting. The Division advances the Department of Correction and Rehabilitation's mission to improve public safety and reduce victimization. It relies on a considerable body of research that demonstrates the cost-benefit advantages of releasing incarcerated individuals through a highly-structured community-based program. *http://www.montgomerycountymd.gov/* (Viewed 25 May 2024.)
Then search **Pre-Release and Reentry Services Division**.

Transition Services Unit (TSU) (Multnomah County, Oregon). The Transition Services Unit provides a comprehensive system of services designed to prepare, equip, and sustain an offender upon their release from jail or prison. The TSU

conducts reach-in visits of prisoners who are going to be released from state prisons back into Multnomah County. The program works on the "housing first" model and coordinates with Multnomah County and the city of Portland's 10-year plan to end homelessness. The program is responsible for linking recently released offenders to services, including prerelease planning, case coordination, housing, transportation, and medical and benefit assistance. The TSU provides transition planning services up to 120 days prior to release from prison or jail and 90 to 180 days post-incarceration. Successful community programs provide the most productive examples of how to complete the transitional process.
https://www.multco.us/dcj-adult/tsu (Viewed 25 May 2024.)

Triangle Residential Options for Substance Abusers, TROSA, is an innovative, multi-year residential program located in Durham, North Carolina. The program enables substance abusers to recover and be productive by providing comprehensive treatment, work-based vocational training, education, and continuing care. Founded in 1994, TROSA is now the largest state-licensed residential therapeutic community in North Carolina. It's widely respected for its innovative therapeutic and entrepreneurial approach to the pervasive issue of substance abuse. TROSA operates a highly structured and disciplined program from several facilities in Durham. It accepts substance abusers on one condition: They must have a strong desire to change their lives. Key elements of the two-year program include vocational training, education, communication, peer counseling, mentoring, leadership training, and aftercare. The program is provided at no cost to the individual.
http://www.trosainc.org (Viewed 25 May 2024.)

Organizations

The National Institute of Corrections provides training, technical assistance, information services, and policy/program development assistance to federal, state, and local corrections agencies. Through cooperative agreements, they award funds to support their program initiatives. They also provide leadership to correctional executives and practitioners as well as public policymakers to influence correctional policies, practices, and operations nationwide in areas of emerging interest and concern. The "Library" section is a wealth of reports and publications.
http://nicic.gov/ (Viewed 25 May 2024.)

The NIC also has an excellent Annotated Bibliography on Offender Reentry: ***https:// nicic.gov/resources/nic-library/all-library-items/reentry-annotated-bibliography*** (Viewed 25 May 2024.)

The National Institute of Justice (NIJ) is the research, development, and evaluation agency of the U.S. Department of Justice. This agency is dedicated to improving knowledge and understanding of crime and justice issues through science. The NIJ provides objective and independent knowledge and tools to reduce crime and promote justice, particularly at the state and local levels. It's committed to being a transformative force in the criminal justice field by meeting five strategic challenges:

1. *Fostering science-based criminal justice practice* by supporting rigorous scientific research to ensure the safety of families, neighborhoods, and communities.
2. *Translating knowledge to practice* by disseminating rigorous scientific research to criminal justice professionals to advance what works best in preventing and reducing crime.
3. *Advancing technology* by building a more effective, fair, and efficient criminal justice system through technology.
4. *Working across disciplines* by connecting the physical, forensic, and social sciences to reduce crime and promote justice.
5. *Adopting a global perspective* by understanding crime in its social context within the United States and globally.

http://nij.gov (Viewed 25 May 2024.)

The National Mentoring Partnership (MENTOR) helps children by providing a public voice, developing and delivering resources to mentoring programs nationwide, and promoting quality for mentoring through standards, cutting-edge research, and state-of-the-art tools. This site is included as a reentry resource, as crime prevention is part of the overall approach to post-release services. ***http://www.mentoring.org/*** (Viewed 25 May 2024.)

The Pew Center on the States is a division of The Pew Charitable Trusts that identifies and advances effective solutions to critical issues facing states. Pew is a nonprofit organization that applies a rigorous, analytical approach to improve

public policy, inform the public, and stimulate civic life. The Pew Center on the States grew from the recognition that America's success and prosperity depends upon the strength of the states. Its purpose is to help build high-performing states that work efficiently and effectively to deliver better results, achieve long-term fiscal health through budget discipline, and make smart investments in programs that provide the strongest returns. Especially helpful is the Public Safety Performance Project: *Policy Framework to Strengthen Community Corrections.*
http://www.pewtrusts.org/en/topics/us-state-policy (Viewed 25 May 2024.)

Quality Enhancement for Nonprofit Organizations (QENO) is designed to improve the capabilities and competencies of nonprofit organizations in New Hanover, North Carolina, and surrounding counties. Hundreds of nonprofit entities are in the counties involved, at vastly differential levels of funding and operational capability. The region experiences dramatic economic, demographic, political, and social change with profound consequences both positive and negative. The University of North Carolina Wilmington is committed to a regional engagement effort. It will enhance the capacity of government, NGOs, and citizen groups to consider issues of social and economic development and organize for effective service, educational, or other activities. This initiative focuses specifically on nonprofit organizations. It utilizes the university and resources in the surrounding area to provide communication, technical assistance, training, or organizational development for nonprofits.
http://www.uncw.edu/QENO/ (Viewed 25 May 2024.)

The Urban Institute gathers data, conducts research, evaluates programs, offers technical assistance overseas, and educates Americans on social and economic issues to foster sound public policy and effective government.
http://urban.org/ (Viewed 25 May 2024.)

Reports and Publications

Bauldry, Shawn, et al. "Mentoring Formerly Incarcerated Adults: Insights from the Ready4Work Reentry Initiative." The Annie E. Casey Foundation, Public/Private Ventures. Viewed 24 May 2024: *https://assets.aecf.org./m/resourcedoc/PPV-MentoringFormerlyIncarceratedAdults-2009.pdf*

Christensen, Gary. "Our System of Corrections: Do Jails Play a Role in Improving Offender Outcomes?" U.S. Department of Justice, the Crime and Justice Institute, and the National Institute of Corrections, August 2008. Viewed 24 May 2024: *http://nicic.gov/resources/nic-library/all-library-items/our-system-corrections-do-jails-play-role-improving*

Crayton, Anna, et al. *Partnering with Jails to Improve Reentry: A Guidebook for Community-Based Organizations.* Urban Institute, September 2010. Viewed 24 May 2024: *https://www.urban.org/research/publication/partnering-jails-improve-reentry-guidebook-community-based-organizations*

Dunworth, Terry, et al. "The Case for Evidence-Based Policy: Beyond Ideology, Politics, and Guesswork." Urban Institute, August 2008. Viewed 24 May 2024: *https://www.urban.org/research/publication/case-evidence-based-policy-beyond-ideology-politics-and-guesswork*

Forensic Taskforce of the NAMI Board of Directors. *Decriminalizing Mental Illness: Background and Recommendations.* National Alliance on Mental Illness, September 2008. Viewed 24 May 2024: *https://www.nami.org/wp-content/uploads/2023/07/FINAL-Hill-Day-17-Leave-Behind-_De-Criminalizing-Mental-Illness.pdf*

Healey, Kerry Murphy. "Case Management in the Criminal Justice System." National Institute of Justice, February 1999. Viewed 24 May 2024: *http://www.ncjrs.gov/pdffiles1/173409.pdf*

Institute on Women & Criminal Justice. "Mentoring Women in Reentry: A WPA Practice Brief." October 2008. Viewed 24 May 2024: *https://ccsme.org/wp-content/uploads/2017/02/Mentoring-Women-in-Reentry-WPA-Practice-Brief.pdf*

International Association of Chiefs of Police. "Building an Offender Reentry Program: A Guide for Law Enforcement." Bureau of Justice Assistance, 2007. Viewed 24 May 2024: *https://bja.ojp.gov/sites/g/files/xyckuh186/files/Publications/Reentry_LE.pdf*

MacLellan, Thomas. "Improving Prisoner Reentry Through Strategic Policy Innovations." National Governor's Association Center for Best Practices, March 6, 2006. Viewed 24 May 2024: *http://www.corrections.com/news/article/6748*

Mellow, Jeff, et al. *The Jail Administrator's Toolkit for Reentry.* Urban Institute, May 2008. *http://www.urban.org/research/publication/jail-administrators-toolkit-reentry*

Office of Research, California Department of Corrections and Rehabilitation. *Evidence-Based Practice in Corrections: A Training Manual for the California Program Assessment Process (CPAP).* Center for Evidence Based Corrections, University of California, Irvine, February 2006. Viewed 24 May 2024: *https://cpb-us-e2.wpmucdn.com/sites.uci.edu/dist/0/1149/files/2013/06/CPAP TrainingManual.pdf*

Pew Center on the States, Public Safety Performance Project. "Policy Framework to Strengthen Community Corrections." December 2008. Viewed 24 May 2024: *https://www.pewtrusts.org/en/research-and-analysis/reports/0001/01/01/ policy-framework-to-strengthen-community-corrections*

Scott, Wayne. "Effective Clinical Practices in Treating Clients in the Criminal Justice System." U.S. Department of Justice and the National Institute of Corrections. June 2008. Viewed 24 May 2024:
https://info.nicic.gov/nicrp/system/files/023362.pdf

Solomon, Amy L., et al. "Life After Lockup: Improving Reentry from Jail to the Community." Urban Institute, May 2008. Viewed 24 May 2024:
https://www.ojp.gov/ncjrs/virtual-library/abstracts/life-after-lockup-improving-reentry-jail-community

Solomon, Amy L., et al. "Putting Public Safety First: 13 Parole Supervision Strategies to Enhance Reentry Outcomes." Urban Institute, December 2008. Viewed 24 May 2024: *http://www.urban.org/research/publication/putting-public-safety-first-13-parole-supervision-strategies-enhance-reentry-outcomes-paper*

Taxman, Faye. "Assessment with a Flair: Offender Accountability in Supervision Plans." Federal Probation, September 2006. Viewed 24 May 2024:
https://www.uscourts.gov/sites/default/files/70_2_1_0.pdf

The United States Conference of Mayors. "Status of Ex-Offender Reentry Efforts in Cities: A 79-City Survey." June 2009. Viewed 24 May 2024:
https://peerta.acf.hhs.gov/sites/default/files/public/uploaded_files/ REENTRYREPORT091.pdf

U.S. Department of Justice National Institute of Corrections. *Implementing Evidence-Based Policy and Practice in Community Correction,* 2nd Ed., October 2009. Viewed 24 May 2024: *https://www.crj.org/assets/2017/07/ CommunityCorrections_BoxSet_Oct9.pdf*

Yoon, Jamie & Nickel, Jessica. *Reentry Partnerships: A Guide for States & Faith-Based and Community Organizations.* New York, New York: Council of State Governments Justice Center, 2008. Viewed 24 May 2024:
https://www.justice.gov/archive//fbci/docs/reentry-partnership.pdf

Data and Analysis

The Bureau of Justice Statistics (BJS), a division of the U.S. Department of Justice, breaks down national trends at the state level for a variety of criminal justice-related issues. For example, the BJS report "Trends in State Parole" compares discretionary and mandatory releases to parole with the parole success rate by state. BJS also provides information on local crime statistics (arrests and reported crimes), investigations and prosecutions, corrections, expenditures, and national reentry trends.
https://bjs.ojp.gov (Viewed 25 May 2024.)

How to Collect and Analyze Data: A Manual for Sheriffs and Jail Administrators. Elias Gail, 2007, Washington, DC: **National Institute of Corrections.** Anyone who needs to gather and analyze data concerning various jail-related issues will find this manual useful. This document provides guidance on how information can fuel policy decision making. Chapters comprising this guide include: Introduction; Good Management Requires Good Information; Information That Should Be Collected; Preparing for the Data Collection; How to Locate and Capture Information; How to Put It All Together; How to Analyze Information; How to Interpret Information; Sharing Information with Others; and Getting the Most from Your Information System. Appendices include: a Glossary of Statistical Terms for Non-Statisticians; Annotated Bibliography; Manual Data Collection Procedures and Sample Forms; Inmate Profile Data Collection; Incident Data Code Book Sample; Transport Data Collection; Tables for Determining Sample Size; Simple Random Sampling; Calculating the Standard Deviation; Calculating Chi Square; and Manual Data Display.
https://nicic.gov/resources/nic-library/all-library-items/how-collect-and-analyze-data-manual-sheriffs-and-jail (Viewed 25 May 2024.)

NIJ's Mapping and Analysis for Public Safety (MAPS) program supports research that helps agencies use GIS (Geographic Information Systems) to enhance public safety. Combining geographic data with police report data and then displaying the information on a map is an effective way to analyze where, how, and why crime occurs. The program examines:

- How to use maps to analyze crime.
- How to analyze spatial data.

- How maps can help researchers evaluate programs and policies.
- How to develop mapping, data sharing, and spatial analysis tools.

https://nij.ojp.gov/topics/articles/maps-how-mapping-helps-reduce-crime-and-improve-public-safety (Viewed 25 May 2024)

The Reentry Mapping Network (RMN) was established in 2002 by the Urban Institute. It's "a partnership of jurisdictions throughout the country that are engaged in mapping and analyzing prisoner reentry and community data to help inform local policies and practices. This report describes the methods underlying the RMN so that other jurisdictions can learn from these experiences and replicate their efforts in the interests of crafting more effective and successful reentry strategies at the community level. These experiences learned are derived from the three RMN partners funded by the National Institute of Justice (NIJ): Washington DC, Winston-Salem, NC, and Milwaukee, WI."
https://www.urban.org/research/pubication/mapping-prisoner-reentry (Viewed 4 June 2024.)

The Reentry Policy Council, a project of the Council of State Governments Justice Center, is a resource for defining the who, what, when, where, and how of using data. Policy Statement 2: Developing a Knowledge Base details the understanding of the nature and scope of local reentry issues and develops familiarity with local release policies, the characteristics of returning prisoners, and the resources and capacities of the communities to which prisoners return.
http://www.reentrypolicy.org/ (Viewed 25 May 2024)

The Serious and Violent Offender Reentry Initiative funded by the **Department of Justice** includes evaluations of a wide range of state programs. It includes basic information about each participating state.
www.svori-evaluation.org/ (Viewed 25 May 2024.)

The Urban Institute has produced portraits of reentry in several states, in addition to numerous publications about reentry from a national perspective.
http://www.urban.org/ (Viewed 25 May 2024.)

The *W. K. Kellogg Foundation Logic Model Development Guide* helps project development. Nonprofits today are being pressed to demonstrate the effectiveness

of their program activities by initiating and completing outcome-oriented evaluation of projects. This guide was developed to provide practical assistance to nonprofits engaged in this process. It aims to give staff of nonprofits and community members sufficient orientation to the underlying principles of "logic modeling" to use this tool to enhance their program planning, implementation, and dissemination activities.
http://www.betterevaluation.org/sites/detault/files/2021-11/Kellogg_ Foundation_Logic_Model_Guide.pdf (Viewed 25 May 2024)

Internet Resources

The Corporation for Supportive Housing (CSH) creates permanent housing with services to prevent and end homelessness. CSH brings together people, skills, and resources. They provide high-quality advice and development expertise, making loans and grants to supportive housing sponsors, strengthening the supportive housing industry, and reforming public policy. Refer to their library of documents concerning ex-offenders.
htttps://www.csh.org (Viewed 25 May 2024)

The Department of Health and Human Services (HHS) Incarceration and Reentry project page. The purpose of this document is to help HHS agencies know the full range of programs and services in the Department that currently address the needs of incarcerated individuals and their families and to understand what research and evaluation efforts are underway to identify evidence-based practices.
https://aspe.hhs.gov/topics/human-services/incarceration-reentry/-0
(Viewed 25 May 2024)

"Improving Prisoner Reentry through Strategic Policy Innovations" was published by the National Governors Association Center for Best Practices (3-6-2006). It describes prisoner reentry issues and challenges and suggests strategies that governors and other state policymakers can use to initiate long-term improvements. A bipartisan organization of the nation's governors, the National Governors Association (NGA) promotes visionary state leadership, shares best practices, and speaks with a collective voice on national policy. Founded in 1908, the National Governors Association is one of Washington, D.C.'s most respected

public policy organizations. Through NGA, governors identify priority issues and deal collectively with matters of public policy and governance at the state and national levels.
www.corrections.com/news/article/6748 (Viewed 25 May 2024)

The Jail Reentry Roundtable, a project of the Urban Institute, John Jay College of Criminal Justice, and the Montgomery County (Maryland) Department of Correction and Rehabilitation, was convened in 2006. The Roundtable's focus was on the 12 million individuals released from local jails each year and the associated challenges faced by individuals, families, and communities around the country. The Jail Reentry Roundtable aims to fill the gap in knowledge on this issue by: commissioning papers; convening a diverse group of practitioners and researchers; conducting a "scan of practice" of jail reentry programs around the country; writing a national report on jail reentry; and developing a training curriculum geared toward jail administrators and correctional staff. This website summarizes the Roundtable's work.
https://www.urban.org/policy-centers/justice-policy-center/projects/transition-jail-community-tjc-initiative/jail-reentry (Viewed 25 May 2024)

The National Institute of Corrections details its "Transition from Prison to the Community" and "Transition from Jail to the Community" initiatives on these websites. The Institute provides training, technical assistance, information services, and policy/program development assistance to federal, state, and local corrections agencies. Through cooperative agreements, they award funds to support these program initiatives. They also provide leadership to influence correctional policies, practices, and operations nationwide in areas of emerging interest and concern to correctional executives and practitioners as well as public policymakers.
https://nicic.gov/resources/resources-topics-and-roles/topics/transition-prison-community-tpc (Viewed 25 May 2024)
https://nicic.gov/resources/resources-topics-and-roles/topics/transition-jail-community-tjc (Viewed 25 May 2024)

Overview and Inventory of HHS Efforts to Assist Incarcerated and Reentering Individuals and their Families. The purpose of this document is to help agencies know the full range of programs and services in the Department of Health and

Human Services (HHS) that currently address the needs of incarcerated individuals and their families. It also explains what research and evaluation efforts are underway to identify evidence-based practices. Although HHS programs don't specifically target incarcerated and reentering individuals and their families, many HHS programs do serve these individuals and families as part of the broader population. Additionally, HHS research, demonstration, and evaluation efforts may be focused on this population because incarceration is an important risk factor for adult and child well-being, as well as the well-being of families and communities. The inventory in the report facilitates stronger intra-agency collaborations to address the many needs of these individuals and families and to improve their well-being. It also serves as an information source for other departments and public and private sector partners. Increasing the safety, security, and well-being of individuals, families, and communities requires the resources of many partners. These partnerships will be stronger when all the partners know what resources are available and activities are already in place.
https://aspe.hhs.gov/sites/default/files/migrated_legacy_files//43516/index.pdf (Viewed 25 May 2024)

The Reentry Policy Council provides researchers with a chart to use when assessing post-release inmates. It is organized by:
 Focus area (e.g., physical health) to view what information should be collected during incarceration or community supervision in a particular focus area over time.
 Timeframe (e.g., prerelease) to view what information should be collected in a particular timeframe across various focus areas.
 "More Detail" to view full descriptions, which includes relevant assessment instruments and program examples from the field.
 Search for **Reentry Policy Council Assessments Chart** for numerous charts.

The Reintegration of Ex-Offenders – Adult Program (RExO), formerly known as the Prisoner Reentry Initiative (PRI), is designed to strengthen urban communities through an employment-centered program that incorporates mentoring, job training, and other comprehensive transitional services. This program seeks to reduce recidivism by helping former inmates find work when they return to their communities and is sponsored by the Department of Labor.
https://www.dol.gov/agencies/eta (Viewed 25 May 2024)

The Safer Foundation believes in an unobstructed road to reentry. From its start in 1972, their mission has been to provide "support, employment, education, and advocacy that empower justice-involved individuals to achieve their true potential." They help clear legal and societal hurdles faced by those reentering their communities.
https://saferfoundation.org/ (Viewed 25 May 2024)

SAMHSA, the Substance Abuse and Mental Health Services Administration, provides a **Data Webpage Help Guide** to assist the public with simple and direct connections to websites that contain information about interventions to prevent and/or treat mental and substance use disorders. The Data Webpage Help Guide provides a list of websites that contain information about specific evidence-based practices (EBPs) or provide comprehensive reviews of research findings.
https://www.samhsa.gov/data/sites/default/files/SAMHSA%20Data%20Webpage%20Help%20Guide.pdf (Viewed 25 May 2024)

ENDNOTES

1. D. Periman, "Prisoner Reentry and the Uniform Collateral Consequences of Conviction Act." University of Alaska Anchorage: *Alaska Justice Forum,* vol. 27, No 4, 2011.

2. National Reentry Resource Center. Viewed 18 May 2024. *http://www.nationalreentryresourcecenter.org/what.*

3. J. Klopovic, M. Vasu, D. Yearwood, *Effective Program Practices for At-Risk Youth: A Continuum of Community-Based Practices.* New York: Civic Research Institute, Inc., 2003.

4. Michigan Prisoner ReEntry Initiative (MPRI). Viewed 23 May 2024: *https://www.michigan.gov/-/media/Project/Websites/corrections/assets/Folder8/THE_MPRI_MODEL_1005.pdf?rev=ce4269c8f7144c638b24ade292b3dc9f.*

5. Ibid.

6. M. Lyman, "Whys and Hows of Measuring Jail Recidivism." Wash., D.C.: Urban Institute, 2006.

7. P. Greenwood, "Preventing and Reducing Youth Crime and Violence: Using Evidence-Based Practices." Sacramento, Calif.: Governor's Office of Gang and Youth Policy, 2010.

8. R. Wolf, "Reentry Courts: Looking Ahead – A Conversation about Strategies for Offender," U.S. Department of Justice, Office of Justice Programs, 2011. Viewed 18 May 2024. *https://www.ojp.gov/ncjrs/virtual-library/abstracts/reentry-courts-looking-ahead-conversation-about-strategies-offender.*

9. Ibid., pp. 3-4.

10. J. Mellow, D. Mukamal, S. LoBuglio, A. Solomon, & J. Osborne, *The Jail Administrator's Toolkit for Reentry.* Wash., D.C.: Urban Institute, 2008. Viewed 22 May 2024. *http://www.urban.org/research/publication/jail-administrators-toolkit-reentry.*

11. J. Jannetta, H. Dodd, & B. Elderbroom, *The Elected Official's Toolkit for Jail Reentry.* Wash., D.C.: Urban Institute, 2006. Viewed 22 May 2024: *http://www.urban.org/research/publication/elected-officials-toolkit-jail-reentry.*

12. Op. Cit., Mellow et al., *The Jail Administrator's Toolkit,* 2008.

13. Ibid., pp. 177-178.

14. Ibid., pp. 81-89.

15. Ibid., p. 1.

16 Op. Cit., Mellow et al., *The Jail Administrator's Toolkit*, 2008.

17 *Second Chance Act of 2007,* PUBLIC LAW 110-199, Apr. 9, 2008. Second Chance Act authorizes federal grants to government agencies and nonprofit organizations to provide employment assistance, substance abuse treatment, housing, family programming, mentoring, victims support, and other services that can help reduce recidivism. Viewed 24 May 2024: *http://www.nationalreentryresourcecenter.org/.*

18 S. Urahn, *State of Recidivism: The Revolving Door of America's Prisons.* Wash., D.C.: The PEW Center on The States, 2011.

19 Op. Cit., Wolf, "Reentry Courts," 2011.

20 According to a 2023 analysis by the U.S. Department of Justice, 82% of people released from state prisons are rearrested at least once within 10 years. On average, state prisoners are rearrested within the first three years after release, at a rate of 68%. The rate increases to 79% at five years and 83% at nine years, whereas LINC Inc. in Wilmington, North Carolina, has a recidivism rate of less than 15%.

21 LINC Inc. in Wilmington, North Carolina, has a recidivism rate of less than 15%. TROSA in Durham, North Carolina, has a very low recidivism rate, is completely self-funded, and saves the state $7.5 million dollars annually.

22 Op. Cit., Urahn, *State of Recidivism,* 2011.

23 Federal Advisory Committee on Juvenile Justice, Annual Report 2010. Viewed 22 May 2024: *https://facjj.ojp.gov/sites/g/files/xyckuh291/files/media/document/2010-facjj-annual-report.pdf.*

24 M. Nelson, M. Tarlow, "Jail Reentry and Community Linkages: Adding Value on Both Sides of the Gate," Jail Reentry Roundtable Initiative, Wash., D.C.: The Urban Institute, 2006; J. Webb, "Why We Must Fix Our Prisons," *Parade,* 30 March 2009.

25 Op. Cit., Urahn, *State of Recidivism,* 2011, p. 22.

26 Op. Cit., Jannetta et al, *Elected Official's Toolkit,* 2006; Reentry Policy Council, *Report of the Reentry Policy Council: Charting the Safe and Successful Return of Prisoners to the Community.* New York: Council of State Governments, January 2005; Op. Cit., Urahn, *State of Recidivism,* 2011.

27 Hagan & Dinovitzer, 1999; Sabol & Lynch, 1997.

28 Op. Cit., Nelson & Tarlow, "Jail Reentry and Community Linkages," 2006.

29 Op. Cit., Jannetta et al, *The Elected Official's Toolkit for Jail Reentry,* 2006; Op. Cit., Mellow et al., *The Jail Administrator's Toolkit,* 2008.

30 Op. Cit., Jannetta et al, *The Elected Official's Toolkit for Jail Reentry,* 2006.

31 J. Carmody, "Effective County Practices in Jail to Community Transition Planning for Offenders with Mental Health and Substance Abuse Disorders," National Association of Counties, Wash., D.C., 2006.

32 Ibid., pp. 4-5.

33 Ibid., p. 5.

34 Durham County N.C. Justice Services Center. Viewed 23 May 2024: *https://www.dconc.gov/county-departments/departments-f-z/justice-services/*.

35 CJRC (Now JSC) Community-Based Corrections 2010-11 Performance Measure. *https://www.dconc.gov/county-departments/departments-f-z/justice-services/*.

36 Leading Into New Communities (LINC). Viewed 23 May 2024: *http://www.lincnc.org*.

37 Triangle Residential Options for Substance Abusers (TROSA). Viewed 23 May 2024: *https://www.trosainc.org/*.

38 Dismas Charities Inc. Viewed 23 May 2024: *https://www.dismas.com*.

39 Op. Cit., Jannetta et al, *The Elected Official's Toolkit for Jail Reentry*, 2006.

40 Adapted from the Reentry Policy Council Report: *https://csgjusticecenter.org/publications* and The Jail Administrators Toolkit: Op. Cit., Mellow et al., *The Jail Administrator's Toolkit*, 2008. Viewed 23 May 2024.

41 A. Solomon, J. W. L. Osborne, S. F. LoBuglio, J. Mellow, D. Mukamal, "Life after Lockup: Improving Reentry from Jail to the Community," 2008. Viewed 28 May 2024. *https://www.ojp.gov/ncjrs/virtual-library/abstracts/life-after-lockup-improving-reentry-jail-community*.

42 Ibid., Solomon et al, "Life after Lockup," 2008.

43 T. Somers, K. Nelson, "Impact of Critical Success Factors Across the Stages of Enterprise Resource Planning Implementations." Proceedings of the 34th Hawaii International Conference on System Sciences, 2001.

44 Op. Cit., Jannetta et al, *The Elected Official's Toolkit for Jail Reentry*, 2006.

45 Method123 Project Management Methodology. Viewed 23 May 2024: *https://www.mpmm.com*.

46 J. Esteves, J. Pastor, "Analysis of Critical Success Factors Relevance Along SAP Implementation Phases," Seventh Americas Conference on Information Systems, 2011; J. Pinto, D. Sleven, "Critical Success Factors Across the Project Life Cycle," *Project Management Journal*, v 19, iss 3, 1988, pp. 67-75.

47 Op. Cit., Somers & Nelson, "Impact of Critical Success Factors," 2001.

48 F. Martinelli, "Building an Effective Board of Directors," 2011. Viewed 23 May 2024: https://www.naco.org/sites/default/files/documents/EncouragingVisionaryBoardLeadership_NCCAE_Oct%202012.pdf.

49 Ibid., Martinelli, 2011.

50 Op. Cit., adapted from Jannetta et al, *The Elected Official's Toolkit for Jail Reentry*, 2006.

51 The National Institute of Corrections, Department of Justice Urban Institute, "Transition from Jail to Community Online Learning Toolkit." Viewed 23 May 2024: https://apps.urban.org/features/tjctoolkit/.

52 Op. Cit., Martinelli, "Effective Board of Directors," 2011, p. 9.

53 University of North Carolina School of Government. Viewed 23 May 2024: http://www.sog.unc.edu/.

54 Op. Cit., Martinelli, "Effective Board of Directors," 2011.

55 Op. Cit., Martinelli, "Effective Board of Directors," 2011; Op. Cit., Jannetta et al, *Elected Official's Toolkit*, 2006.

56 Reentry Policy Council 2005, *Report of the Re-entry Policy Council: Charting the Safe and Successful Return of Prisoners to the Community.* New York: Council of State Governments, January 2005. The Report of the Reentry Policy Council, which was authored by the Council of State Governments and 10 project partners, reflects the results of a series of meetings among 100 of the most respected workforce, health, housing, public safety, family, community, and victim experts in the country. Viewed 24 May 2024: https://csgjusticecenter.org/publications/report-of-the-re-entry-policy-council.

57 Ibid., *Report of the Reentry Policy Council*, 1999.

58 J. Lynch, W. Sabol, *Prisoner Reentry in Perspective.* Wash., D.C.: Urban Institute Justice Policy Center, Crime Policy Report, v 3, Sept. 2001.

59 Ibid.

60 Op. Cit., Jannetta et al, *The Elected Official's Toolkit for Jail Reentry*, 2006.

61 K. Kolat, B. Grosshans, R. Margolies, J. Dipko, A. Loftus, "Statutes, Policies, and Practices Affecting Prisoner Reentry in Wisconsin," 2011. Viewed 24 May 2024: https://evidence2impact.psu.edu/wp-content/uploads/2023/05/s_wifis26c.

62 Ohio Department of Rehabilitation and Corrections. Viewed 24 May 2024: https://drc.ohio.gov/web/reentry_resource.htm.

63 Op. Cit., Reentry Policy Council 2005, Report.

64 Suggested by ChatGPT.

65 Op. Cit., Mellow et al, *The Jail Administrator's Toolkit,* 2008.

66 J. Mellow, G. Christiensen, K. Warwick, J. Willson, *Transition from Jail to Community: Online Learning Toolkit.* Wash., D.C.: The Urban Institute, revised May 2011.

67 Op. Cit., Mellow et al, *The Jail Administrator's Toolkit,* 2008.

68 Ibid.

69 Op. Cit., Mellow et al., *Transition from Jail Toolkit,* 2011. Adapted from Module 4: Data-driven Understanding of Local Reentry, pp. 7-8.

70 C. McNamara, "Basics of Developing Mission, Vision and Values Statements," 2011. Viewed 24 May 2024. *https://managementhelp.org/strategicplanning/mission-vision-values.htm#anchor521412.*

71 Op. Cit., Reentry Policy Council 2005, Report.

72 Op. Cit., McNamara, "Mission, Vision," 2011.

73 Urban Institute, *Transition from Jail to Community Online Learning Toolkit,* 2010, Section 3, p. 11. Viewed 24 May 2024: *https://apps.urban.org/features/tjctoolkit.*

74 Op. Cit., Reentry Policy Council 2005, Report.

75 E. Rhine, "The Ohio Plan for Productive Offender Reentry and Recidivism Reduction." Columbus, Ohio: The Ohio Department of Rehabilitation and Correction, 2002. Adapted from Rhine 2002, p. 8. Viewed 24 May 2024: *https://drc.ohio.gov/systems-and-services/2-reentry-services/reentry-programming/reentry-programming.*

76 "Criminal Justice Resource Center Annual Report FY10," Durham County Government. Viewed 23 May 2024: *https://www.dconc.gov/county-departments/departments-f-z/justice-services/.*

77 J. Bush, B. Glick, J. Taymans, *Thinking for a Change: Integrated Cognitive Change Behavior Program,* National Institute of Correction, Wash., D.C, 1997, revised 2/02. Viewed 24 May 2024: *https://nicic.gov/resources/resources-topics-and-roles/topics/thinking-change.*

78 G. Zimmerman, C. Olsen, M. Bosworth. "A 'Stages of Change' Approach to Helping Patients Change Behavior," *American Family Physician,* 1 March 2000. Viewed 18 May 2024. *http://www.aafp.org/afp/2000/0301/p1409.html.*

79 Op. Cit., Mellow et al., *Transition from Jail Toolkit,* 2011.

80 Solomon et al. 2008, p. 178.

81 QENO, Quality Enhancements for Nonprofit Organizations, an initiative designed to improve the capabilities and competencies of nonprofit organizations located at the University of North Carolina, Wilmington. Viewed 18 May 2024: https://www.uncw.edu/QENO.

82 While *holistic* and *wholistic* are used interchangeably, there is a subtle but important difference. Holistic emphasizes *interconnectedness* and integration of the parts. Wholistic emphasizes *completeness*. Both suit Capacity Building, in which integration of services is important *and* the whole becomes greater than the sum of the parts.

83 M. Robinson, G. White, "The Role of Civic Organizations in the Provision of Social Services: Toward Synergy." Helsinki, Finland: UNU World Institute for Development Economics Research, 1997.

84 A. Crayton, L. Ressler, D. Mukamal, et al, *Partnering with Jails to Improve Reentry: A Guidebook for Community-Based Organizations*. Wash., D.C.: The Urban Institute and the John Jay College of Criminal Justice, 2010. Viewed 24 May 2024: https://www.urban.org/research/publication/partnering-jails-improve-reentry-guidebook-community-based-organizations.

85 L. M. Najavits, *Seeking Safety: Treatment Innovations*. Viewed 24 May 2024: https://www.treatment-innovations.org/seeking-safety.html. Also: https://www.samhsa.gov/resource/dbhis/seeking-safety.

86 TROSA – residential recovery program. Viewed 24 May 2024: trosainc.org.

87 SAMHSA Evidence-Based Practices Resource Center. Viewed 24 May 2024: https://www.samhsa.gov/resource-search/ebp.

88 Ohio Department of Rehabilitation and Correction. Viewed 24 May 2024: http://www.drc.ohio.gov/web/ipp_criminogenic.htm.

89 D. L. Sackett, W. M. Rosenberg, J. A. Gray, et al, "Evidence Based Medicine: What It Is and What It Isn't," 1996. Viewed 25 May 2024: https://pubmed.ncbi.nlm.nih.gov/8555924/.

90 Pennsylvania's Juvenile Justice System Enhancement Strategy, p. 5. Viewed 24 May 2024: https://www.court.co.lancaster.pa.us/143/Juvenile-Justice-System-Enhancement-Stra#:~:text=.

91 Bureau of Justice Statistics. Viewed 24 May 2024: http://bjs.ojp.usdoj.gov/index.cfm?ty=tp&tid=17.

92 Transformational Capacity Building, informed by *chat.openai.com*. (Accessed 10-23)

93 Op. Cit., Reentry Policy Council 2005, "Report of the Reentry Policy Council Charting the Safe and Successful Return of Prisoners to the Community, Policy Statement 8: Development of Intake Procedure," pp. 114.

94 Ibid., pp. 114-15.

95 With kind permission, adapted from a Durham County, N.C., Criminal Justice Resource Center Memorandum of Understanding.

www.ingramcontent.com/pod-product-compliance
Lightning Source LLC
Chambersburg PA
CBHW042358030426
42337CB00032B/5139